LIVING THE EDGES

A DISABLED WOMEN'S READER

LIVING THE EDGES

A DISABLED WOMEN'S READER

edited by Diane Driedger

INANNA Publications and Education Inc.
Toronto, Canada

Published in Canada by
Inanna Publications and Education Inc.
210 Founders College, York University
4700 Keele Street, Toronto, Ontario M3J 1P3
Telephone: (416) 736-5356 Fax (416) 736-5765
Email: inanna@yorku.ca Website: www.yorku.ca/inanna

 Canada Council **Conseil des Arts**
for the Arts **du Canada**   ONTARIO ARTS COUNCIL
CONSEIL DES ARTS DE L'ONTARIO

The publisher gratefully acknowledges the support of the Canada Council for the Arts and the Ontario Arts Council for its publishing program.

The publisher is also grateful for the kind support received
from an Anonymous Fund at The Calgary Foundation.

Printed and Bound in Canada.

Front Cover Artwork:
Anjali Dookeran, "untitled," 2006, watercolour, 22" x 30".
Cover Design: Val Fullard
Interior Design: Luciana Ricciutelli

Library and Archives Canada Cataloguing in Publication:

      Living the edges : a disabled women's reader / edited by
Diane Driedger.

Includes bibliographical references.
ISBN 978-1-926708-17-1

      1. Women with disabilities--Canada. 2. Discrimination
against people with disabilities--Canada. 3. Sex discrimination
against women--Canada. 4. Sociology of disability--Canada.
I. Driedger, Diane, 1960-

HV1569.3.W65L58 2010   362.4082'0971   C2010-905701-5

Dedicated to the memory of
Kathleen Guy, Elizabeth Semkiw and Marie-Louise Gagnon

CONTENTS

ACKNOWLEDGEMENTS

THANK YOU TO ALL the women who contributed to this reader. Without you, there would be no book. I also appreciate the vision and hard work of Luciana Ricciutelli, Editor-in-Chief of Inanna Publications and Education, in making this reader a reality. Thanks, Luciana!

DIANE DRIEDGER

INTRODUCTION

I HAVE SPENT THE last year looking for pieces for this book. Now that I see them all in one place, I feel awe for the strength, resilience, and dignity of women with physical and mental, visible and invisible disabilities in Canada. This book, *Living the Edges: A Disabled Women's Reader*, is a vehicle for women with disabilities to share experiences with other disabled women, and with the public at large. We are silent no longer. This is the first reader of its kind that is Canadian.

Women with disabilities inform society about our lives through organizations such as the DisAbled Women's Network Canada and through writings, such as those that I have been involved in melding into books (Driedger and Gray; Driedger, Feika and Girón Batres; Driedger; Driedger and Owen). I have believed it is so important for disabled women's voices to be heard. Just being able to say something about what is happening to us empowers us as women who have dignity and worth. I have believed this since 1992 when I co-edited *Imprinting Our Image: An International Anthology by Women with Disabilities*. At that time, there were few voices of disabled women present in written form or even in organizations of people with disabilities. The women are always the last heard—but we are persistent.

WHO ARE WE?

Women with various types of disabilities account for the majority of people with disabilities in Canada at 13.3 percent of the population. Men living with disabilities comprise 11.5 percent (Government of Canada). Poverty is much more pronounced for Canadian women with disabilities than for men. A disabled man's average income from employment is $19,250 a year, while women with disabilities' employment income is $8,360 (DAWN Ontario). And women who have more severe disabilities tend to have lower incomes than women whose disabilities are less severe (CRIAW). We are women who are wheelchair users, crutch users, deaf or hard of hearing, blind or visually impaired. We are women who have chronic illnesses such as fibromyalgia, chronic fatigue, diabetes, colitis, arthritis, depression, and anxiety. Some women's disabilities are visible, and some are invisible.

WHY WRITE ABOUT WOMEN?

Women with disabilities are disadvantaged because we are women and because we are disabled. Thus, the disabled women's movement in Canada has coined the phrase "double jeopardy" to refer to the lives of women with disabilities. When other factors, such as race, sexual orientation or ethnicity, are added a woman may experience more than double jeopardy. That is, a woman may experience discrimination because she is a woman, disabled and Aboriginal, for instance.

Women with disabilities deal with issues that men with disabilities usually do not deal with, such as a greater risk of emotional, physical and sexual abuse. This is as a consequence of being women. On the other hand, women in general may not have as many situations where others may abuse them, as disabled women do, especially if they rely on assistance from caregivers to assist them in the activities of daily life, which may include toileting and dressing.

The DisAbled Women's Network (DAWN) Canada has led the movement for change for women with disabilities since 1985. From the outset, DAWN recognized the dual oppressions that disabled women face and set out to make them known to the women's movement, the disability movement and society at large. The women's movement has largely overlooked the needs of disabled women through the years and DAWN has been there to remind them of the need for accessibility for women with various types of disabilities.

In like manner, DAWN Canada has worked with the larger disability rights movement to educate them about the issues of women who are disabled. For a long time, the disability rights movement was concerned with issues that were relevant to both disabled men and women, such as transportation and employment; however, the unique needs of women were not taken into account. The leadership of the organizations tended to be men in the early years of organizing in the 1970s. They did not think of the need for childcare for women with disabilities to participate in events or to obtain employment. They did not discuss the issues of violence against women with disabilities, as the awareness was not there.

EDITING THE EDGES

An opportunity to promote more awareness about the lives of women with disabilities presented itself when Luciana Ricciutelli from Innana Publications and Education asked me in 2008 to edit a Canadian disabled women's reader. I immediately said yes. She explained to me that the feminist journal *Canadian Woman Studies/les cahiers de la femme* had published a special issue on "Women and Disability" in 1993, and that it had long been out of print. Luciana said that there were still a lot of requests for this back issue from university professors and researchers. She wanted to publish a disabled women's reader as a book, using the 1993 issue as a base. I looked at the articles, poems, and artwork, and have included about half of the original pieces. Some articles were dated, so I asked women with disabilities to submit articles, as well artwork and poetry, on topics that are timely to the 2010s.

The work in this reader reflects the diversity of women with disabilities. Aboriginal women make a strong contribution to this reader. Women from ethno-racial backgrounds are not as well represented as they should be. Lesbians with disabilities have made several contributions to this anthology also. The women are from all over the country, from West to East and one from the North. However, there are many contributors from Manitoba. This may be because I reside in Manitoba and know more of the women with disabilities here personally. It could also be that disabled women have very strong voices in this province. The DisAbled Women's Network Manitoba has been in existence for the last four years, after years of there being no voice of women with disabilities in the province. Women with all types of disabilities are reflected in the pieces I have chosen. Women with intellectual disabilities have contributed several articles to this book, for which I am very happy. It is not often that women with intellectual disabilities have their own ideas and writing published. Women from many walks of life have contributed pieces. Overall, though, the women tend to be well educated.

I thought about the title for this book long and hard. Should it be a "disabled women's reader" or "a reader by women with disabilities?" I decided on a disabled women's reader—I see it as a political statement: yes, we're disabled, and we're women, so what? Just as there are Aboriginal women, African women, lesbian women, there are disabled women. We are a distinct group that some would argue have a culture that arises from our lives, from our presence in the world.

At the same time as I've been editing this book, I have been living my own life with several chronic illnesses that are also disabling to me and thus I identify as having disability. I've lived life without disability (until age thirty-two) and with disability for the last eighteen years. To me, I have felt the many edges of my disability, most of them not self-imposed, but encountered as social, physical, and economic barriers that, when I least expect it, take a swipe at me, or I run into, like a sharp stick on the hiking trail.

The opportunity to edit this book has been a gift to me. Learning about the lives of other women with disabilities in this book has provided me with these women as companions as I, too, am "living the edges." What does that mean? The title is from Charlotte Caron and Gail Christy's article, "Living on the Edges" in Section 1 of this book. I started thinking about the word "edges" which in itself is a noun. I decided to use it as a noun; there are many edges out there. One thinks about being out on the edge, being on the cutting edge of an issue, looking over the edge, balancing on the edge, sharpness of edges. All of these meanings are reflected in this collection. I have divided the book into sections that explore the multifaceted lives of women with disabilities living those edges.

Section 1, *Who We Are on the Edges*, introduces the reader to women with disabilities and who we see ourselves to be. There may be images of disabled women out there that are of passive women who accept handouts, or who need care all the time. This section tells us that being a woman with a disability is a complex business. We think a lot about who we are too, because society often perceives us as weak and as women to be acted upon, looked after, told what to do and there are misunderstandings about our disabilities.

Section 2, *Naming the Edges: Barriers*, discusses the nature of the edges which are social, economic, and attitudinal barriers to participating in society as full citizens like everyone else, disabled or nondisabled. I am utilizing the social model definition of disability in this reader. That is, how society disables us through physical, social, and economic barriers is what we are discussing (Oliver).

In Section 3, *Violence on the Edges*, women with disabilities discuss the emotional, mental, physical, and sexual abuse that we have encountered while living the edges. This abuse arises from social attitudes that perceive women with disabilities as weak, vulnerable and not having a voice. These issues have been discussed since the 1980s and, unfortunately, abuse has not gone away. In the end, though, women with disabilities continue to encounter this very sharp edge in their lives, and some tell us how they have coped.

Section 4, *With Us on the Edges: Relationships and Sexuality*, discusses our lives as women who have many types of relationships and who are sexual beings. There has been a prevailing myth that disabled women are "asexual" because we are "damaged goods", we do not measure up to the body beautiful aesthetic that is portrayed everywhere in our society. The women in this section proclaim, we are women, we are sexual, we have relationships, we have families, we have children. And in the end, we have ourselves and our own perceptions and feelings about our sexuality.

Challenging the Edges, Section 5, looks at how women with disabilities are working to blunt the edges, the barriers, in their lives. We are on the cutting edge here—organizing together to understand our lives and to move forward in society. And we also find ways to challenge the status quo through art and reflection.

Overall, I hope you will glean from this reader that our lives as women with disabilities are in process. We encounter edges, most not of our making, that are social, physical, and attitudinal barriers. In the end, we sometimes struggle and we sometimes have successes—it's all part of living like everyone else, whether one is disabled or nondisabled. It's all part of our resiliency.

REFERENCES

Canadian Research Institute for the Advancement of Women (CRIAW). *Fact Sheet: Women and Poverty.* Toronto: CRIAW, 1995.

DisAbled Women's Network (DAWN) – Ontario. "Fact Sheet." 2007. Online: <http://dawn.thot.net/fact.html>.

Driedger, Diane. *The Mennonite Madonna: Poems.* Charlottetown: gynergy books, 1999.

Driedger, Diane and Susan Gray, eds. *Imprinting Our Image: An International Anthology by Women with Disabilities.* Charlottetown: gynergy books, 1992.

Driedger, Diane and Michelle Owen, eds. *Dissonant Disabilities: Women with Chronic Illnesses Explore Their Lives.* Toronto: Canadian Scholars' Press/Women's Press, 2008.

Driedger, Diane, Irene Feika and Eileen Girón Batres, eds. *Across Borders: Women with Disabilities Working Together.* Charlottetown: gynergy books, 1996.

Government of Canada. *A Profile of Disability in Canada, 2001.* 2001. Online: <www.statcan.ca/english/freepub/89-577-XIE/index.htm>.

Oliver, Michael. *The Politics of Disablement: A Sociological Approach.* New York: St. Martin's Press, 1990.

WHO WE ARE ON THE EDGES

SHARON DALE STONE

MUST DISABILITY ALWAYS BE VISIBLE?

The Meaning of Disability for Women

I ONCE COMPLAINED TO my mother about how different I felt on account of my (largely invisible) impairments, and she pointed out to me that practically everyone has something wrong with them. As a case in point, she drew attention to the large number of people suffering from poor eyesight. That silenced me for a while, but lately I have begun to ponder what it means to identify as disabled. If impairment is so widespread that it is the individual with the perfectly functioning body who is truly remarkable, then why is it that we speak of disabled people as though they constitute a minority?

For some time now I have been grappling with the question of what it means for a woman to identify as disabled; I still find that the questions are more numerous and come more easily than the answers. I don't pretend to have definitive answers to the question of what disability means for women, but I do think that the following ideas suggest a way into the problem and bear serious consideration.

References to physical or mental impairments call attention to the body. This is because no matter how diligently our culture[1] works to convince us that mind and body are separate, they are not separate. Indeed, the intimate relationship between mind and body was explicitly recognized in the nineteenth century as compulsory schooling for children was being promoted (Prentice 29-30). At the time, the school promoters argued that one must train the body in order to train the mind. It is for this reason that physical education was introduced into the curriculum and has remained there to this day. In the nineteenth century, these men did not argue that the mind and body were of equal value; they were quite adamant that the body was inferior. Moreover, their recognition of the intimate relationship between mind and body was used primarily to justify the assumption that someone with a feeble body must therefore have a feeble mind. Contemporary culture has retained this noxious assumption, yet seems to have forgotten the premise upon which it was once based: that mind and body are not separate.

When thinking about disability, it is useful to notice that in our culture, notwithstanding the fleeting recognition of mind/body unity that appears every now and then, the theoretical separation of mind and body is centuries old. Equally old is the idea that the mind is more valuable than the body. Today these ideas are increasingly being questioned, yet our culture continues to assume that mind and body may be regarded as separate and unequal. As Lois McNay says:

> This [mind/body] dualism privileges an abstract, prediscursive subject at the center of thought and, accordingly, derogates the body as the site of all that is understood to be opposed to the spirit and rational thought, such as the emotions, passions, needs. (126)

Thus, our culture encourages us to "rise above" and transcend the body, to pretend that it does not really exist. Much of this, of course, is at bottom tied to a fear of death, and can be seen as an attempt to deny the inevitability of death. Nevertheless, we are not encouraged by our culture to pay attention to whatever aches and pains we may suffer. Rather, we are encouraged to ignore them and go about our business as though our bodies had nothing to teach us. Indeed, it is because our culture holds the body in such contempt that we are able to find ourselves living in a world that is structured, as Susan Wendell has pointed out, "as though everyone can work and play at a pace that is not compatible with any kind of illness or pain" (111). Those who are best at denying the limitations of the body reap monetary rewards (e.g. the workaholic executive, the supermom, the sports athlete), while those who either refuse to ignore or are unable to ignore their bodily limitations reap no rewards from our culture.

Our culture does not pretend that no one ever suffers. Everyone is allowed, on occasion, to have a headache, an upset stomach, or the common cold. But no one is allowed to let such ailments interfere with daily tasks. Our culture admires those hardworking individuals who, despite sniffles, bleary eyes and a temperature of 101 degrees Fahrenheit, go to work and get things done. Similarly, our culture admires the individual who has, for example, a persistent pain somewhere in the body yet refuses to go to a doctor. Such individuals, our culture implicitly asserts, are to be valued for an ability to rise above the body and, indeed, ignore it. Our culture teaches us that "a pain in the neck" may be felt physically as well as recognized metaphorically, but "a pain in the neck" ought to be regarded as a minor inconvenience to be overcome, not something that puts a stop to the achievement of goals.

In this manner, disability becomes unspeakable. Those who dare to call attention to their bodily "imperfections" are shunned. Their demonstrated inability or refusal to "rise above" the body is taken as evidence of their inferiority, and they are not taken seriously. Those who cannot conceal their impairments are encouraged to remain out of sight—whether in an institution or in a private home matters not, so long as the general population does not have to deal with their presence.

Those who can conceal their impairments, however, are welcome to mingle with the general population, but only to the extent that they are successful in concealing their impairments. Thus, the old woman with arthritis is allowed on the street but she is assumed, because of her advanced age and the difficulty she may have with walking, to be incompetent. She can be easily dismissed because of her inability/refusal to conceal her bodily "imperfections." Her age alone is enough to make her "other" (Posner) and so whatever impairments she might have acquired in the process of living may also be considered "other." To the extent that young women take notice of her, they may comfort themselves that arthritis is a disease of the old, and this thought prevents them from identifying with the old woman.

Arthritis, however, is not a disease exclusive to the old, and is often present in the bodies of children. What happens when it is a young woman who has arthritis? If a young woman complains of not being able to walk far because of arthritis, she too is looked down upon. No one can use her age to dismiss her, but she is looked down upon because she is seen to be giving in to the infirmities of the body. She is regarded as inferior in her inability to withstand pain. She may be told that she must keep moving, for it is only with continual movement that the joints may stay oiled and supple, she may be told by someone else that she is not exercising properly, and she may be told by still another person that if she pays too much attention to her body, she'll never get anything done.

In this manner, the young woman with arthritis is encouraged to "normalize" her suffering (Abberley 17). She is asked to participate in maintaining the huge silence surrounding the existence of impairments in young bodies. Suffering is part of the human condition, she may be told philosophically, and so there is nothing unusual about her pain. From this perspective, she has no cause for drawing attention to her "imperfect" body. She should get on with life, grin and bear it. Above all, she is not encouraged to identify herself as disabled.

In our culture, disability is equated with incompetence and inferiority. The woman (or, for that matter, the man) who says she is disabled is understood to be announcing her own incompetence and inferiority. It is on this basis that well-meaning friends may counter her announcement of disability with the statement, "But I don't think of you as disabled." Intended as a compliment, the statement is meant as an affirmation of her ability to participate in social life. Sometimes, the statement is uttered in an attempt to deny that the woman who says she has impairments has any limitations beyond those that are considered normal, and thus the statement is meant to deny her ability to define her own reality. At other times, the statement is uttered as an affirmation of the essential incompetence and inferiority of disabled people.

The body is not something with which women are trained to feel comfortable. In our culture, women learn that their value resides in the attractiveness of their bodies. It is small wonder, then, that even women who are conventionally attractive are continually alert to the slightest of bodily "imperfections." And it is small wonder that we have a huge cosmetics industry that caters to women who are terrified of drawing attention to the imperfections which they perceive in their bodies. In our culture, women learn at an early age that it is incumbent upon them to do their utmost to conceal their "imperfections." Women learn that there is nothing about an "imperfect" body to celebrate; such a body is cause for shame.

Perhaps the lengths to which women in our culture will go to deny the widespread existence of impairments can be illustrated with the following anecdote: Several years ago, I read an article about a lesbian organization in which I used to be active. Written by Becki Ross, the article was based on interviews with a number of lesbians who had been involved in the organization. Of everything that was said in the article, one particular line has stuck in my mind. That is, Ross discussed the kinds of women who used to attend events there, and stated that: "No one that I interviewed remembers ever seeing a disabled lesbian" there (81). Had I been interviewed, Ross would not have been able to write that line, but what is more interesting to me is that I was not the only lesbian there who was disabled.

I note that in the article Ross did not conclude that there were no disabled lesbians there, only that her informants do not remember any. This gives me pause for thought, and prompts me to wonder exactly what counts as being disabled. I wonder if one must sit in a wheelchair in order to be recognized as disabled, or at least use crutches for walking. If these highly visible pieces of equipment are required in order to be recognized as disabled, then it is not surprising that no one remembers seeing disabled lesbians at that organization, because meetings and social events were held in a very inaccessible building. But as anyone with any knowledge about impairments knows, there are all kinds of impairments and many of them are not obvious. It would have been more correct for Ross's informants to have stated that they did not see any lesbians with impairments that were so visible they could not be hidden.

Although I have been disabled since childhood, either my impairments are not usually apparent or else others assume that any clumsiness on my part or any disinclination to do certain things can be ascribed to some amorphous strangeness. For a very long time, I was not inclined to enlighten others about my impairments and, in fact, worked hard at trying to forget that they are part of who I am. Certainly, I was not interested in identifying as disabled during the period that Ross wrote about in her article, and I have written about this elsewhere (Stone).

Yet, I have to wonder why the lesbians who Ross interviewed assumed that impairments are always visible, or at least that if they had seen a disabled lesbian, they would have recognized her as such.

Off the top of my head, I can think of two other lesbians with invisible impairments who were often present at that organization's meetings and/or events. One had diabetes and another was mobility impaired. These two were lesbians that I personally knew about, and I did not know about them because they went around announcing their impairments to one and all. Regarding the lesbian with diabetes, I only knew about her because I heard her speak at a meeting for women with diabetes which I had attended with my lover who was diabetic and, by then, blind as well (my partner had also been to the lesbian organization in question, but was not actively involved). Regarding the lesbian who was mobility impaired, I knew about her because she told me one evening when the two of us were trading personal stories that we did not usually talk about. Then, there was also the lesbian who was epileptic and had a seizure in front of a group of us. My point is that I am sure that there were all kinds of lesbians who had impairments that were not usually apparent and which, like me and others I knew about, they did not talk about.

This is not intended to blame those who don't remember seeing any disabled lesbians for their lack of awareness, and it is not to blame those of us who did not speak up about our impairments. All of us were doing nothing more than conforming to and reinforcing the cultural myths about disability with which we were familiar. By not noticing or denying the presence of disabled lesbians, we were doing what women in our culture are supposed to do (deny the existence of bodily "imperfections").

We did not challenge the theoretical separation of mind and body, and we did not challenge the belief that disability must always be immediately visible. That we were unable to break out and challenge cultural myths about disability is a testament to the strength of those myths. Ultimately, this points to one more area where feminists need to do a lot of work.

Originally published in CWS/cf's *issue on "Women and Disability," 13 (4) (1993): 11–13. Reprinted with permission.*

[1]Where the essay refers to "our culture," this should be read as shorthand for the dominant culture of late twentieth-century North America.

REFERENCES

Abberley, Paul. "The Concept of Oppression and the Development of a Social Theory of Disability." *Disability, Handicap & Society* 2 (1): 5-19.

McNay, Lois. "The Foucauldian Body and the Exclusion of Experience." *Hypatia* 6 (3): 125-39.

Posner, Judith. "Old and Female: The Double Whammy." *Aging in Canada.* Ed. Victor W. Marshall. Toronto: Fitzhenry & Whiteside Limited, 1980. 80-87.

Prentice, Alison. *The School Promoters.* Toronto: McClelland and Stewart, 1977.

Ross, Becki. "The House That Jill Built: Lesbian Feminist Organizing in Toronto, 1976-1980." *Feminist Review* 35 (Summer 1990): 75-91.

Stone, Sharon Dale. "Notes Toward a Unified Diversity." *The More We Get Together: Women and Disability.* Eds. Stewart Houston, Beth Percival and Elizabeth R. Epperly. Charlottetown: gynergy books, 1992. 21-28.

Wendell, Susan. "Toward a Feminist Theory of Disability." *Hypatia* 4 (2): 104-124.

LAURA HOCKMAN

A LONGER JOURNEY OF REFLEXIVITY
Becoming a Domesticated Academic

COMPLETING MY MASTER'S IN Arts (Interdisciplinary Studies) was a lifetime goal I never thought possible. My research, "A Longer Journey: An Exploration of Individuals' Experiences with Employment Programs in Vernon, B.C.," was designed to explore one question: how do people with disabilities experience their employment journey in the current political context that emphasizes results-based employment programs? When I began to review the literature for my thesis, I quickly realized the daunting task I had undertaken to explore employment and people with a variety of disabilities. However, I underestimated the personal understanding I would gain on the academic journey of my research. The purpose of this article is to demonstrate how my experiences in education shaped aspects of my identity, and ultimately, impacted how I position myself in my thesis research. I will first share key moments in school that shaped my view of education. This will provide a foundation to explain why I chose the three paradigms used in my "A Longer Journey" research. I will then outline two invisible influences in my practice as a social worker and as a researcher. The article will conclude with a discussion of the multiple intersections of my identity as an Aboriginal woman with disabilities. Throughout the article I will also acknowledge the many women who I admire and who have shaped my life.

IMPOSTER COMPLEX

In my experience throughout elementary school, I was singled out by teachers, isolated in learning assistance and listened to school counsellors asking me "to apply myself more." This resulted in me constantly feeling that I was not smart enough to keep up and my thought process was misunderstood. One moment in particular shaped my view of education. Being one of two Aboriginal children in my grade three class helped to single me out. One day our class was told everybody would be checked for lice. Of all the kids in the class, another Aboriginal boy and I were kept the longest in the office to check for lice. I remember sitting in the office and desperately trying to think of an excuse to tell my friends about why I was kept longer. This experience was made more humiliating because neither of us had lice. What this experience taught me was to try to blend in with other kids and to not draw attention to myself. I was a low to average student academically, but a model student behaviourally who knew how to keep the attention away from myself.

By high school, I had mastered the art of blending in, making high school more positive for me, socially and academically. I never questioned the material I was taught or protested about deadlines etc. throughout my schooling. This ensured I blended in with others. The positive response I got from high school teachers and counsellors encouraged me to pursue post-secondary education. Completing my Bachelor of Social Work degree in 1999, I am still very passionate about being a social worker, working with marginalized groups and advocating for social justice. As I reflect on my practice, social work seems to be a perfect fit as a career option, but during my time in the social work program I was constantly full of doubt. The focus of the curriculum toward child welfare, aging, clinical practice with individuals, families, and groups brought up those feelings of inadequacy, the need to blend in and being misunderstood front and centre. While I never questioned any of the material presented in the program, I always felt like something was missing from the interaction between client and social worker. I could never picture myself being able to "pull off" the role of a social worker in a clinical or child welfare setting, making me feel like an "imposter." My "imposter complex" was at its peak once I became the Executive Director of Independent Living Vernon (formerly Vernon Disability Resource Centre) in 2001.

Learning there was a name for the feeling I had all my life was very empowering. I met an amazing woman, successful in her profession, incredibly compassionate and enthusiastic about the non-profit sector, who stunned me when she described having an "imposter complex" as well. The best description of the imposter complex I have come across was Catherine Porter's column in the *Toronto Star* on January 16, 2010:

> The imposter complex. It's a familiar anxiety for women in the police force, law firms, Bay Street—any place that has for years been the domain of our brothers, fathers and husbands, but not us. We quietly suspect we don't have what it takes and that we've scammed our way in like that Virginia couple crashing Obama's first state dinner. We expect to be exposed as frauds at any moment, tarred, feathered and frogmarched to the gallows of public opinion.

This description highlights the constant worry caused by the imposter complex, which adds stress and fatigue to women's careers. I know for myself, this complex did not start once my physical and emotional disabilities worsened; therefore it is important to note this complex is not just relevant to women with disabilities or Aboriginal women. My imposter complex continues as I write this article, but to a more manageable degree for two reasons. First, I accept my disabilities. I acknowledged the severity of my depression and anxiety and the need to use medication to help manage these disabilities. If I was a diabetic, there would be no stigma attached to needing insulin, so I take the same attitude to my anti-depressants and anti-anxiety medications. With my physical chronic pain worsening, I needed to reach out to my doctor for support and answers, which were provided without hesitation.

The second and most important reason for my imposter complex being reduced happened in the first course of my Master's degree in May 2006. My first course was part of an inaugural Indigenous Summer Institute. The Aboriginal instructor summed up my educational experience in the first ten minutes of the session. She affirmed the influence of my upbringing and my Aboriginal heritage on my attitude, values, and ethics. She confirmed that even though I did not grow up on the reservation, the influence of my culture and use of "rez English" from the maternal side of my family is strong. She suspected many of the Aboriginal students, who grew up off reserve, would have been in learning assistance or had been screened for Fetal Alcohol Syndrome (now referred to as Fetal Alcohol Spectrum Disorder). I sat in stunned silence as she described my experience from elementary to post-secondary education, despite this being the first time we had met each other.

In the months that followed, with each new course in my Master's program, my whole conception of myself changed, personally and professionally. I had always thought I wanted to do a Master's of Social Work, but could not find a program without a clinical focus that would allow me to explore diversity areas, such as Aboriginal culture and critical disability studies. This is why I will always be forever grateful to my Master's supervisor, Dr. Rachelle Hole, Ph.D., Assistant Professor at University of British Columbia Okanagan and Co-director for the Centre for Citizenship and Inclusion at the University of British Columbia Vancouver, who encouraged me to do a Master in Arts (Interdisciplinary Studies).

Interdisciplinary Studies was the answer I had been looking for to examine the areas I was interested in and gain research skills, which would add more marketable skills to my curriculum vitae. However, I never anticipated the insight I would gain about myself by learning the skill of reflexivity. Reflexivity is defined by Dorothy Horsburgh as the acknowledgement by the researcher that his/her own actions and decisions will inevitably impact upon the meaning and the context of the experience under investigation. Reflexivity is not a point in time event; reflexivity is a process that occurs throughout the research.

Being a social worker, self-reflection after an event was not a new concept. However, understanding reflexivity as a process throughout research was a new way of practice. The journal I kept during my graduate program was originally meant as a place to express issues as they arose during the research process. Issues included ethical considerations, difficulties and delays with data collection, and initial impressions of topics covered in the interviews and how they linked to the review of academic and government literature. The research journal was also the place to track any decisions and the justification for making such decisions in the research process. But this journal also became the place to express new insights about myself and how I viewed the world and the true impact of my research.

PARADIGMS

A paradigm can be described in plain language as a worldview. Discovering paradigms that fit my view of the world and the research question of "A Longer Journey" was an empowering feeling; it was the first time I had felt understood in an academic setting. The worldview of "A Longer Journey" research was informed by three paradigms: Independent Living, pragmatism, and an emancipatory paradigm.

The Independent Living paradigm emerged out of the Independent Living movement of people with disabilities which is founded on the right of people with disabilities to live with dignity, to participate in all aspects of their lives, and to control and make decisions about their own lives (Shannon). As I am the Executive Director of Independent Living Vernon, which adheres to and promotes the Independent Living Philosophy (IL), IL was the primary paradigm that guided my research.

The Independent Living paradigm differs significantly from its rehabilitation counterpart in defining outcomes. While self-care, mobility and employment are stressed in the rehabilitation model, Independent Living stresses a much larger constellation of outcomes, including the importance of living arrangements, intimate relationships, consumer knowledge and assertiveness, and outdoor and out of home activities (Gadacz). The IL paradigm represents the emergence of a new value system and an entirely new lifestyle for people with various disabilities.

Complementing the IL paradigm, a pragmatist paradigm also informs my methodology (Rocco, Bliss, Gallegher and Perez-Prado). Pragmatism fits with an IL approach for two reasons. Firstly, pragmatic principles emphasize using whatever paradigm or methodological approach works for the particular research question under study (Rocco et al.). This concept of using "whatever works" addresses one main concern of researchers conducting disability research—the issue of full participation and accessibility (e.g. the option to conduct interviews in a setting of the participant's choice). In any research project that involves people with disabilities, ensuring full participation is crucial. This includes addressing needs such as plain language, physical access for people who use wheelchairs or other mobility devices, and assistive technology needs. Secondly, the pragmatist paradigm emphasizes consideration of the practical consequences of ideas (Johnson and Onwuegbuzie). Thus, I was attracted to this paradigm for the possibilities it could offer for advancing the rights of people with disabilities and their inclusion in society.

In his article, "Changing the Social Relations of Research Production?," Mike Oliver called for the development of a new research paradigm: the emancipatory paradigm. This paradigm is also congruent with the IL and pragmatist paradigms. As the name suggests, it "is about the facilitating of a politics of the possible by confronting social oppression at whatever level it occurs" (110). Emancipatory research requires the transformation of the material and social relations of research production. This means people with disabilities should have control of the research process, including the funding and the research agenda (Barnes 2001). This emphasis on control is in alignment with the IL paradigm and its emphasis on control by people with disabilities. For research to be truly emancipatory, the entire research process must be accessible to people with disabilities, and there must be a workable "dialogue" established between the research community and people with disabilities to facilitate the empowerment of people with disabilities (Barnes 1992). Once a dialogue is established and working relationships built, in addition to producing new knowledge, research can "actively seek change rather than hoping that the right people read the work and act upon it" (Kitchin 44).

While the entire process of "A Longer Journey" research was not truly emancipatory as outlined by Oliver, I initiated my research because of the questions and frustrations expressed by people I had met with who had a variety of disabilities. Further, the research question and design focused on the experience of people with a variety of disabilities. Lastly, as a researcher who identifies as a person with a disability, I brought an intimate knowledge of disability, the need for accommodation and disability supports, and the considerations needed to ensure accessibility.

DELICIOUSLY SUBVERSIVE

These paradigms were not the only influences on my "A Longer Journey" research. Now I will share the influences in my research which were "deliciously subversive," to borrow from Catherine Frazee (a writer, educator, and researcher whose work focuses on the rights and well-being of persons with disabilities). This phrase resonated loudly with me when I heard Frazee use it in the 2006 documentary *Shameless: The Art of Disability.*

Earlier in the article, I had shared how I never questioned any material taught to me. I learned what I needed to make it successfully through school. This learned coping mechanism continued during my Master's program, but only to a minimal degree. A Master's degree allowed me to explore areas about which I was very passionate. I had a supportive academic supervisor who encouraged me to take risks; thus, I did not feel the need to blend into the crowd.

Two additional influences on my research are Enowkin and post-modernism. Enowkin is a conflict resolution approach developed by the Okanagan people. I was introduced to this approach in the beginning of my Master's program. This approach, in action, means, "I challenge you to give me the opposite perspective to mine. In that way I will understand how I need to change my thinking to accommodate your concerns and problems" (Jensen). What really attracted me to Enowkin was the emphasis on the minority voice. The minority voice is the most important because it is most likely to demonstrate what is going wrong, what is not being looked after, or what is not being done (Stone and Barlow).

This has particular relevance to my social work practice, to my role as a researcher, and to myself as a person with disabilities. Often in society the voice or experience of people with disabilities is discounted or viewed as an insignificant concern. Even within the disability community, certain groups of people with specific disabilities are emphasized versus others (Shannon). Diane Driedger and Michelle Owen highlight how people with chronic illnesses have been encouraged to not talk about the changing nature of their bodies within the disability community (2).

I did not consider post-modernism a fit for me until I read Fiona Williams' "Post-modernism, Feminism and Question of Difference" in Nigel Parton's book *Social Theory, Social Change, and Social Work.* According to Williams, post-modernism provided a major challenge to the universalism of social and political theories by pointing out that there are a "myriad of different subjectivities and different realities" (63). Elaine Power clarifies further that the "pursuit of 'the truth' has been replaced by the search to understand multiple, localized, contextual truths" (859). For me, learning about post-modernism was the first time that my and my family's traditions and values were not discarded. I did not have to feel guilty about using other ways to develop relationships with people in my social work practice. Post-modernism allowed me to justify my practice based on the merit of traditional ways of knowing versus clinical skills learned in the social work field.

The documented academic paradigms were more specific to "A Longer Journey" research, whereas the subversive ones are always in my practice, research, and personal roles. To deepen the illustration of my paradigmatic position, I will share my own "situated knowledge" of being a woman, Aboriginal, and having disabilities (Haraway).

SITUATED KNOWLEDGE

The multiple intersections of being an Aboriginal woman with disabilities has been described as triple jeopardy or multiple jeopardy (Demas). For me, this description does not fit. First, it oversimplifies the intersection of my multiple identities and, second, these terms assume oppression is experienced due to all of my identities.

In a literature review, Deborah Stienstra highlights the work of Maria Barile, who suggests those in "multiple minority groups" experience more unequal treatment than those in single minority groups. Stienstra emphasizes that being from a multiple minority group challenges our theoretical understanding of how to work collectively for change. Even with membership in five or more "groups" the individual's needs are not necessarily met because the groups are designed to address a single identity or minority status.

It is critical not to view any aspect of identity through only one lens. For example, the social model of disability focuses on the barriers in society that prevent people with disabilities from participating fully. This focus on the social construction of disability and related barriers emphasizes only one aspect of a person's experience: disability. Identity as a person with a disability may not always be the key defining characteristic of the person; the way they define themselves depends on place, time and context (Bransfield 401). This emphasis on one aspect of a person's identity is not unique to the disability movement.

The fundamental problem is that each oppressed group focuses on a single system of oppression, believing it to be the primary cause of discrimination (Vernon). It is not possible to "simply prioritize one aspect of our oppression to the exclusion of others" (Begum 61).

The concept of multiple oppression has been used to illustrate the complexity of issues surrounding people with disabilities (Vernon). However, it can be misleading because it implies that aspects of identity and different dimensions of inequality can be separated "as if they can be compartmentalized in everyday experience and then added together in an overall balance sheet" (Barnes and Mercer 61). The idea of multiple oppression has been referred to as interlocking inequalities (Dish), interlocking oppressions (Razack), and overlapping oppressions (Wendell). Ayesha Vernon claims that the issue of multiple oppression is treated as though it is an issue which concerns only a minority of people with disabilities. The majority of people with disabilities consists of cultural groups (African, Aboriginal etc.), women, lesbian, gay, bi-sexual, trans-gendered, older people, and those from the working class, all of whom experience the negative effects of being rendered a multiple "other." Leonard Davis emphasizes that "the solution to the problem of identity is not the inclusion of disability to the roster of favoured identities" (537), because the list of identities will only grow larger.

While I am familiar with subtle and explicit forms of discrimination and oppression as an Aboriginal woman growing up off reserve in an urban setting, it was not until college that I realized the discrimination and oppression experienced by women and by people with disabilities. In my immediate and extended family, there were always many people of all ages with various disabilities. These family members had various roles or duties to fulfill, and many times I was able to assist them with personal care and assistance. They were not isolated or left without a purpose. Once in college, I was shocked to learn how people with disabilities were treated and that their contributions were not valued by society.

As my disabilities began to worsen, from repeated sports injury, overworking myself despite severe fatigue, physical pain, and stress, I struggled with the attitudes from others about disability. But I found acceptance and understanding from my family and within the Independent Living Movement.

Being from a matriarchal clan system, I always felt very empowered as an Aboriginal woman. Once in college, I was unprepared for the attitudes of young women about feeling oppressed and discriminated against because they were women. They talked about being feminists. Women close to me in age would comment about how "domesticated" I was, or how I reminded them of "Suzy home-maker" because I did the housekeeping, cooking, baking, gardening, crafts, preserving, and made lunches for my partner. Some even went so far as to imply that my partner was controlling me by making me do these chores. These activities and skills are not chores. Being able to care for family and friends and to provide good hospitality to guests is an enormous responsibility and a way of showing respect to others. Needless to say, this wasn't a great first impression of feminism, but that is another story. Within my family, hospitality to family, friends, and guests is a way of life and a skill learned early to show respect and to ensure people felt welcome and comfortable. Viewing the world through this lens is primarily why I felt like something was missing when learning about clinical social work, where there was a lot of focus on defence mechanisms, how to avoid transference, or maintaining calm and open body language. This was the complete opposite of how I was brought up.

When I am with people, my primary focus is to ensure that they are comfortable and feel welcome. This will then allow them to share their feelings, stories, and current joys or difficulties. Therefore, I ask if they need something to drink or a snack, is the temperature too warm or too cool, or do they need to use the washroom? I always ensure the person knows they can take their time, stretch or move around as they need to in order to relieve pain or stiffness. If needed, we can re-schedule another appointment if they get too overwhelmed. I use this approach in my social work practice and as an executive director I encourage a welcoming atmosphere for staff, volunteers, and visitors of Independent Living Vernon. This has earned IL Vernon the reputation of the "loudest office in the building." I see this as a compliment; it means people feel welcome and able to express themselves. My hospitality role model is Traci Walters, former National Director of Independent Living Canada. She built a feeling of family within the Independent Living Movement in Canada, and in my opinion that is what separates Independent Living from all disability organizations.

To conclude, writing this article has provided me with the closure I needed after "A Longer Journey," which was filled with hesitation, tears, pride, and surprise. This is the first time I have shared parts of this story. The intellectual, emotional, and physical journey of reflection has brought me to a new identity, the domesticated academic, whose favourite colour is red.

Many thanks to Diane Driedger for the opportunity and the encouragement to share this story.

REFERENCES

Barnes, C. "Qualitative Research: Valuable or Irrelevant?" *Disability, Handicap & Society* 7.2 (1992): 115-124.

Barnes, C. "Emancipatory Disability Research: Project or Process?" Paper presented for public lecture at City Chambers, Glasgow. 24 October 2001.

Barnes, C. and G. Mercer. *Disability*. London: Polity Press, 2003.

Begum, N. "Mirror Mirror on the Wall" (1994). *Disability*. Ed. C. Barnes and G. Mercer. London: Polity Press, 2003.

Bransfield, F. "The Disability Movement: A Movement of Disabled People – A Response to Paul S. Duckett." *Disability & Society* 14.3 (1999): 399-403.

Davis, L. J. "Identity Politics, Disability, and Culture." *Handbook of Disability Studies*. Ed. G. L. Albrecht, K. D. Seelman and M. Bury. Thousand Oaks, CA: Sage Publications, 2001. 535-545.

Demas, D. "Triple Jeopardy: Native Women with Disabilities." *Canadian Woman Studies/les cahiers de la femme* 14.3 (1993): 53-55.

Dish, E., ed. *Reconstructing Gender: A Multicultural Anthology*. 3rd Ed. Boston: McGraw Hill, 2003.

Driedger, D. and M. Owen, eds. *Dissonant Disabilities: Women With Chronic Illnesses Explore Their Lives*. Toronto: Canadian Scholars' Press Inc./ Women's Press, 2008.

Gadacz, R. *Re-Thinking Dis-Ability: New Structures, New Relationships*. Edmonton: University of Alberta Press, 1994.

Haraway, D. "Situated Knowledges: The Science Question in Feminism and the Privilege of Partial Perspective." *Feminist Studies* 14 (1988): 575-599.

Horsburgh, D. "Evaluation of Qualitative Research." *Journal of Clinical Nursing* 12 (2003): 307-312.

Jensen, D. *Conversations About Nature, Culture, and Eros: Jeanette Armstrong.* San Francisco: Sierra Club Books, 1995.

Johnson, R. B. and A. J. Onwuegbuzie. "Mixed Methods Research: A Research Paradigm Whose Time Has Come." *Educational Researcher* 33.7 (2004): 14-26.

Kitchin, R. "The Researched Opinions on Research: Disabled People and Disability Research." *Disability and Society* 15.1 (2000): 25-47.

Oliver, M. "Changing the Social Relations of Research Paradigm?" *Disability, Handicap & Society* 7.2 (1992): 101-114.

Oliver, M. and C. Barnes. "All We Are Saying is Give Disabled Researchers a Chance." *Disability & Society* 12.5 (1997): 811-813.

Porter, Catherine. "Porter: Six women ready to 'take that power'." *Toronto Star* 16 January 2010. Online: <http://www.thestar.com/news/canada/article/751568--porter-six-women-ready-to-take-that-power>.

Power, E. "Toward Understanding in Postmodern Interview Analysis: Interpreting the Contradictory Remarks of a Research Participant." *Qualitative Health Research* 14.6 (2004): 858-865.

Razack, S. *Looking White People in the Eye.* Toronto: University of Toronto Press, 1998.

Rocco, T. S., L. A. Bliss, S. Gallagher and A. Perez-Prado. "Taking the Next Step: Mixed Methods Research in Organizational Systems." *Information Technology, Learning & Performance Journal* 21.1 (2003): 19-29.

Shameless: The Art of Disability. Screenwriter and Dir. Bonnie Sherr Klein. Producer. Tracey Friesen. DVD. National Film Board of Canada, 2006.

Shannon, D. *Six Degrees of Dignity: Disability in an Age of Freedom.* Ottawa: Creative Bound International Inc., 2007.

Stienstra, Deborah. "The Intersection of Disability and Race/Ethnicity/Official Language/Religion." Paper presented at the "Intersections of Diversity" Seminar, Canadian Centre on Disability Studies, University of Winnipeg, 8 March 2002. Online: <http://canada.metropolis.net/events/diversity/Disability_stienstra_e.pdf>. Accessed June 1, 2010.

Stone, M. and Z. Barlow. *Enowkin: Decision-Making as if Sustainability Mattered: Ecological Literacy.* San Francisco: Sierra Club, 2005.

Vernon, A. "Multiple Oppression and the Disabled People's Movement." *The Disability Reader: Social Science Perspective.* Ed. Tom Shakespeare. London: Cassell, 1998. 201-210.

Wendell, S. *The Rejected Body: Feminist Philosophical Reflections on Disability.* New York: Routledge, 1996.

Williams, F. "Post-modernism, Feminism and Question of Difference." *Social Theory, Social Change, and Social Work.* Ed. N. Parton. New York: Routledge, 1996. 61-76.

DIANE DRIEDGER

"Self-Portrait with Bandaged Breast (After Van Gogh's Self-Portrait with Bandaged Ear)"

"Self-Portrait with Bandaged Breast (After Van Gogh's Self-Portrait with Bandaged Ear)," 2010, watercolour, 18.25" x 21.5".

DIANE DRIEDGER

PROLIFERATION

there is an arms build up
I open the cabinet every morning
and there are more pills
pills and pills
spill
onto my hands
pop in my mouth
it's quite a thrill
to take so many pills
so cancer will not kill

DIANE DRIEDGER

MEDICATION REACTION

trembling
chattering
twitching
anti-nausea
medication
24 hours
to pass through

stop taking that
says the pharmacist
my words
            follow
                    my chat
tering
jaw
pacing floor
of bedroom

never knew 24 hours
could pass
without doing anything
thinking anything
but survival

soul speaking
all
one moment

DIANE DRIEDGER

RADIATION

long crucifixion
31 days
arm in the air
the buzzing machine
me in the vault
door closed
steel treatment table
my jaws steel

elevator panel reads zero floor
radiation room
had no merit
had a naught
as a number

this is not
fun
not what I do everyday

this is not
how I want to spend time

LIVING ON THE EDGES

CHARLOTTE CARON AND GAIL Christy are members of the Barbwire Collective, a group of nine women who, over the past three years, have been writing about living with disabilities and chronic illnesses and the spiritual resources that help us and that emerge out of our experiences. Gail has lived with mobility impairment since birth and reflects on how faith has been a sustaining dimension of her life. Charlotte lives with chronic illness. She reflects on how theologies of the Christian church have influenced her life. Both are members of Christian churches and Charlotte is also active in feminist spirituality groups. The article is written in two voices to show our different experiences and perspectives.

SOME EFFECTS OF DISABILITY/CHRONIC ILLNESS ON HOW WE THINK ABOUT/ EXPERIENCE SPIRITUALITY

Gail: My disability dates from the time of my birth so my experience of the world was never typical. I have the gift of being sensitive to my environment. This meant that from a young age, I experienced both the goodness and unkindness of people. When I think of unkindness, I recall laughter and pointing fingers and snowballs thrown at me when I could not move out of their path. But this same awareness that caused me to notice derisive laughter also enabled me to remember and treasure the acts of kindness that have been part of my journey. I knew, deep within me (even at the age of six) that God was ministering to me through people.

Charlotte: Unkindness and the fact that people do not always think about the consequences of their words and actions angers me. But being part of a liberal Christian church has meant that I learned from a young age to be nice rather than to be angry. Most white, middle-class North American women are taught to be passive instead of angry. The risks are very high for women with chronic illnesses and disabilities to express their anger, especially those dependent on attendants, care givers, families, and friends. Isolation is a constant possibility. Thus anger is often repressed, or turned in on oneself. Anger can, however, be the motivator to get creative power moving toward changes so that we all have access to the resources we need to participate freely and fully in the community.

Gail: Participation in community is really important to me. I think this was due to my disability and to the community that surrounded me. As a youngster, beginning at the age of five, I spent considerable time in hospital and I attended a special school. These are rarely regarded as positive events. But I knew and experienced God's love through the staff of these institutions. The other kids were wonderful friends and we helped each other manage our problems. For example, the boy who was blind chummed with the child who was deaf and the girl in the wheelchair was often seen with a girl who was ambulatory but whose speech was impaired. We were a grand community full of life and joy!

Charlotte: Living with chronic illness has pushed me to a new understanding of diversity. The range of disabilities that people experience and the kinds of impairments created by living with chronic illnesses mean that we have to work together if we are all going to have our rightful place in the world.

Disability is a socially constructed phenomenon. It is constructed to create hierarchies—to keep a powerful few in control of the resources that are needed by others for basic survival and for a full and free life. It is based on keeping some people invisible and powerless. Thus those desiring power seek homogeneity—they seek to be as much like those in power as possible.

Women with chronic illnesses and disabilities cannot succeed in such a system. The norm has to be diversity and acceptance of difference for us to belong. I believe that what makes communities spiritual is the capacity to integrate diverse realities, to connect people to each other, and to seek justice and safety for those who hold the least power in society.

For diversity to be a reality, each person must be able to communicate her/his reality. People have been taught that respect is not asking about disabilities. This habit of ignoring disabilities denies how hard our lives are and inhibits dialogue about how these attitudes and practices affect us. It is especially important for those of us who live with the uncertainties and unpredictability of chronic illness to be able to make some choices. To do that we need voice—we need to be able to speak about our lives as they really are, the struggles and frustrations of living in a society that disables us, and the wisdom we gain from viewing the world through this particular lens.

Gail: I used to think the process of being spiritual was closed to me because I experienced too much physical pain. This pain means I am not able to sit for long lengths of time in contemplation nor can I concentrate for too long because the discomfort of my body impinges on my concentration. Now I know that my encounters with God do not have to be lengthy to be meaningful.

I think that the emphasis on the "other worldliness" of spirituality has done a disservice to those who live with disability and chronic illness. Pain is often a major reality of our lives. Yet I was once advised to "surrender all pain to the universe."

This may be a wonderful idea but for people living with chronic illness or disability, it denies the reality of our world and sends messages that pain is not really all *that* terrible—just a momentary thing. For many of us, it is not like that. Rather, pain is like a heart-beat, always there. The plus side of living with this pain is that my endurance skills have been superbly honed.

Charlotte: Part of our spiritual strength is learning from our pain. All of us know pain—some physical and mental pain, some the pain of loss, some the pain of rejection, humiliation, and discrimination, some the pain of despair. Ways to live with pain are spiritual gifts much needed by our world. Spirituality is one of the ways of seeking hope and courage in the midst of pain and despair.

Certain strains of Christian theology have suggested that God gives pain and suffering to provide meaning and that we simply must search for that meaning. Some New Age philosophies stress that we choose our illnesses and disabilities because we have something to work out in this life. Both of these formulas blame the victim. Susan Wendell is much more helpful when she states, having experienced a crisis of meaning in my body, I can no longer assume that even powerful bodily experiences are psychologically or spiritually meaningful.... With chronic pain, I must remind myself over and over again that pain is meaningless. (120)

I find it constructive to believe that there is no inherent meaning in suffering, chronic pain, chronic illness, or conditions of the body that are disabling. They simply exist as part of the diversity of creation. Not everything has meaning.

We need endurance as a spiritual resource. Eleanor Haney says that endurance shows that the human spirit is tough. It enables people to lead complex lives in incredibly difficult conditions. It is her contention that theological and ethical literature often ignores endurance focusing on what we should do in situations rather than on the question "how much longer can I hold on doing what I have to do?" She suggests that hanging on shows "a self exercising responsibility, a self of often tremendous moral courage" (15). Endurance is a spiritual and moral resource for the boring, exhausting and uncertain times.

Gail: The concept of "dwelling" is important to me. Maria Harris in her book, *Dance of the Spirit,* suggests that there are four places where women can dwell at different times in their lives: desert, garden, city, and home. I have moved among these dwelling places of spirituality and my disability influences these places. It can influence the length of my stay, and the depth of my feelings. Harris describes the desert as a "place of sorrow, emptiness, and ending" (93). I know these feelings well because the world has isolated me in my difference. I sorrow a lot because sometimes to live with disability is "cruel and unusual punishment" in a world where movement for others is easy and effortless. The desert is not an easy place to be but my disability had led me to know it well. Sometimes it feels like a place of endings and no beginnings.

Harris describes the dwelling place of the city as symbolic of reaching out to others. Relationship is its important focus. The assumption is that we actively do the reaching out, that we initiate and sustain relationships. As someone living with a disability, I have come to welcome initiatives, and first learn to "be" in relationship, rather than always to "do." My disability does not exclude me from the spirituality of the city dwelling. I just have to acknowledge my value as someone through whom others can also know their dwelling in the city. My being open to people who want to assist me answers a need for both of us. Again we reflect on the benefits of mutuality—something that living with a disability teaches well.

My garden times grow out of my ability to be nurtured by my physical environment, even though that environment may seem pretty limited, for example, to the chair I am sitting in. When I was encased in total body casts, I honed these garden time skills. From my bed, I learned to appreciate skies of different hues and tree tops whose dress changed with the seasons. This legacy serves me well now. I cannot do lengthy walks but I can go in my imagination, or I can focus on something close to where I sit—a leaf or a scurrying ant. Anything in creation reminds me of God. Living with a disability has made me aware of the sacred in the midst of life. I think, too, because I have had to be sedentary, I am more able simply to be. I am content to dwell where I am.

HOW HAS SPIRITUALITY AFFECTED HOW WE THINK ABOUT/ EXPERIENCE DISABILITY/CHRONIC ILLNESS

Gail: When I first thought about this question, I became quite annoyed that I have a mobility impairment. The practice of spirituality had always been associated, in my mind, with gentle, effortless, movement. I cannot move that way. Thus I thought that I was closed off from the "normal" expressions of spirituality. I once left a women's spirituality group because I could not tolerate the isolation I felt when they moved about in graceful dancing circles. However, reading and reflection have taught me that there is much more to spirituality than moving your feet and raising your arms. You actually can be spiritual while sitting still.

The fact that one can experience God though the gift of our senses has made me grateful to God for the care that is lavished upon us. I may have a disability, but that does not limit my access to God, does not limit my spirituality. My deep awareness of God, through the agency of other people, nature, and hard learnings that have enriched my soul, has led me to regard my disability (at least at times) with thanksgiving. I have learned deep truths by witnessing both the goodness and unkindness of people. I have learned lessons about acceptance and rejection. And I have learned that no matter what, I am a beloved child of God.

Charlotte: Christianity asserts all people are equal and are made in the image of God. But I think it is hard for women with chronic illnesses to keep strong self-esteem, to know we are loved and loveable. Frequently we have experienced situations in which we are demeaned and humiliated. If our needs vary from day to day, we are seen as unreliable. If our disabilities or illnesses are not clearly visible, we are seen as imposters.

Yet "all people" includes those with disabilities and chronic illnesses. Whatever God/dess is like, we are a part of that. To live in the image of God/dess means self-respect, acceptance, and using our unique gifts creatively and courageously in this world.

Many people suggest God is a source of comfort in rough times. I personally have not often found the comfort of God. More often I have known the presence of God when I needed the courage to do/ speak for right when injustice and discrimination were present. When we have a disability or chronic illness, we have the mixed advantage of living on the edges—never quite fitting, but also not caught into the contradictions of privilege of the powerful. The edges do not always provide us with the safety we need, nor are our survival needs always well met. Yet from the edges we can name injustice and stand in solidarity with others who do not have privilege and power in society. From the edges we can question everything and express the doubts and outrage embodied in our faith. We can speak out for the rights of those who are oppressed and disadvantaged by society, knowing that the presence of God is in the midst of people's suffering and that God's bias is for the oppressed. All need to participate if the community is to be whole.

THE SPIRITUAL FOR US

As women with disabilities and chronic illnesses, we need to tell our stories honestly, to be accompanied by people who love us, to dwell in just and compassionate communities of mutuality where we can participate fully and freely, where endurance is valued, and where we offer wisdom on how to live with suffering and pain. Our spiritual lives are strong when we believe ourselves to be made in the Divine image, when we see ourselves mirrored in the Holy, and accept ourselves as loved unconditionally by that Creative Spirit.

Originally published in CWS/cf's *issue on "Female Spirituality," 17 (1) (Winter 1997): 86–88. Reprinted with permission.*

REFERENCES

Haney, Eleanor H. *Vision and Struggle: Meditations on Feminist Spirituality and Politics.* Portland, ME: Astarte Shell Press, 1989.

Harris, Maria. *Dance of the Spirit: The Seven Steps of Women's Spirituality.* New York: Bantam, 1991.

Wendell, Susan. "Feminism, Disability and Transcendence of the Body." *Canadian Woman Studies/les cahiers de la femme* 13.4 (Summer 1993): 116-22.

MARIE ANNHARTE BAKER

CRY NOT CRAZY LADY

1. MYSELF AS A PERSON I'D LIKE TO KNOW

I SLIP OFTEN ENOUGH into experimenting with a preferred genre—fragment writing. Personal journal writing reflects inner angst and has been a starting point for the dialogue with myself. I become both interlocutor and witness to the inner struggle to express myself. The memory of my deceased mother helped. As a spirit, my mother was a guardian. For most of my life though she had been only a missing statistic which no one cared to investigate. Now I am part of a larger sisterhood of women who have lost parents because of the residential schools. Understanding the neglect, abuse, and abandonment of our mothers because they were casualties of that system allows us to honour and respect them as survivors of a holocaust that has until now been denied, ignored, or forgotten by Canadians.

At the occasion of the Prime Minister's apology in 2008, to Canada's First Nations People for imposing the Canadian residential school system, I was in a room with others who called themselves survivors. A box of tissues was handed around but when it came to me, I just passed it on. I made the resolve that I was not going to cry because I decided to fight whatever atrocities were associated with the disappearance of my mother. It is genocide and I am witness to the countless human rights violations my mother's generation suffered during the 1930s and '40s. While I cannot totally idealize my mother because she is a disappeared woman, I can take on her fight for justice.

Part of getting to know myself was to perform an inquiry into a tortuous identity passed onto me by her absence. Her disappearance has haunted me since I was nine years old and last saw her. Yet, I do savour the memory of times when I was out in the bush with both my parents. I see my mother then as being happy. She was a true Bush Lady. Her alcoholism and subsequent probable murder was a mystery. As a child, I was waiting for her return. I searched for my mother in other people, especially as a young adult. Marriage to a violent and abusive husband was only another step in my journey through a historic trauma cycle. I was dominated in marriage and almost took up violence as a way to get back, get even, and get out of that painful existence. As I struggled to free myself from depression, I countered the returning suicidal thoughts by envisioning my son suffering the loss and shame of his mother. I did not want to bring that fate on him. I now take responsibility for his incurring vicarious violence and his experience of post-traumatic stress disorder. I have also faced the legacy of a disappeared mother without much hope or dignity.

2. I DON'T WANT TO THINK I AM THE ONLY PERSON DOING ALL THE TALKING

In becoming a writer, I opened myself up to ancestral voice that now informs any or all creative efforts and experience. Involvement with the street scene fine-tuned perceptions that inform my work. From this place, I first heard the voices of women singing to me. They were sitting on the riverbank passing a jug in a brown paper bag. I wrote down the chanting that I heard. It took the form of verse. I sang and chanted out loud what I heard. I knew they had taken pity on me. I first thought they saw me as one who would listen. I was not afraid because when they spoke to me in this inner vision, they asked me not to despair because they had horrific stories too. They encouraged me to not to feel sorry for myself because of what happened to them.

I began to compose a first volume of poetry just after I returned to live in Canada from the U.S. Prior journal writing courses helped to rebuild myself. After suffering a shame-based mentality, I eventually found a better sense of purpose and dignity in a prouder Anishinabekwe (Ojibway woman) self. While impossible to copy the generic First Nation woman role, at least I was truly grateful for a right to Indigenous heritage through my mother's line. I wanted to be a whole person yet I was put down for being a "half breed" or "mixed blood" person, too hybrid ndn and not enough of a pure one, by Natives and non-Natives, friends and relatives, organizations and institutions. That travail was dealt to me because of the *Indian Act*, because my mother lost her status when she married my father. Bill C-31 made me a member of the Little Saskatchewan First Nations. Since 1985, I am a status Indian. This legislation allowed me to have medical and dental benefits as well as educational assistance. I was less of a self-identified Native and now had legal recognition of heritage I have my mother to thank for her spirit of resistance. I remember my mother and others talking about running away from the residential school. I have talked to others about inheriting the anger and rage of our mothers. Her generation was silenced. I cannot help but consider a need to document and bear witness to the treatment of First Nations women which comes from what I see as the blood price paid for any of our cultural productions to have survived the onslaught of 500 years of domination and attempts to wipe out our spirituality, our land base, and our oral literature/language.

3. HOARDING: AN IDENTITY NOT WANTED

Several bouts of severe depression led me to admit I had a hoarding problem. Depressed after losing another dream job I sunk into a state that only might be termed hoarder horribilus. A decision to reform had me getting informed about the "clutter" condition. I had to tackle the identity blast of coping with being a "hoarder" as I sank to the bottom of a clutterer's secret closet self. Then the scary stories, "Cat Woman found with 68 cats" etc. flooded the brain pan. If it was not just animal hoarders that gripped one's fancy, it was disclosure of yet another incidence of "senior squalor." The term "hoarder" is a loaded expression. Ever notice the uncomfortable giggle response in others? It's probably damn scary sounding, but a lucky moment for those in denial who put on the false face of appearing mildly interested. The real chill factor is that the hoarder disorder (I like the sound of that) might be linked to OCD (Obsessive Compulsive Disorder). My PTSD (Post Traumatic Stress Disorder) had progressed.

What removes the stigma is when a person regularly communicates and connects with those who know what it means to live in clutter. Ah, the relief that is a peer group support! Who would ever admit to being into CHAOS? It's the "can't have anyone over syndrome." Obvious to any sometime visitor is realizing I am also called a "Pack Rat." It is a comment about the mounds of boxes, papers, and old clothes that fill my home. Unforgivable is the observation "you have so much stuff!" So the choice to be hermit-like results because most people are uncomfortable in hoarder surroundings. Again, a reality check must be made. *Who has room for visitors!*

Sometimes a co-venture out with a few other "ratties" to get more help on how to de-junk our lives is a beginning of the dehoard recovery cycle. The big cure is the organized life: once we begin downsizing there is room for more fun, creativity, and self-respect in our lives. Being ass-deep in clutter and wanting better housing, a person has to make the painful decision to abandon beloved crap! Ouch, it is going to hurt but with help there is support, especially when relapse happens. It is not an overnight activity. Even if someone else cleans up the mess, the hoarder might still go back to binge shopping. Is this why reality television shows make hoarding a spectator sport? Even an Oprah intervention might not stop it!

Meanwhile back at the rubble, junk or recent acquisitions accrue. It's hard to trust any advice when rooms almost automatically fill with accumulated Sally Ann throwaways. Arggghhhhh! I am used to getting nowhere but deeper into my extremely messy adobe hacienda. Once after I cleared up a dish drainer rack, the cat found it to be a great nesting place! Oooh, that was devious! The project to have a clean sink in the kitchen was puzzling enough. I was very accustomed to the weekly pile up called Mt. Dishmore. The cat conspiracy was just more sabotage besides my slippery moon walking steps.

Someday I will clear up the sty that is currently my residential nightmare. However, I have compounded a prevailing disinterest in housework easy enough to make me obsessive about dehoarding (a bit focused in other words). Someday my transformation into a "tosser" will come! Removing and sorting just one handful at a time may work. Then did I mention my short-term memory is shot? I even forget to take the pills that destroy it!

4. DISABILITY AND DIVERSITY: TAKES TWO TO TANGLE

More research is needed to find out what is the unique diversity of Aboriginal/Indigenous women with disabilities in Winnipeg. While this group shares a common legacy of marginalization and oppression with other groups in Canadian society, the literature continues to be dominated by an extremely limited range of issues, specifically matters touching on health and healing, violence and abuse and even the criminal justice system. Perhaps, residence in Winnipeg itself might prove to be a prime factor in the disregard and exclusion from services that Aboriginal/Indigenous women face. Many service providers insist they do not have barriers to access and even those managed by Aboriginal/Indigenous people may also discriminate on the basis of class, race, and age. Existing studies have not focused on the salience of the household and community as key sites of action. Yet, some disAbled women demonstrate an exceptional lifestyle of self-reliance or know ways to get their needs met within even the most dysfunctional families.

The purpose of fostering connections among disAbled Aboriginal/Indigenous women with others who are researchers, community members, and students would be an intended result of community representation. With few exceptions, services directed toward Aboriginal/Indigenous women have been described as dominated by a singular, negative orientation. A balanced approach to helping strategies is not often detailed because of the highly problem-focused approach that has pathologized and disempowered women's agency and realities. Aboriginal/Indigenous women are more than survivors of their complex realities; they are also capable of contributing to community-based research initiatives. Ensuring that academic research methodology respects language and cultural differences would permit any study to demonstrate more unique data gathering. How actual multiple disabilities interplay within the wide range of myriad challenges faced by disAbled Aboriginal/Indigenous women in a community as opposed to an institutional setting might detail survival strategies. Again, the possibility of strengthening the ability and opportunity for women to advocate for their collective needs is part of a continuing vision in the improvement of their healing and spiritual advancement. Government stances prefer to endorse and fund those who claim to be representative of all Aboriginal/Indigenous women yet do not monitor elite leaders so that the disAbled women are, in fact, representing themselves. They may be supported by caregivers but also need to voice their own issues about healthcare delivery.

In March 2001, *A Profile of Manitoba First Nations People With a Disability,* was prepared for the Assembly of Manitoba Chiefs by Brenda Elias and Doreen Demas (Advisor on Disability Issues). The recent study by Don Shackel, *Persons with Disabilities Living within First Nations Communities in Manitoba,* identifies the continued jurisdictional wrangling and offloading by levels of government. This denial of services to disabled First Nations peoples has been labelled as a significant human rights violation and a profound violation of human dignity. In his work with the Manitoba First Nations Education Resource Center and continued consultation with Doreen Demas, Don Shackel has advocated to eliminate exclusion for special needs students who do not receive services that are available to non-Aboriginal parents. First Nations children with disabilities are often forced to leave their communities to get help, and some of the children are placed in care. They don't have access to a continuum of care, so the relocation and the forced involvement with Child and Family Services result in wrangling over jurisdictional problems and funding responsibilities. Further, the lack of accesses to essential medical supports and services violates the rights of these children according to certain sections of the *Canadian Charter of Rights* and international human rights conventions, such as the Convention on the Rights of the Child. Children are unnecessarily kept in hospitals and other institutional environments so their physical and psychological integrity is severely affected. Physiotherapists or occupational therapists are seldom available to children living on reserves compared to hundreds of publicly-funded specialists working in other areas of Manitoba. The Assembly of Manitoba Chiefs are considering a suit against the Canadian government for failing to provide adequate health care to Native children.

With federal and provincial agencies and agendas, double talking and double dealing will compound to more than double trouble for disabled Aboriginal/Indigenous women. Health officials are trying to hammer out a solution to emerging crises for families, yet often Indigenous women are not invited to be present at the discussion table. Instead, they face the mismanagement of resources that happens when non-Native agents of the Aboriginal Service Industry, such as caregivers, health care professionals, lawyers, consultants, and anthropologists, are involved. Those who thrive on our segregated policy approach to

First Nations people generate tens of billions of dollars in funding by a manipulation of Native people.

5. VAGINA MONOCLE

How are we to dialogue about women and madness? Does it downsize into monologue mode when we share experiences with each other? Remember the book called *The Vagina Monologues*? It seemed a good idea at the time to substitute "monocle" for monologue. Picture it, eh? If and when it was asked "Look who's talking?", we might need to assume an objective stance by donning the monocle to examine ourselves from a plethora of perspectives. All argumentation must rest on the authority of the personal narrative. Before we may begin to converse, we have to counter the awkward obstacles to our own stories. The gender angle dangles before us much like the phallocentric pendulum of knowledge or philosophic bent of the European male. So when we peer through the "madness" monocle, we must surely spout the usual avoidance of clandestine commentary with exclamations such as "Oh, Dear" or even the shock response of "Poor Dear" as we arch our back to feign the formal distance in a polite discussion. *Time out for a spot of tea, dearie?* The right/rite of prompting our inner dialogue is to carry on the endless depictions of abuse—misdiagnoses that surround the "mad woman," "crazy bitch," or "sicko cunt." Maybe it's time to take off the glam tiara and replace the eye/spy glass with more mumbles. Slide off and throw down the over-elbow gloves! Rip off the gown! Beat the non-hairy chest! Time to vent volatile! Quite a maddening venture to take on!

In any appreciation of who is a mad woman and why, how, what did she do this time, the person who cares must confront the many locks or dreads on the Medusa head of modern mental health practices. Oops, excuse the inept designation of "modern" because what is out there is a tad pre-medieval. Not aged like a fine wine or cheese even! More cheesy whine? Perhaps. Now get the visual picture of a line up at the church police station where witches need to be branded with labels such as Depressed, Bi-Polar, Borderline and Etc. A good guess is that this ahistoric moment is happening in the present. Feminist writers have examined the various and particular women's "ailments" in the early 1900s such as neurasthenia, hysteria and anorexia nervosa. They have boldly asserted that madness was a way out of oppression for women. Gender-assigned roles in the family remained constant and restrictive in spite of the mass demographic changes in that time, i.e. urbanization and industrialization. Charlotte Perkins Gilman's prison environment was a woman's own room where she becomes disturbed by the décor. In "The Yellow Wallpaper," the unnamed heroine suffers from a malady called "melancholia." She fights the terror of social conformity as she witnesses a woman trapped behind the wallpaper. While Freud is credited with the onset of the "talking cure," his legacy of ordering disorders also cemented the concept that "hysteria" was exclusive to the female population. Phyllis Chesler's book *Women and Madness* documents the disparity of the treatment of women versus men in the mental health field, and she does confront the dogma. Her work as a feminist psychologist has helped many women understand the social construction of madness in which women who do not conform to societal standards of sanity are targeted. So this century begins with a solid link between women and madness defined by the practice of misogyny. The various mental disabilities and medications available today still spin on the same nervous and hysterical axis projected upon women since medieval times and before. Poor women and even uppity rich women might share a somewhat similar fate of misdiagnosis and mistreatment but slight similarities do not forge a sisterhood of sanity/insanity.

Having met Phyllis Chesler at a conference on mental health and women in Toronto in the early eighties, I was impressed with how accessible she was as an authority on women and madness. She invited me to join her for dinner and we began to chat about mutual interests. She was writing about the loss of parental rights for women that would drastically affect especially those women diagnosed with mental health conditions and I shared my experience as an advocate in the child welfare sixties scoop scandals that affected First Nations women in Canada (and which still happen). I had worked in Winnipeg and northwestern Ontario to prevent the apprehension of Native children and advocated for a service delivery system that would help Native parents prevent loss of custody or regain custody with adequate parenting support programs. To find an ally like Phyllis Chesler does prompt an inner dialogue for me because I had always wondered what happened to my own mother who was hospitalized and given shock treatment in the mid-forties. I had not considered that my mother might have been abused by the mental health system, as all I knew was that "it ran in the family." I knew that sexism and racism contributed to women and madness stereotypes which limited self-potential, later actualizing in the women's liberation trend. In 2002, the book *Women and Madness* had been in the bookstores for thirty years. In an interview upon that occasion, the author quipped, "men were still driving women crazy." That accusatory finger did switch directions as, at the time, it had mostly pointed to mothers as the source of all social evils and illnesses. Those were confusing times and recently the book has been called a "pseudo-medical exploration" because it is limited by a lack of deep historical research and a failure to take actual mental illness into account. I had been reluctant to accept the feminist analysis because of the lack of cross-cultural research. Bea Medicine, Lakota cultural anthropologist, however, has written about how First Nations women have suffered from the misunderstanding about how addictions play out in various urban and reservation/reserve communities. Her work does bridge the gap between the universal of "all women in the world" to "Indigenous women" in particular. I do find the obsession with goddesses to be a peculiar bias in the reconstruction of the history of women. The Medusa head image of writhing snakes does make me pale at the prospect of inquiry into any quagmire of guesses about women and madness. Will it prompt just more of a "crazy bitch" rant from me and others like me?

No! I want to conjure my own uniqueness so that when I look in a mirror I do not cringe.

6. EVEN WINNIE THE PIG DON'T LIKE ME

If I were to choose to be born, it wouldn't be in this city. My first fiction would be that I was born in another century and in a place of my own choosing. Dropped on moss. Wiped off. Fast delivery. I'd be up and on the trail again riding in the tikinagin *on my mother's back. She would have been making ready for me. I wouldn't be placed in a crib or any jail type of contraption. She'd put me in a moss bag and carry me around until I damn well chose to jump off her back. I had picked the spot, the exact spot to touch the earth. Maybe we discussed it while I was in the womb. I got frantic when the moment came to be. Now, mom. It is time, mom. Let me down, mom.*

The above excerpt is taken from a fragment written to record the last time I saw my mother. I chose the name Nitanis as this means "daughter" in Ojibway. Maybe it was less painful for me to write in third person. *She ran home from school but found her mother had been taken away by the police. She knew her mother was sick and needed her.*

I am not going to give up on her. She will come back. I know she is coming back. She's not always there waiting for me but I will wait for her. She usually comes back after awhile.

The vulnerable child voice is interspersed with the "little mother" tone that Nitanis must assume so she will be able to survive without her mother.

Death mother. Dirt mother. Always the talk of an Earth Mother. But nobody talks about what happened to her. She was treated like dirt. She went to residential school. Maybe that is what actually killed her spirit. She's just lying down somewhere in the Earth being a typical Earth Mother. Dirt in her eye sockets. Dead leaves covering what would be called a corpse if she was ever found. She had to be an Earth Mother now.

I include this last fragment of my writings to illustrate how deep the damage might be for me. I have been told by countless people both Indigenous and non-Indigenous that I have to get over it. I am encouraged to accept an apology from the government for taking my mother away and making her a political child prisoner. They will not compensate either her or me nor will they be sure that adequate health services are available. I want others to know that there is much left to do to address the genocide that Indigenous people have experienced and no simple governmental apology will benefit those who have lost parents or relatives. While I await justice, I keep on conjuring an identity of safety and solace consistent with my being a grandmother or "coo coo." This Ojibway name is derived from the more formal title

"Nokomis" or "Kookum." So when and if I am called "coo coo," which sounds like cuckoo, I know I really am.

REFERENCES

Chesler, Phyllis. *Women and Madness*. Hampshire, UK: Palgrave Macmillan, 2005.

Demas, Doreen and Brenda Elias. *A Profile of Manitoba First Nations People With a Disability*. Winnipeg: Assembly of Manitoba Chiefs, 2001.

Ensler, Eve. *The Vagina Monologues*. New York: Villard, 2007.

Gilman, Charlotte Perkins. *"The Yellow Wallpaper" and Other Stories*. Minneapolis: Filiquarian Publishing LLC, 2007.

Medicine, Bea. "American Indian Women: Mental Health Issues Which Relate to Drug Abuse." *Learning to Be an Anthropologist & Remaining "Native": Selected Writings*. Eds. Bea Medicine and Sue-Ellen Jacobs. Urbana: University of Illinois Press, 2001. 197-206.

Shackel, Don. "Persons with Disabilities Living within First Nations Communities in Manitoba." Master's thesis, University of Manitoba, Winnipeg, 2009.

KELLY-JO DORVAULT

"Post-Kelly Re: Constructed Reality"

Kelly-Jo Dorvault, "forked connection," 2010, photo-still digital print.

My most recent project, "Post-Kelly Re: Constructed Reality," is a photo-still animation that deals with topics society might deem to be sins of living or unconventional medical problems that are not openly discussed in most conversation areas.

The above scene deals with the frustrations of dealing with the brain-gut disorder of Irritable Bowel Syndrome. The fork represents the stabbing pain, which occurs during digestion, and an impulse to try and cut out the pain from the outside. The homeopathic medicine is what I take to cope with the pain, along with managing controllable factors such as diet, exercise, and proper sleep.

Mental health is directly linked to this problem, and the two conditions work in a cyclical effect on each other that can manifest into being unable to function in daily routines. The game, "Connect Four" and the bicycle reference these connections and also the importance of play, even for adults.

Kelly-Jo Dorvault, "slow pitch," 2010, photo-still digital print..

This still is an image portrayed from the "Anxiety" scene. This is one of the most complicated images, as that seems to be the nature of how anxiety seems to be crippling even when it can be predicted. Trigger points can be identified and used to work through to find coping mechanisms, but occasionally they do not work. The way that things build up and fall are how anxiety rolls in and out, and the empty awkward space around the central action indicates the agonizing discomfort.

There are multiple photos of myself throughout my life to show that time does not exist and all experiences are inter-twined. Baseball has been a passionate influence and core strength in dealing with my problems. The animals are part of this as I feel a strong connection to them and the importance of treating them with respect and proper living conditions.

RENEE NORMAN

ARTHRITIC DREAMS II

first to go
the neighbourhood walk
down to a brief turn
of several blocks
woosh
then driving up the youngest
on a field trip
poof
baseball in the park
gone
doing the dishes
(no real loss there)
if you don't mind the crumbs
no one but me ever sees

I could catalogue
the changes
bed rest   Epsom salts
by the gallon
ice packs
sitting down to peel potatoes

the most difficult to bear
a disappointed look
in the eyes
when I have to say no

i can't
it's too hard
poof

Originally published in CWS/cf*'s issue on "Canadian Feminism in Action,"
25 (3,4) (2006): 183. Reprinted with permission.*

SUSAN WENDELL

FEMINISM, DISABILITY
AND TRANSCENDENCE OF THE BODY

IDEAS OF TRANSCENDING THE body have generally been rejected by feminists, including feminist theologians, because they are seen to originate from philosophies and/or religions which devalue the body (especially women's bodies) and bodily experience. For example, Naomi Goldenberg describes the notion of transcendence in traditional theology as "a wish for something beyond body, beyond time, and beyond specific relationships to life" and "a notion of perfect safety ... probably motivated by a characteristically (but not exclusively) male fear of being merged with matter" (Goldenberg 211).

Feminist theorists have criticized the mind-body dichotomy and the intellectual denigration of the body, both of which make important contributions to motivations for transcending the body, and both of which are prevalent in the history of Western thought. We can see their philosophical roots in such ancient ideas as those of Plato and Aristotle, where abstract forms are superior to material things, and reason is superior to the appetites which originate in the body. Feminists have also argued that the dominant forms of Christian theology strengthened these ancient views by representing the body as a major source of the desires and weaknesses that lead to sin, and seeing transcendence of the body as an essential ingredient in moral perfection.

Yet feminist theory has so far failed to appreciate the strength of another motive for wanting to transcend the body. We need to recognize that much of the appeal of philosophies of life which recommend some form of transcendence of the body lies, not in elevation of the mind and denigration of the body, but in the desire to make one's happiness, or at least one's sense of self, independent of illness, pain, weakness, exhaustion, and accident. We have not recognized this because feminist writing about the body has not fully confronted experience of the negative body.[1] This is partly because feminism's primary concern has always been to identify and change social arrangements that cause preventable suffering, and we have applied this approach to the body. But it is also because we have focused the rest of our attention on alienation from the body and on bodily differences between women and men. These emphases have not been conducive to developing a feminist understanding of bodily suffering.

One of the central concerns of feminism has been men's control of women's bodies, especially women's sexuality and reproductive processes, through violence and coercion, law, economic relations, religion, custom, and institutionalized medicine. Outrage over the injustice of this control and the many ways it hurts women led to the long-established movement to increase women's own control of their sexuality, reproductive lives, and health care. Because this movement has always sought to increase women's power to make decisions about their own bodies and to prevent or reduce their bodily suffering, and because there is still so much that needs to be done toward both these goals, it does not foster discussion of experiences of bodily suffering that cannot be controlled or prevented.

Another direction of feminist discussion of the body has been particularly concerned with how men's and women's alienation from their bodies contributes to women's oppression, and how women are alienated from their bodies by male-dominated society. Understandably, alienation from the body is a very negative concept in these discussions; it is something to be overcome by re-uniting culture and people with bodily experience.

Dorothy Dinnerstein and Susan Griffin are the major developers of the view that alienation from the body contributes to women's oppression. Both focus upon the desire to escape the vulnerability of the body, especially its vulnerability to unfulfilled need, which is experienced by infants in relation to their mothers. They argue that this desire is a primary motive for creating and maintaining cultures and ideologies which objectify, rage against, and attempt to control women. Because Dinnerstein and Griffin want us to see the pathology of cultures which are pitted against the bodily experiences of men and women, it makes sense that both discuss only the experiences of healthy bodies in relatively favourable physical circumstances. However, for those of us who find their theories persuasive (as I do), there is a potential difficulty that arises from ignoring negative adult experiences of the body: we may come to believe that all will be well between us and our bodies if we can overcome cultural alienation from them.

Other feminist discussions of the body have explicitly focused on overcoming women's social and cultural alienation from our bodies. A major concern of feminists has been the re-description, by women, of bodily experiences unique to women. Because the Western tradition particularly de-valued women's bodies and appropriated the authority to describe bodily experiences unique to women, feminist writings about experiences of the body tend to focus on sexuality (heterosexual, lesbian, and bi-sexual), the changes of monthly cycles, pregnancy, birth, and mothering. Also in reaction to this tradition and its consequences, feminists have celebrated the body, emphasizing aspects of bodily experience that are sources of pleasure, satisfaction, and feelings of connection. These two understandable and valuable reactions, however, have led feminists to overlook or underestimate the fact that the body is also a source of frustration, suffering, and even torment. One consequence is that women with disabilities may feel that feminists have an ideal of the female body or of female bodily experience in which they cannot participate any more than they can in the idealized images of sexist society, and that their experiences cannot be included in feminist understandings of the body.

Nevertheless, although feminists have often ignored the suffering body in their theorizing, they have not ignored other aspects of the negative or rejected body. They have always drawn attention to and criticized body image ideals that alienate women from our own bodies and function as instruments of social control. There have been feminist critiques of fashions in body type and clothing, of the cult of youth, of the tyranny of slimness, of standards of femininity that require restricted movement, extensive grooming and use of makeup, and of growing cultural pressures on women in wealthy countries to alter their bodies by "cosmetic" surgery, to name but a few. Traditionally, these critiques have encouraged women to cultivate more positive and realistic body images in resistance to the idealizations with which they are pressured, and to reduce their alienation from their bodies by focusing on bodily experience and competence rather than appearance. (For more discussion of these issues, see Bartky). These are important aims for women with disabilities as well as for women without them. But, as in the other feminist treatments of alienation, there is little room to examine bodily suffering when the goal is to restore women's appreciation of embodiment. Recent work along these lines has taken another direction, urging women to adopt a playful, mocking stance toward standards of beauty and femininity, using their own bodies to resist and comment upon these standards (see, for example, Wolf and Morgan). Here the emphasis moves away from subjectivity altogether and toward a kind of taking control of how one is objectified. I believe the latter line of thought is influenced by feminist postmodernist treatments of the body, which are a development of feminist inquiries into the significance of women's bodily differences from men.

Feminist attention to women's bodily differences from men began with arguments that, contrary to long scientific and popular traditions, these differences do not by themselves determine women's social and psychological gender (or the more limited "sex roles" we used to talk about). These arguments still go on, especially among biologists, anthropologists, and psychologists; understandably, they have little or nothing to say about bodily suffering. But the view that gender is not biologically determined has taken a much more radical turn in feminist "post-structuralist" and "post-modernist" criticism, where the symbolic and cultural significance of women's bodily differences from men are closely examined. Here "the body" is often discussed as a cultural construction and "the body" or body parts are taken to be symbolic forms in a culture. In this latter development, experience of the body is at best left out of the discussion, and at worst it is precluded by the theory; here feminist theory itself is alienated from the body. As Carol Bigwood says,

A body and nature formed solely by social and political significations, discourses and inscriptions are cultural products, disemboweled of their full existential content. The poststructuralist body ... is so fluid it can take on almost limitless embodiments. It has no real terrestrial weight. (59)

A body which is experienced has both limitations and weight.

I was particularly struck by the alienation from bodily experience of some recent forms of feminist theorizing about the body when I read Donna Haraway's exciting and witty essay, "A Manifesto for Cyborgs." The view she presents of the body as cultural and technological construct seems to preclude the kind of experience I have had. When I became ill, I felt taken over and betrayed by a profound bodily vulnerability. I was forced by my body to reconceptualize my relationship to my body. This experience was not the result of any change of cultural "reading" of the body or of technological incursions into the body. I was infected by a virus, with debilitating physical and psychological consequences. Of course, my illness occurred in a social and cultural context which profoundly affected my experience of it, but a major aspect of my experience was precisely that of being forced to acknowledge and learn to live with bodily, not cultural, limitation. In its radical movement away from the view that every facet of women's lives is determined by biology, feminist theory is in danger of idealizing "the body" and erasing much of the reality of lived bodies. As Susan Bordo says: "The deconstructionist erasure of the body is not effected, as in the Cartesian version, by a trip to "nowhere," but in a resistance to the recognition that one is always somewhere, and limited" (145).

Feminism's continuing efforts to increase women's control of our bodies and prevent unnecessary suffering tend to make us think of bodily suffering as a socially curable phenomenon. Moreover, its focus on alienation from the body and women's bodily differences from men has created in feminist theory an unrealistic picture of our relationship to our bodies. On the one hand, there is the implicit belief that, if we can only create social justice and overcome our cultural alienation from the body, our experience of it will be mostly pleasant and rewarding. On the other hand, there is a concept of the body which is limited only by the imagination and ignores bodily experience altogether. In neither case does feminist thought confront the experience of bodily suffering. One important consequence is that feminist theory has not taken account of a very strong reason for wanting to transcend the body. Unless we do take account of it, I suspect that we may not only underestimate the subjective appeal of mind-body dualism, but also fail to offer an adequate alternative conception of the relationship of consciousness to the body.

At the very least, we must recognize that awareness of the body is often awareness of pain, discomfort, or physical difficulty. Since people with disabilities collectively have a great deal of knowledge about these aspects of bodily experience, they should be major contributors to our cultural understanding of the body. I propose to demonstrate this, in a modest way, by discussing some interesting aspects of pain and some of the effects that bodily suffering has on our desire to identify with our bodies. I hope to open a new feminist discussion of transcendence of the body, one which will eventually take full account of the phenomenology of bodily suffering.

Virtually everyone has some experience of physical pain. Drew Leder gives a good phenomenological account of acute or non-chronic pain. He points out that our experience of it is episodic, that it always demands our attention, that it constricts our perception of space to the body and of time to the here-and-now, that the goal of getting rid of it becomes the focus of our intentions and actions, that it often renders us alone psychologically by cutting us off from other people's reality, and that it causes some degree of alienation of the self from the painful body (70-79). All this seems to me true. Nevertheless, I believe our understanding of pain can be greatly enriched by experiences of chronic pain. By chronic pain, I mean pain that is not endured for some purpose or goal (unlike the pain of intense athletic training, for instance), pain that promises to go on indefinitely (although sometimes intermittently and sometimes unpredictably), pain that demands no action because as far as we know, no action can get rid of it.

From my own and other people's experiences of chronic pain, I have learned that pain is an interpreted experience. By this, I mean not only that we interpret the experience of pain to mean this or that (we do, as Leder points out, and I shall discuss the meaning of pain later), but also that the experience of pain itself is sometimes and in part a product of the interpretation of sensations. For example, it is a fascinating paradox that a major aspect of the painfulness of pain, or I might say the suffering caused by pain, is the desire to get rid of it, to escape from it, to make it stop. A cultivated attitude of acceptance toward it, giving in to it, or just watching/observing it as an experience like others, can reduce the suffering it usually causes. People with chronic pain sometimes describe this as making friends with their pain; I suspect they have achieved a degree of acceptance that still eludes me, but I think I know what they mean. (See, for example, Albert Kreinheder's description of his relationship to the severe pain of rheumatoid arthritis in Kreinheder, Chapter 6.)

I want to make it clear before I continue that my descriptions of living with chronic pain do not apply to everyone and are certainly not prescriptions for anyone else. Living with pain is a very complex and individual negotiation; successful strategies depend on such factors as how intense the pain is, where it is in the body (for instance, I find pain in my head or my abdomen much more demanding than pain in my back, arms or legs), how much energy a person has, whether her energy and attention are drained into worries about money, family, medical treatment or other things, what kind of work she does, whether her physicians and friends encourage and help her, how much pleasure she has, what she feels passionate about, and many other factors. (For a sample of strategies, see Register.) In other words, it is important to remember that pain occurs in a complex physical, psychological, and social context which forms and transforms our experience of it.

For me, pain is no longer the phenomenon described by Leder. I have found that when focused upon and accepted without resistance, it is often transformed into something I would not describe as pain or even discomfort. For example, my disease causes virtually constant aching in the muscles of my arms, upper chest, and upper back. I know this, because any time I turn my attention to those parts of my body, I experience pain; I think of this pain as similar to a radio which is always playing, but whose volume varies a great deal. When the volume is low, or when I am doing something that absorbs my attention very fully, I can ignore it, but when the volume is turned up high, it demands my attention, and I cannot ignore it for long. I focus my attention fully on the pain, in which case I must stop doing everything else. I am usually able to relax "into it," which is a state of mind difficult to describe except by saying that I concentrate on remaining aware of the pain and not resisting it. Then the experience of being in pain is transformed into something else—sometimes a mental image, sometimes a train of thought, sometimes an emotion, sometimes a desire to do something, such as lying down or getting warmer, sometimes sleep. Perhaps if I remained focused upon it in this way, I would rarely suffer from pain, but I do not want to devote

61

much conscious attention to this process. Other things interest me more, and this is, for me, the problem of pain.

I must balance the frequency of attention to how my body feels that is required by the constant presence of pain with whatever attention is required by something else I am doing. It surprised me to find that I could learn to do this, and that I got better at it with practice. (Of course, it requires structuring my life so that I can rest and withdraw my attention into my body much more than healthy people my age normally do). But the most surprising thing about it is that my ability to think, my attitudes and feelings seem to me less, not more, dependent on the state of my body than they were before I became ill.

Thus, before I had M.E.[2] I would never have considered setting to work at a difficult piece of writing if I woke up feeling quite sick, not only because I knew that I should rest in order to recover, but because I thought I could not possibly write well, or even think well, unless my body felt fairly good. Now I do it often, not because I "have to," but because I know how to do it and I want to. This outcome is the opposite of my expectation that paying much more attention to my bodily experience would make every aspect of myself more dependent on its fluctuating states. In a sense, I discovered that experiences of the body can teach consciousness of a certain freedom from the sufferings and limitations of the body. I shall return to this subject later, after discussing some strategies of disengagement from the body.

Attempting to transcend or disengage oneself from the body by ignoring or discounting its needs and sensations is generally a luxury of the healthy and able-bodied. For people who are ill or disabled, a fairly high degree of attention to the body is necessary for survival, or at least for preventing significant (and sometimes irreversible) deterioration of their physical conditions. Yet illness and disability often render bodily experiences whose meanings we once took for granted difficult to interpret, and even deceptive. Barbara Rosenblum described how a "crisis of meaning" was created by the radical unpredictability of her body with cancer:

> In our culture it is very common to rely on the body as the ultimate arbiter of truth.... By noticing the body's responses to situations, we have an idea of how we 'really feel about things.' For example, if you get knots in your stomach every time a

certain person walks into the room, you have an important body clue to investigate.... Interpretations of bodily signals are premised on the uninterrupted stability and continuity of the body.... When the body, like my body, is no longer consistent over time ... when something that meant one thing in April may have an entirely different meaning in May, then it is hard to rely on the stability—and therefore the truth—of the body. (Butler and Rosenblum 136-137)

Chronic pain creates a similar (but more limited) crisis of meaning, since, to a healthy person, pain means that something is wrong that should be acted upon. With chronic pain, I must remind myself over and over again that the pain is meaningless, that there is nothing to fear or resist, that resistance only creates tension, which makes it worse. When I simply notice and accept the pain, my mind is often freed to pay attention to something else. This is not the same as ignoring my body, which would be dangerous, since not resting when I need to rest can cause extreme symptoms or a relapse into illness that would require several days of bedrest. I think of it as a re-interpretation of bodily sensations so as not to be overwhelmed or victimized by them. This process has affected profoundly my whole relationship to my body, since fatigue, nausea, dizziness, lack of appetite, and even depression are all caused by my disease from time to time, and thus all have changed their meanings. It is usually, though not always, inappropriate now to interpret them as indications of my relationship to the external world or of the need to take action. Unfortunately, it is often much easier to recognize that something is inappropriate than to refrain from doing it.

For this reason, I have found it important to cultivate an "observer's" attitude to many bodily sensations and even depressive moods caused by my illness. With this attitude, I observe what is happening as a phenomenon, attend to it, tolerate the strangeness of, for example, feeling depressed or nauseated when there is nothing obviously depressing or disgusting going on, accommodate to it as best I can, and wait for it to pass. This is very different from the reactions that come most easily to me, which have to do with finding the causes of these feelings and acting on them. I find it hardest to adopt an observer's attitude toward depression, since although in the past I had brief illnesses that cause the other symptons, I had never experienced severe depression without something to be depressed about. Thus, my first, easiest response to depression was to search my life for something that might be depressing me. Since my world (like virtually everyone's) is full of things that, if focused upon, might cause depression, I increased and prolonged my depressions with this habitual response. Learning to regard severe depression (by this I mean, not the lows of everyday living, but the sorts of feelings that make you wish you were dead) as a physical phenomenon to be endured until it is over and not taken seriously, has greatly reduced my suffering from it and may have saved my life. Register describes a similar strategy used by a man who suffers from recurring depressive illness (280).

In general, being able to say (usually to myself): "My body is painful (or nauseated, exhausted, etc.), but I'm happy," can be very encouraging and lift my spirits, because it asserts that the way my body feels is not the totality of my experience, that my mind and feelings can wander beyond the painful messages of my body, and that my state of mind is not completely dependent on the state of my body. Even being able to say: "My brain is badly affected right now, so I'm depressed, but I'm fine and my life is going well," is a way of asserting that the quality of my life is not completely dependent on the state of my body, that projects can still be imagined and accomplished, and that the present is not all there is. In short, I am learning not to identify myself with my body, and this helps me to live a good life with a debilitating chronic illness.

I know that many people will suspect this attitude of being psychologically or spiritually naive. They will insist that the sufferings of the body have psychological and/or spiritual meanings, and that I should be searching for them in order to heal myself (Wilber). This is a widespread belief, not only in North America but in many parts of the world, and I have discussed some of its consequences for people with disabilities and/or terminal illnesses elsewhere (Wendell). I do not reject it entirely. I too believe that, if my stomach tightens every time a particular person enters the room, it is an important sign of how I feel about him/her, and I may feel better physically if I avoid or change my relationship to that person. But, having experienced a crisis of meaning in my body, I can no longer assume that even powerful bodily experiences are psychologically or spiritually meaningful. To do so seems to me to give the body too little importance as a cause in psychological and spiritual life. It reduces the body to a mere reflector of other processes, and implicitly rejects the idea that the body may have a complex life of its own, much of which we cannot interpret.

When I look back on the beginning of my illness, I still think of it, as I did then, as an involuntary violation of my body. But now I feel that such violations are sometimes the beginning of growth, in that they force the self to expand or be destroyed. Illness has forced me to change in ways that I am grateful for, and so, although I would joyfully accept a cure if it were offered me, I do not regret having become ill. Yet I do not believe that I became ill because I needed to learn what illness has taught me, nor that I will get well when I have learned everything I need to know from it. We learn from many things that do not happen to us because we need to learn from them (to regard the death of a loved one, for example, as primarily a lesson for oneself, is hideously narcissistic), and many people who could benefit from learning the same things never have the experiences that would teach them.

When I began to accept and give in to my symptoms, when I stopped searching for medical, psychological or spiritual cures, when I began to develop the ability to observe my symptoms and reduced my identification with the transient miseries of my body, I was able to re-construct my life. The state of my body limited the possibilities in new ways, but it also presented new kinds of understanding, new interests, new passions and projects. In this sense, my experience of illness has been profoundly meaningful, but only because I accepted my body as a cause. If I had insisted on seeing it primarily as reflecting psychological or spiritual problems, and devoted my energy to uncovering the "meanings" of my symptoms, I would still be completely absorbed in being ill. As it is, my body has led me to a changed identity, to a very different sense of myself, even as I have come to identify myself less with what is occurring in my body.

People with disabilities often describe advantages of not identifying the self with the body. For those who are ill, the difficulty of living moment-to-moment with unpredictable, debilitating symptoms can be alleviated by having a strong sense of self which negotiates its ability to carry out its projects with the sick body (Register, Chapter 9). This sense of self and its projects provides continuity in lives which would be chaotic if those who led them were highly identified with their bodies. The anthropologist Robert Murphy, who is quadriplegic and has been studying the lives of people with paralysis, describes another motive for disembodying the self: "The paralytic becomes accustomed to being lifted, rolled, pushed, pulled, and twisted, and he survives this treatment by putting emotional distance between himself and his body" (100-101).

In addition, people with disabilities often express a strong desire not to be identified with their bodily weaknesses, inabilities or illnesses. This is why the phrase "people with disabilities" has come to be preferred over "disabled people." When the world sees a whole person as disabled, the person's abilities are overlooked or discounted. It is easy to slip into believing other people's perceptions of oneself, and this can take a great toll on the self-esteem of a person with a disability. Those people with disabilities who still have impressive and reliable physical abilities can counteract people's misperceptions by asserting those abilities. For those of us whose remaining physical abilities are unimpressive or unreliable, not to identify ourselves with our bodies may be the best defence. It is good psychological strategy to base our sense of ourselves, and therefore our self-esteem, on our intellectual and/or emotional experiences, activities, and connections to others.

Robert Murphy, whose paralysis is steadily increasing as a tumor in his spinal column slowly grows, writes eloquently about the consequences of losing the ability to move. He says of himself: "My thoughts and sense of being alive have been driven back into my brain, where I now reside" (102), and: "Like all quadriplegics, I have a great fear of being left stranded and helpless, but my sense of self is otherwise shrunken to the confines of my head" (193). Although Murphy does not shrink from recognizing what he has lost by this, he describes vividly what he has gained:

> I have become a receptor in physical things, and I must continually fight the tendency for this growing passivity to overcome my thoughts. But there is a certain security and comfort in returning to my little cocoon every night, enswathed in a warm electric blanket, settled into a micro-environment consisting of one's essentials. It is a breach of communication with the toils of social ties and obligations, a retreat into a private cerebral world. And it is at these times

that my mind wanders furthest afield. In such deep quietude,
one indeed finds a perverse freedom. (193-194)

I do not want to give an exaggerated impression of the degree to which
people with disabilities rely upon strategies of disembodiment. For all
the advantages that some degree of disembodying the self may have in
coping with illness or disability, the process of coming to identify with
a sick or disabled body can play an important part in adjusting to it. For
many of us who have become ill or disabled as adults, reconstructing
our lives depends upon forging a new identity. An important aspect
of this process is what Register calls "acceptance: ability to regard the
illness [or, I would add disability] as your normal state of being" (31).
This could also be described as learning to identify with a new body
as well as, for most of us, a new social role. For me, this had many
advantages: I stopped expecting to recover and postponing my life until
I was well, I sought help and invented strategies for living with my sick
body, I changed my projects and my working life to accommodate my
physical limitations and, perhaps most important, I began to identify
with other people with disabilities and to learn from them. Thus, I do
identify with my sick body to a significant degree, but I also believe that
my thoughts and feelings are more independent from my experiences
of it than they ever were from my experiences of my well body.

What has all this to do with transcendence of the body? That,
of course, depends on what we have in mind when we speak of
transcendence. The forms of independence from the body's sufferings
that I have described are partial and mundane. They are strategies of
daily living, not grand spiritual victories. Perhaps some people might
even regard them as forms of alienation from physical experience. I
think that would be a mistake. Alienation, as we usually understand it,
reduces freedom, because it constricts the possibilities of experience.
If we spoke of being alienated from suffering, I think we would mean
being unable to face up to and undergo some necessary, perhaps
purposeful, pain. To choose to exercise some habits of mind which
distance oneself from chronic, often meaningless, physical suffering
increases freedom, because it expands the possibilities of experience
beyond the miseries and limitations of the body.

It is because they increase the freedom of consciousness that I am
drawn to calling these strategies forms of transcendence. It is because

we are led to adopt them by the body's pain, discomfort or difficulty, and because they are ways of interpreting and dealing with bodily experience, that I call them transcendences of the body. I do not think that we need to subscribe to some kind of mind-body dualism to recognize that there are degrees to which consciousness and the sense of self may be tied to bodily sensations and limitations, or to see the value of practices, available to some people in some circumstances, which loosen the connection. Nor do I think we need to de-value the body or bodily experience to value the ability to gain some emotional and cognitive distance from them. On the contrary, to de-value the body for this reason would be foolish, since it is bodily changes and conditions which lead us to discover these strategies. The onset of illness, disability or pain forces us to find conscious responses to new, often acute, awareness of our bodies. Thus, the body itself takes us into and then beyond its sufferings and limitations.

In conclusion, by defending some notion of transcendence of the body I do not mean to suggest that strategies of disembodying the self should be adopted by people without disabilities. Instead, I want to demonstrate how important it is to consider the experiences of people with disabilities when theorizing about the relationship of consciousness to the body. One thing is clear: we cannot speak only of reducing our alienation from our bodies, becoming more aware of them, and celebrating their strengths and pleasures; we must also talk about how to live with the suffering body, with that which cannot be noticed without pain, and that which cannot be celebrated without ambivalence. We may find then that there is a place in our discussion of the body for some concept of transcendence.

Originally published in CWS/cf's issue on "Women and Disability," 13 (4) (1993): 116-122. Reprinted with permission.

[1] I use the terms "negative body" and "rejected body" to refer to those aspects of bodily reality (such as illness, disability, weakness, and death), bodily appearance (usually deviations from the cultural ideal of the body), and bodily experience (including most forms of bodily suffering) which are feared, ignored, despised, and/or rejected in a culture and society.

[2] M.E. stands for myalgic encephalomyelitis, which is a debilitating illness

that affects the muscles and nervous system. Its cause is still unknown, but it usually begins with a severe viral infection like influenza.

REFERENCES

Bartky, Sandra Lee. *Femininity and Domination: Studies in the Phenomenology of Oppression.* New York: Routledge, 1990.

Bordo, Susan. "Feminism, Postmodernism, and Gender-Scepticism." *Feminism/Postmodernism.* Ed. Linda J. Nicholson. New York: Routledge, 1990. 133-156.

Bigwood, Carol. "Renaturalizing the Body (With a Little Help from Merleau Ponty)." *Hypatia: A Journal of Feminist Philosophy* 6.3 (1991): 54- 73.

Butler, Sandra and Barbara Rosenblum. *Cancer in Two Voices.* San Francisco: Spinsters Book Company, 1991.

Dinnerstein, Dorothy. *The Mermaid and The Minotaur: Sexual Arrangements and Human Malaise.* New York: Harper, 1976.

Goldenberg, Naomi R. *Returning Words to Flesh: Feminism, Psychoanalysis, and the Resurrection of the Body.* Boston: Beacon Press, 1990.

Griffin, Susan. *Pornography and Silence: Culture's Revenge Against Nature.* New York: Harper, 1981.

Haraway, Donna. "A Manifesto for Cyborgs: Science, Technology, and Socialist Feminism in the 1980s." *Feminism/Postmodernism.* Ed. Linda J. Nicholson. New York: Routledge, 1990. 190-233.

Kreinheder, Albert. *Body and Soul: The Other Side of Illness.* Toronto: Inner City Books, 1991.

Leder, Drew. *The Absent Body.* Chicago: University of Chicago Press, 1990.

Morgan, Kathryn. "Women and the Knife. Cosmetic Surgery and the Colonization of Women's Bodies." *Hypatia: A Journal of Feminist Philosophy* 6 (3) (1991): 25-53.

Murphy, Robert F. *The Body Silent.* New York: W.W. Norton, 1990.

Register, Cheri. *Living With Chronic Illness: Days of Patience and Passion.* New York: Bantam, 1987.

Wendell, Susan. "Toward a Feminist Theory of Disability." *Hypatia: A Journal of Feminist Philosophy* 4.2 (1989): 102-124.

Wilber, Ken and Treya Wilber. "Do We Make Ourselves Sick?" *New Age Journal* (September/October 1988): 50-54, 85-90.

Wolf, Naomi. *The Beauty Myth.* Toronto: Vintage Books, 1990.

"Untitled Painting"

"Untitled," 2006, mixed media, 8" x 10".

MARIE ANNHARTE BAKER

BLACK THREAD AROUND

hard stare at an Inuit carving
                shaman pose with black
                        thread tied to tooth
strong yank
                        suspended animation
one look in a mirror after clean jerk
troubling tooth extraction
                shows vacancy
                tentative tongue
                explored cavity
then I was just a kid
toothless being temporary
heartless faceless disability
commands if the eye offends
pluck it out of body or mind
                throb bleed ache
                disfigure disorient
                cause more trouble
who is to blame for residual
                anguish hysteria
                anxiety angst?
should a shaman snare
whip off offensive visage
wriggling smiles half
apology aided abetted
wrinkles scowls frowns
forehead lined furrows

prefer cosmetic surgery
a botox fill in lieu of face
pulled off by black thread
shamanic string continues
captures angina symptom
removal tug heart immediate
preventive actions not taken
                        could not repair it
                        in time had to face
give up on compassionate
self care but not right way
slow last murmur to beep
flatline wait for final thump
as if turtle heart devoured
in youth would prevent onset
deadly lonesome heart beat

NAMING THE EDGES: BARRIERS

CHERYL GIBSON

MARGINS ARE NOT FOR COWARDS

D OES BEING A WOMAN and having a disability somehow marginalize me? I don't think so, except when I'm having a really bad day. Like the time I wanted to take my children on a holiday and found that Via Rail refused to accommodate me. Or the time I tried to attend a conference for Health and Welfare Canada and Via Rail informed me that the train was fully booked months ahead with tourists and they didn't have to keep any seats for people who couldn't travel any other way. The time I was in a wheelchair and asked for a cup of tea, only to be told to get my own tea on the other side of a wheelchair inaccessible room, has to near the top of the pathos scale. Major setbacks or minor insensitivities can make even a tough "cripple" like me wonder if it is all worth it.

What does it mean to be marginalized? According to my dictionary, it is derived from the Latin "merg" which means a boundary; it can also mean "a lower standard or limit of a certain quality." Perhaps these two have blended to imply that people who can't meet a certain standard are expected to stay outside the boundaries of civilized society. That is certainly how it feels to discover that the things I used to take for granted are now out of reach. What is even more frustrating is when society thinks they should be beyond my expectations.

I wasn't born with my disability. It is the result of a failed back operation, so I still have the expectation that I will be able to do the same things and go the same places—because I am very stubborn, I thought it was just a matter of figuring out how. The reality of a world that is made for the average person's needs is slowly sinking into my conscious mind. It is my subconscious that keeps insisting that there has to be a way around, over or through any obstacle or problem.

Either that, or it is just a habit I developed early in life and have yet to outgrow. Whatever the cause, the effect is the same: I never stop trying to live a full life and am surprised when the rest of the world thinks I should be content with something less.

Before I had my operation, I was oblivious to the barriers that are created when a society is geared towards providing services for the majority. I didn't purposefully restrict the activities of women who could not walk, but I did wonder if all those handicapped parking spaces were really necessary. I assumed people who couldn't walk were fortunate to have ramps and wheelchairs and shouldn't aspire further than an accessible washroom.

At first, I fought the idea of a wheelchair, of a scooter and of two canes. Only when my "back was against a wall," because my legs wouldn't function, did I admit that I needed help. It was humbling to realize that I could no longer live my life on my terms. My mother claims that I was born on my own and have been on my own ever since, so the thought of using an "orthotic appliance," as they are euphemistically labelled, was admitting defeat.

It was even more difficult for me to resolve my feelings about depending on other people than it was to admit that I had to use a wheelchair. In my mind, a grown woman should be able to stand on her own two feet in every sense of the word. When a feminist who has spent all of her life insisting that she could do as well or better than any man has to ask for help, or worse yet, accept it graciously, then it is time to rethink all her assumptions about life.

I can be marginalized by my own attitude or by the constraints of a world designed around the needs of those people who can sit and walk and carry things. Those of us who have to spend a great deal of time lying down would have been better off in the Roman Empire; in this century we need to drive cars, ride in trains, or work at a desk. My internal struggle to come to terms with a disability is different from the external struggle of fitting into society.

My philosophy, which grew out of the turmoil of facing a permanent disability, rests on the cornerstones of interdependence and balance. I still, especially as a woman with a disability, need to feel self-sufficient, competent, and useful. Being thought of as attractive wouldn't be bad either, but I'm not sure if society is ready to see people with disabilities as sexual beings.

Interdependence requires a delicate balance of pride and humility, common sense and resilience. Last month, I was staying in a hotel with my daughter, Jennifer, who is hearing impaired. We were in town for her hockey tournament and had to haul hockey equipment plus the usual luggage into the hotel. When we were looking for a place to park, we noticed that someone had parked in the handicapped parking spot without a permit. Jennifer went to the desk and confronted the manager about not enforcing the parking by-law and about having only one space. The manager found a parking spot for us. Later, Jennifer decided to watch a movie on TV and asked me to phone the manager to find out if they had closed captioning for deaf customers. I did and they didn't, but the hotel at least became aware that it was an important issue for some people. This is a classic example of being interdependent. I was able to help her when she couldn't use the phone and she was able to help me when I was in too much pain to confront anyone.

Balance is something which is very hard for me to achieve because it means leaving things out or paying for them later. That is a difficult choice for someone who used to want it all. There are times when I choose to do something, like going to my daughter's graduation, even though I know I will be in more pain at the time and for several days after the event. I have discovered that trying to do things that I used to take for granted is impossible unless I am willing to give up something else. It is a lesson that all women learn, but it is more brutal for some of us. Living a balanced life is crucial to accomplishing anything. I am always asking myself "How much do I need this and am I ready to pay the price?"

My work used to give meaning to my life. It defined me as a mother and a psychologist. Not to work is to become invisible, so I have created projects to occupy my mind. There are times when I get frustrated and have to admit that the work is too physically draining, but then I remember that I really should be grateful because two years ago I couldn't write at all. Trying to work within my own limits puts me completely out of step with the rest of society, but not working renders me obsolete.

My struggle to find meaning in my new life as a woman with a disability has taken time. I needed to understand, at the deepest level, that there were real limits which I couldn't wish away. Then I had to find a way to incorporate those limits into my life without becoming dehumanized.

Creative expression in writing poetry, prose or in art became my route to wholeness. I learned that I can avoid being marginalized in life if I refuse to recognize that margins exist. I still get irritated when I can't do something that everyone else takes for granted, but I'm also grateful that I have the opportunity to live a full rich life within the parameters that I have been given. I can create meaning within my life. Finding joy and possibilities takes greater creative effort when the options are limited, but it also provides greater satisfaction. I suspect that most women have had to face this restriction of opportunities at some time in their lives. When society defines us as marginal, for whatever reason, it can be a signal to fight back. Margins are not for cowards.

Originally published in CWS/cf's *issue on "Women and Disability," 13 (4) (1993): 14-15. Reprinted with permission.*

"Me, Myself and I"

"Me, Myself and I," 1993, oil on canvas, 61 x 76 cm.

DOREEN DEMAS

TRIPLE JEOPARDY

Native Women With Disabilities

I T IS ESTIMATED THAT in some Native communities, more than 40 per cent of the population lives with a disability of some kind. In Northern Canada, otitis media is a persistent problem. In many communities this middle ear infection affects 80 per cent of the individuals at some time during their life. This infection is a major cause of hearing impairment. Fully one-third of all deaths among Status Indians and Inuit are alcohol related, while over 60 per cent of the Native children in care arrive in that situation as a direct result of alcohol abuse. The number of Native children who attend school until the end of secondary level is 20 per cent, compared with the national rate of 75 per cent. Native unemployment is about 35 per cent of the working age population, and in some areas it reaches as high as 90 per cent.

People with disabilities are disadvantaged in the areas of education, access, transportation, housing, employment opportunities, recreation, cultural opportunities, etc. Women with disabilities speak of double jeopardy. I believe that Native women who have a disability are in a situation of triple jeopardy. You may be familiar with many of the concerns that Aboriginal people in Canada have—poor housing conditions, lack of adequate medical care, and substance abuse. When you add disability and being female to this, you have a situation of extreme disadvantage.

As an example, when it was time for me to start school, I had to leave my home in Manitoba to attend a special school for visually impaired children in Ontario. Not only did I have to leave my family, but I was in a different culture with its own language and norms. Like all the children there, I experienced the negative effects of being educated in a segregated institution, but for me there was the additional burden of being in a different culture. This is still happening today. There are many Native children from remote communities in the North who must come to the South for educational or rehabilitative services.

WHO WE ARE

Native people are not a homogeneous group. Just as you cannot talk about "the disabled" with any clarity, you must remember that Canada's Aboriginal population can be divided into the following groupings— Status, Non-status, Treaty, Metis, and Inuit. Aboriginal people are urban and rural dwellers; some live on a reserve while others live off the reserve; and many still live in the North. This means that there are many varying circumstances and realities for Canada's Aboriginal population.

SELF-GOVERNMENT

Self-government is the number one priority for Aboriginal people. It is seen as the best way to improve their status in Canadian society. While Native persons with disabilities are in agreement with self-government, there is the concern that their needs as persons with disabilities may not be included in the process of self-government. I saw evidence of this when doing the interviews which comprise the Coalition of Provincial Organizations of the Handicapped (COPOH) report "Disabled Natives Speak Out."

JURISDICTIONAL PROBLEMS

It is often said that for disadvantaged groups, education is the key to escaping poverty, dependency on welfare, unemployment, etc. Natives with disabilities are being denied access to the services that would enable them to get the education that assists in obtaining employment. Employment is crucial if an individual is to have an independent and financially secure lifestyle. What is denying us that access?

That access is being denied by jurisdictional quagmires. For those of us who have status or treaty rights, we have always been viewed by service agencies as being the responsibility of the federal government.

This means that provincial rehabilitation resources that are available to other Canadians with disabilities are not always available to us. For example, in Manitoba, the Society for Manitobans with Disabilities, formerly the Society for Crippled Children and Adults, does not include people with Status in their mandate. This makes it very difficult for Native people to get needed services.

I have my own personal example in this area. I was told by one worker at the Canadian Institute for the Blind (CNIB) in response to my request for a closed circuit TV reader, which I needed for my education, that as a Native person with status that I was not eligible for VRDP allocated equipment, and that VRDP students had first priority to these devices. The worker told me that as a Native person I was not eligible for VRDP and as a status Indian I was the responsibility of Indian Affairs and it was to them that I should make the request. However, not more than two days prior to that I had been told by someone from the education department of Indian Affairs that there was no money in their budget for these devices and that I was registered with the CNIB and that I should make my request to CNIB. This is just one example of a situation where the lack of clarity and the bureaucratic-run-around prevents Natives with disabilities from getting adequate services.

Now that Native people have started to set up their own education services, the whole situation has become just that much more complex. Despite the fact that Indian Affairs has a policy on Native people with special needs, this policy is not clear or well understood by many of these organizations. As a consequence, they do not know how to access the funds that are theoretically available to meet the rehabilitation needs of Native persons with disabilities. So who is the loser in all this? It is ultimately the person with the disability, of course.

Just as there is a lack of clarity in the education area, there is a lack of clarity in the area of Medical Services. I have come across many situations where a person with a disability whose health is stabilized and who is eligible for assistance from other programs is rejected by those programs because those programs assume that Medical Services should be taking care of all their needs. We are running up against the domination of the medical model. This is something that non-Native people with disabilities were fighting in the early 70s when the consumer movement was born. Native people with disabilities are still fighting that battle. Often, these people end up going home to their reserve with nothing, because none of the programs would accept responsibility for them.

These are just a few examples of the bureaucratic problems which Native people with disabilities encounter when they attempt to access necessary services. Add to that coming from a different culture, speaking a different language, having to deal with non-Native bureaucrats, and you will get an idea of some of the obstacles encountered by Native people with disabilities and why I am talking to you about a situation of triple jeopardy.

ISOLATION

Recently, I attended a conference which focused on the concerns of parents of children with disabilities from the North. There were a number of women at the conference who were single parents. These women felt that their needs, and the needs of their disabled children were not being met. For the most part, these women were living in poverty and it was difficult for them to meet the dietary needs of a child with a disability. At this conference, I heard many accounts from parents whose children were living in Southern institutions. These children have come from Northern isolated communities to Southern settings to get needed services which are unavailable in the North. I heard about how these children lose contact with their families and their communities. The length of time spent away from family and community can be months and even years. The only way for parents to see their children is to fly down. Flying from North to South is very expensive. It is impossible to make frequent trips. This is particularly true if you have a low income or are on social assistance. The end result is that you lose contact with your child. You have really no choice in that matter, because there are no services in your community. If the child is to get those services, she/he must come South.

TRANSITIONS

People can become disabled as children or it can happen later in life. If you have a disability as a child and you have to leave your community to get access to services or for education, the more time spent away from your community and family the more assimilated into white culture you become. Earlier I made a reference to going away to school. I spent six and a half years of my childhood away from my family and community, and during that time I lost most of my language, a lot of my cultural roots, and perhaps the most devastating to me was the loss of family contacts and bonds. While language and culture are important, these are something I think one can re-learn. But not growing up in a family atmosphere is not something that you can make up for in later years. Being assimilated into another culture makes you a stranger in your own culture, but it does not make you belong in the other, so in a sense you belong in neither culture. Ultimately, if you have different norms and values than that of your family, it makes it harder for you to be part of your own family, so you tend to be isolated.

When you are disabled as an adult, you have to learn to adjust to your disability while simultaneously adjusting to white culture in order to receive services. If you need services to assist you with these adjustments, they are very difficult to find. There are very few service providers who have the necessary understanding of both the cultural factors and the disability factors to assist a person in coping with the transitions they are experiencing in their life.

Non-Native disability organizations do not always have culturally appropriate programs to help people who are Native. Native organizations do have these programs, but they often do not have the understanding of disability issues. We need to aim some of our attention at Native women's organizations, so that they become sensitive to the issues and concerns of their Native sisters who have disabilities.

CONDITIONS ON RESERVES

I have met a number of Native women and men with spinal cord injuries at Ten Ten, which is a housing project in Winnipeg for disabled people. These women and men were preparing for a life in Winnipeg, because there are no options at home on their reserves. There are no accommodations on their reserves to assist them to live in that setting with their disability—ramps into buildings, modified living units that are accessible, accessible transportation, etc. The condition of existing facilities on reserves can make independent living difficult. For example, gravel roads that are poorly maintained are difficult to travel on when using a wheelchair. These individuals had no choice but to live in the city.

People who live in isolated communities in the North get into the community either by winter road or by air. During spring when the ice is breaking up there is total isolation, because the winter roads are not usable and you can't fly in. So you are stuck either in or out. That makes it difficult for a person with a disability. It doesn't make it easy for you to live in your community. Situations such as this also force people into urban settings.

SUBSTANCE ABUSE

It is well known that the high rate of substance abuse leads to disabilities. For example, children born with fetal alcohol syndrome can have learning disabilities. People become disabled in accidents that are brought on by substance abuse. Furthermore, drug dependency does not end with disablement. Many treatment facilities are inaccessible. This is particularly true when it comes to women's treatment facilities. We need to work to see that these facilities become accessible and have programs which are culturally appropriate for Native women with disabilities.

Substance abuse is a contributor to domestic violence. There are many Native women who are survivors of violence. As the DisAbled Women's Network (DAWN) report indicates, violence can lead to disability. Shelters for abused women need to be made aware of the needs of Native women with disabilities. Non-Native shelters for abused women need to be encouraged to have culturally appropriate programs for Native women with disabilities.

MEDICAL CONDITIONS

Native people are susceptible to certain kinds of diseases and medical conditions such as diabetes which can cause loss of limbs, blindness, etc. These medical conditions are exacerbated and triggered by poor living conditions on reserves—i.e. malnutrition, poor housing, etc. Many reserves still have poorly constructed houses which lack plumbing, water systems, and adequate heating systems. These living conditions make it difficult for a person with a disability to live independently, and it is particularly difficult for women who are raising children. You can imagine how difficult it is for a Native woman who is a wheelchair user to raise her children in a house which does not have indoor plumbing. Inadequate health services on reserves compound the problem. There are examples of people who are more disabled than they need to be because they were treated by people who were poorly trained, underqualified, etc. in limited facilities with poor diagnostic equipment.

It would seem to me that clarity of jurisdiction, clear lines of responsibility, and a better internal understanding of the lines of responsibility would improve the situation immensely. Some recommendations are as follows:

•Clarify methods for accessing services and make this information well known at the individual level. If people understand better how to access services, it is easier for consumers to get the services for which they are looking.

•Decentralize services. Services should be available on reserves so the people living there would not have to leave their community.

•Improve access on reserves. For example, schools could be made accessible.

•Make access to people with disabilities a priority everywhere— including on reserves.

•Develop information programs, so that the people who need this information can get access to it. Native organizations need to have an understanding of their funding process so they can get the funds to provide the services they require.

We must do public education with Native women's organizations, so they become aware of the issues and concerns of Native women with disabilities. We must also encourage non-Native women's organizations to provide culturally appropriate programs which meet the needs of Native women with disabilities.

Originally published in CWS/cf's issue on "Women and Disability," 13 (4) (1993): 11-55. Reprinted with permission.

JANE FIELD

COMING OUT OF TWO CLOSETS

I FEEL IT IS very important for dykes and gay men with disabilities to be "out" in terms of both their disability and their sexual orientation. The other day someone remarked to me that there are a number of people with disabilities, particularly paraplegic men, who attempt to "pass" in the non-disabled world, who want nothing to do with disability groups, especially consumer-run groups. I chuckled a bit at the picture that this conjured up in my head of people in wheelchairs covered with trench coats, furtively wheeling around, attempting to hide their disability.

Of course people who have invisible disabilities are more able to hide their disabilities, if they choose to do so. It's a bit ridiculous for a wheelchair user like myself to consider hiding the fact. But it leads me to wonder why I would want to. Why wouldn't I want people to know that I have a disability, that I accept it as part of who I am and that I am proud of who I am? Why wouldn't I want anyone to know that I confront physical and attitudinal barriers every day of my life and that I identify with strong individuals who are part of the disability rights movement? And why would I deny myself the opportunity to be part of consumer-driven groups like the DisAbled Women's Network?

I don't hide my disability and I don't "overcome" it either. It's just something I live with. I am not handicapped. Society is handicapped when it shuts out people like me. I am not physically challenged. Tri-athletes and mountain climbers are physically challenged. And I'm certainly no more differently-abled than anyone is from anyone else. No. I just simply have a disability. I don't deny it, or hide it. I'm "out."

Being "out" as a person with a disability is a conscious choice, whether or not one's disability is visible. For the way others view us is closely connected with the way we view ourselves. Choosing to see disability as a part of who we are and recognizing our strengths and abilities, is all part of "coming out." Realizing that having a disability is not a negative thing is an important first step in this process.

My disability is only one part of me. I am also a lesbian, and as a lesbian, I am also "out." It took me a while to come to terms with my sexuality, just as it did for me to accept my disability. I am proud of being a lesbian and I see my sexuality as a very important part of who I am. I wonder why I wouldn't want people to know that. Why wouldn't I want people to know I am actively involved in the struggle for lesbian and gay rights?

Recently, I met two women in North Bay who thought that they had never met a lesbian. They said, "Of course you have those kinds of people in Toronto, but we don't have any in North Bay." Not only were they astonished to learn that I was a lesbian, but they were also greatly surprised when I told them that I could introduce them to at least two lesbians who lived right in North Bay. Their eyes opened even wider when I continued: "Maybe you don't know these lesbians are right here in your own community, because they don't feel it's safe for them if people know. And what is it about your little community that would make them feel that way?"

It makes me feel very sad that for many lesbians the closet is safer than the community. And people won't change their attitudes if they continue to think they are not affected. The "we don't have that problem here" mentality leads to isolation, misunderstanding, stereotypes, and prejudices.

We must be "out" both in terms of our sexuality and our disability, so that people will know that we do belong and that we occupy a rightful place in the community as a whole – not just in the disabled community, or in the lesbian community.

Sometimes, however, we are not "invited" to be part of our own gay community. This happens when events are not accessible, when there are no lesbian bars that are wheelchair accessible, when only part of a bookstore can be accessed, or when our fellow lesbians and gay men assume that we don't exist and can't even conceive of having a relationship with us. We are in a sense "handicapped" by the inaccessibility of the gay community and by the attitudes of others. Our full participation as "out," practising homosexuals may be limited by these barriers. We have to do our best to make sure the gay community knows we are here, that we belong and have much to contribute, if we can just get in.

Similarly, as lesbians and gay men in the disability movement, we need to feel validated and recognized. We need to feel comfortable discussing our issues and concerns as gay people in the context of our disabilities. This is not always easy either. Although the disability community may be readily physically accessed, there are just as many attitudinal barriers and misconceptions about our sexuality in this community as there are in society at large.

As lesbians and gay men with disabilities, our struggle lies not just in being accepted in society, but also in being accepted for who we are in both the gay community and the disability community.

I am reminded of a store-owner who once remarked to me that his store didn't need a ramp because "people in wheelchairs don't come here." Right! And there is no homophobia in North Bay, because homosexuals or "people like that" apparently don't live there! Well, of course they do, but they may not be "out" because people's attitudes are as inaccessible as an unramped store. There is no obvious invitation to be "out."

Invitation or not, I think we have to be "out" in all of our communities. We have to be proud of who we are as dykes with disabilities, or gay men with disabilities, and invite others to get to know us.

Originally published in CWS/cf's issue on "Women and Disability," 13 (4) (1993): 18-19. Reprinted with permission.

JULIE DEVANEY

PERFORMING MY LEAKY BODY

> Women are out of control, uncontained, unpredictable, leaky:
> they are, in short, monstrous. Set against the more familiar and
> unthreatening parameters of feminine passivity, the anxiety
> provoked by the female body with its putative power to disrupt
> must alert us to the inadequacy of any attempt to confine
> corporeal difference to the place of the other. (Shildrick 31)

O N OCTOBER 19, 2003, in my hospital bed, my knees tightly
pressed to my chest, my body began writing itself with ink
and paper. The process of meaning-making had begun much
earlier, with much less visible manifestations. Since 2001 I had been
experiencing painful and often debilitating symptoms as a result of
an autoimmune disease called Ulcerative Colitis. In October of 2003,
after all attempts to achieve bodily stability with medication proved
ineffective, a surgeon removed my entire large intestine. In the days
following this operation I began to write consciously and reflectively,
in prose and rants, the dialogues and scenes as they appeared from
my position. The physical act of writing my body was a site of intense
complexity with layered meanings. To inscribe any single motive onto
myself from this current distance would be contrived and false. What
I do recall is the experience of profound anger spilling out of me and
onto the page, a raging sense that I needed "to render noisy and audible
all that had been silenced" (Minh-Ha 259).

I began performing *My Leaky Body* as a last resort because suddenly
I just couldn't function any other way. After four years of being in and
out of hospitals, propped up on examining tables and in bed in pain for
weeks and months at a time I went back to grad school. My schedule

looked like this: I had class one day and taught undergraduates the next day. Then back to bed. And I was supposed to be writing and talking about disability and the politics of health policy in the abstract, when all I wanted to do was sit on the table in my hospital gown and read the things I wrote while I lay on those stretchers and in those beds. So it was kind of a joke when, in 2006, I applied to two big conferences, proposing a performance piece where I undressed, put on a hospital gown and sat up on the table reading from my hospital chart. Much to my surprise (and horror) it was accepted at both conferences, the first in Toronto, the second in Washington, DC. My supervisor, Margrit Shildrick, was both theoretically inspiring with her work *Leaky Bodies and Boundaries* and practically supportive about me taking this work on as my Master's Project. I began all academic performances of this work with the Shildrick quote at the beginning of this introduction.

I went on to do it at a conference in the United Kingdom and soon people were requesting more performances in Toronto. Since then I've been invited to perform and do workshops for medical professionals, patients, disability activists and students across the country and internationally. I now recognize that performance in my hospital gown is always a performance, whether I am feigning deference in an emergency room or sitting on a makeshift stretcher at a conference. I realize that it is equally important to bring my undressed body into a formal academic space as it is to bring my academic analysis to the imagined/recounted scene of the hospital.

***

SCENE 1 – "SNAP!"

Hospital gown on chair. Sheet, pillow, hospital chart on bed. Julie enters, puts on hospital gown, and "snaps" on rubber glove.

Julie: it occurs to me that the manufacturers of latex gloves should do something about that haunting elastic sound that happens when rubber meets flesh. The warning shot.

The Vancouver Emergency Room doctor is exhausted, worn to shreds. He looks at me, feels my abdomen and says,

"Your tummy is soft, what do you want me to do?"

I am strung too high on pain, undernourishment, and fear to edit the words that flood out.

"Well, I'm in a great deal of pain. I've had twelve bloody bowel movements in the last sixteen hours. I came here because I thought *you* might know what to do."

"Fine."

"I'll order you some Demerol and Gravol and call the GI guys."

Julie takes glove off.

After he leaves, my partner Blair and I have The Talk: "Julie Julie, it's not fair, and you really shouldn't have to do this, but you have to make them feel like they know more than you. They can't handle the way you speak to them, you have to let *them* think that *you* think that *they're* in charge. Because unfortunately, they are."

I practice mock tones of weakness and deference.

"Doctor, I feel so sick, oh please, Doctor, please, please, I'm just a little girl, please bestow your wisdom on me…"

We laugh, and then fall asleep on the stretcher. Blair, who later denies having fallen asleep, is snoring when the nurse comes by. She and I make conversation about the fact that we live near each other and talk about our dogs.

Finally, I work up my nerve and ask her,

"The way the doctor spoke to me, I really felt like he thought … he thought I wasn't sick enough to be here, that I shouldn't have come. Do you think I shouldn't be here?"

I brace myself, waiting for her to agree with him and give me a lecture about wasting hospital resources.

She leans in and says very clearly and seriously,

"I just tested your urine. You're metabolizing protein, that's dangerous. You were right to come in. We're just having a *really* bad night; it's not about you."

And I understand what she means, that it's not about me. I'm supposed to be speaking on a panel with the president of the Hospital Employee's Union the next day, I know how bad their working conditions have become with the massive cuts to health care. But when political economy is being meted out on my body, it *is about me.*

SCENE 2 – PATIENT HANDBOOK

I understand now, that despite the nurse's opinion, to get admitted into hospital you need to either have a high fever, a distended abdomen, or uncontrollable vomiting. If only I'd read the getting-admitted handbook. The doctors wouldn't have sent me home for another week so that my joints were so swollen I could only crawl to the bathroom fifteen times a day in searing pain, trying to force down *Ensure* at Blair's insistence as he watches me wither away, my hair falling out from malnutrition—covering my pillows and coming out in chunks in my hands.

I phone the gastroenterologist who sent me home from the hospital. His only insight is,

"Really, colitis shouldn't be causing you this much pain."

The following Saturday I am being wheeled back into the same ER. I make a mental note to add this to the patient handbook that I am now planning to write: Being wheeled in gives you credibility—you may be awarded a gurney in the hall. Frighteningly low blood pressure also contributes to the speed of attention you can expect.

A doctor comes to see me in the waiting room and sits down next to me,

"I'm so sorry that there's nowhere else to talk to you."

She looks at my chart.

"I have a cousin with Ulcerative Colitis. It's a terrible disease. Oh, look at your joints, and your skin. This is a really serious flare-up, you need to be admitted."

SCENE 3 – EXHIBIT A SPEAKS LATIN

At this point I am so dehydrated they are ready to put a central line into my neck. I refuse, so they finally settle on a vein deep on the inside of my elbow, after poking and stabbing around and through my inflamed hands, ankles, wrists, and feet. I am now lying on the gurney, pushed up against the wall of a hallway near the waiting room, with IV poles at my side. The nurses repeatedly apologize as they come by.

"Everyone's talking about you in the nurses' station. We're all trying to figure out where else to put you. We feel awful."

I can't have any pain medication because the specialist is concerned that it will slow my bowel down and cause a blockage. So now I am not even eligible for the oblivion I had enjoyed, however briefly, in my previous ER experiences. And here the worst part begins, the lowest drama, the highest torment … the waiting.

"I wanna be sedated" by The Ramones plays in background.

Except it's worse than that. Cuz the Ramones are only in my head. The highlight is the doctor who brings his class of medical students crowding around me, half-naked, curled up on the gurney.

"Do you mind showing us your erythema nodosum?"

The swollen purple and red bumps that are covering my legs and elbows are fascinating to the medical students. I excel at the development of extra-intestinal side-effects, which also includes the arthritis now plaguing my peripheral joints. But I think what fascinates and amuses them even more is my ability to pronounce Latin and articulate the features of my illness. *Exhibit A Speaks Latin.*

When I am finally moved from the actual hallway I end up in a part of the Emergency ward that just feels like a giant hallway. Rows upon rows of patients lined up like wilting, limp plants, waiting to be watered. A young woman with Hepatitis B is across the hall from me. Her whole family is crowded around her crying. I have sent Blair home by now, so I am alone.

Lifting up arm for pulse, sticking out tongue, etc. looking up, as if towards nurse.

"Do you have any idea when I might get be getting a bed in a room?"

Looking down, feeling own wrist as if nurse.

"Some people have been down here for five days. The problem is that although there are beds upstairs, there isn't enough staff to take care of seriously ill patients, so you have to stay in Emerg with us so we can monitor you."

Looking at audience.

I find this deeply ironic. A week ago, I was sent home because I wasn't sick enough to be admitted to hell, and now I am too sick to get a bed, and I am stuck in *hospital* purgatory.

SCENE 4 – PURGATORY WITH TOMMY DOUGLAS

I finally fall asleep. I wake up to my stretcher being moved at about 2:00 in the morning. They need my rectangle of space for someone else. I am moved into a storage space in the emergency ward for people admitted for psychiatric treatment. Restraining devices are stored on shelves all around me with needles and tubing. The washroom is a good trek around corners and through doors. It consists of two stalls to share with the entire emergency room, patients and visitors.

I manage to read my chart at one point when I am being taken for tests on my stretcher. I feel like I am in grade three, surreptitiously trying to read my report card through the sealed envelope before I get home to deliver it to my Mum. I get top marks for hygiene, which is exciting. My friend who is in med school tells me that this hospital is known in Vancouver as being the "downtown" hospital, reputedly packed out with homeless people with drug addictions. The hygiene checklist is a code. *She's clean. Not one of "them."*

Some people get songs stuck in their heads. I get political chants from demonstrations. This time it was one from the G8 demos in Calgary a month earlier.

"Suharto, Bin Laden and Pinochet ... all created by the CIA!"

Repeat, fading out.

It occurs to me that if anyone hears me muttering the names of foreign dictators and accusing the CIA of things while lying on a gurney my status might be advanced from closet-tenant of the mental health unit to committed patient. As I look at the restraints on shelves all around me I have a sense of how very thin that line might be.

I'm thinking about this as a flood of light descends from the ceiling.

Spotlight comes down onto bed.

I blink several times, trying to clear my eyes of the black and purple spots now floating in my field of vision. They don't go away. In fact they start to congeal, into a sort of blob. And this blob starts to take form. First I see neatly coifed hair and glasses. I start to make out lapels on a suit jacket, and a little tie. Definitely 1940s style. I'm very confused as the voice rings out,

"What on earth is going on here?!"

"Um, I'm sick."

"Well I can see that, but what are you doing in the closet?"

"There's nowhere else for me."

"Good grief! What's been going on? Did the doctors go on strike? Are we back to private medicine? Are you too poor to pay?"

"Are you Tommy Douglas? Seriously, as in the father of Canadian medicare?"

"Yes, right. Right then, okay, climb on."

"Oh my god. Is that a wing? Really? Where are we going?"

"To the fully-funded facility of both of our dreams…"

"Nice … wow, so Tommy, are you like, an angel now? So when you met God, she was a socialist?"

"You ask way too many questions."

"That's what you get for rescuing a grad student."

Climbs down, moves to podium, look at audience.

At the same time as I am infuriated with the way I am being treated as a patient, my history as a political activist and academic training in political economy add a new lens to my absorption and insights. Almost as a reflex, I see the meting out of political structure onto my body and the bodies of my over-worked caregivers.

Lying on the stretcher I embody the contradiction between my political support for the funding of public healthcare and my profound opposition to the violence with which I am treated.

SCENE 5 – BASTA! AM I SEXY?

The next scene begins, as all healthcare encounters do, in the Waiting Room. As I enter the hospital, my music floods out all hospital sensation, drowning out my anxiety—*Asian Dub Foundation* blasting political sentiment that exactly echoes my feeling on the medical establishment, the illness, my colon—"basta, basta, basta, basta!" *enough, enough, enough.* I'm not allowed to have anyone with me because it's during the SARS scare in Toronto and only people with appointments are allowed in the hospital.

I'm feeling emboldened, confident, and, terrified.

A nurse greets me.

"You can just sit right over here."

She leads me to an examining table in a room where there is scope equipment looming about threateningly. I can feel the machines and hoses looking at me, I try to stare them down but there are too many of them and they are just too powerful. After several years of colitis and endless painful scopes of my very inflamed and bleeding bowels, I can't even look at the machines when they're off.

I venture into the hall to find a trashy magazine to bring back to the room. It's now about forty minutes after the time my appointment is scheduled for.

Shania Twain is on the radio. I consider the possibility that in my weakened, vulnerable state my pretensions may fade away long enough to find some innocent enjoyment in "Man! I Feel Like a Woman."

Julie sings and dances badly.

No such luck. The intensity of the cringe just increases. Coolness is such a curse.

I pick up a pamphlet about the surgery I'm going to have—the one about sex. It is all about having an "understanding" partner and suggesting that I should not worry if I do not feel like having sex for 3 or 4 months after the surgery. There is no discussion of why a bowel surgery would have this drastic libidinal impact. And I'm terrified by this random, unsubstantiated statistic. I am overwhelmed by my desire to be desired, to have my sexuality acknowledged.

Enter the young Dr. Leonard. One of the nice ones. Matter-of-factly describing the surgery, what happens afterwards, the drugs, the cutting, the next surgery, the … But me, all I want to know is, will I be sexy? Am I SEXY? And the annoying thing is that I don't think he's sexy. He's not bad but it's not like I'm fantasizing about jumping the doctor.

So I ask about drugs and milligrams and adrenal glands and amphetamines and steroid withdrawal depression… "Like depression, don't you get it … Will I be SEXY?"

"Answer!"

But if there's anyone in the world who won't answer internal dialogue it's someone who's gone through medical training. They rarely deign to answer explicit questions.

SCENE 6 – "IN HER GENTLY CUPPED HANDS…"

So now it's time to meet the surgeon. She comes over to my chair and shakes my hand,

"Hi, I'm Athena."

She pulls the chair that Dr. Leonard sat in toward me at a safe and objective distance. She opens my chart in her lap,

"Wow, you've really had a hard time of it."

We talk about my Masters' program in Women's Studies and my university. She shows me her medical books, describing in detail everything she is going to do.

"So we'll start the procedure laproscopically, meaning we can just cut little 'key holes' and insert cameras inside of you. We perform the surgery with long tools so you'll only be left with tiny scars. But after all the inflammation and the steroid medication, your colon might just be mush, in which case it could be dangerous to continue. In that case, we have to cut."

At this point she looks at me and cups her hands,

"Because I would rather be able to hold it, and see exactly what we're doing if that's the case."

I feel really safe for the first time in all the chaos and medical mayhem. She is going to hold my colon in her gently cupped hands.

And so the appointment ends and the stoma nurse starts. Her job is to pick the best spot for the bag, the external appliance that will hold my stool after the surgery. She wants to draw the spot where my intestine will be pulled out of my stomach and into the bag with a green marker.

She has cartoons about stomas on her door.

"So have you thought about where you want it?"

She makes me sit with my steroid-cushnoid colitis-bloated tummy hanging out of my pants. She pokes and asks. Forwards and backwards. It needs to sit on top she says. And I picture skinny girls with no top on and she says,

"Do you know where you want it?

And I say, "I DON'T WANT IT."

And she says "I know and here's my card and call me if you want to talk about it" and I say "I don't want to talk and I'm not going to think about it until it's there and then I'll pretend that it's not there."

And she says, "that's okay, that's one way to deal with it, but call me if you change your mind" and I don't. I meet my friend in a bar and drink some rum. It doesn't help.

SCENE 7 – INFLAMED, IN FLAMES

I schedule my surgery. The surgeon wants to do it sooner, but there is simply no time in the schedule. When I leave the building I am on fire. Inflamed, in flames. Part of me thinks "of course this is the best thing, I'll get through this surgery, no problem." Another part of me thinks, maybe this is it. Maybe I'll go under the anesthetic and that's it. It's over. And what will I have missed? It's a remarkably easy question to answer: Mexico City. Like any young, self-respecting Canadian graduate student would do—I want to see Frida Kahlo's house. I want to feel Mexican sun warming my skin in a thriving, buzzing urban centre. Mad markets and bright colours. *Viva la revolucion!* I dip very heavily into the overdraft on my bank account with the reasonable thought that if there is anytime to feel no remorse about spending money I don't have, this is it. Once the ticket is booked no one argues with me ... Friends offer support, if reluctantly. Spanish lessons and advice on where to stay. I tell my Mum that I'm going to Montreal to an antiwar conference with my friend Martine. I like the alliteration. Montreal with Martine, Mexico with me. Blair reluctantly drives me to the airport.

SCENE 8 – CERTAIN WOMEN BLEED

Mexican music plays as Julie takes off hospital gown and turns it into a wrap-around skirt.

The plane lands. I put on my small backpack and find a cab. The driver takes me to the centre of the city, the *Zocolo*. Saturday afternoon, it's heaving with people, cars, markets. I have memorized all the Spanish I might need with possible responses. I walk a few blocks to the hotel I have picked out in the guidebook. It's now a warehouse clothing store. I quickly find somewhere else to stay. I go to my room, unpack some of my things, and go out in search of groceries. Dry bread and bottled water are the safest route to digestive comfort. Walking back to the hotel I see a sign that says "Colon." I'm shocked, I do a double take. It's a clothing store. Called Colon. Two weeks before surgeons hack mine out. The store is just a block away from where I am staying.

I go back to my room and suddenly have no idea what to do. I am overwhelmed by a wave of complete helplessness. I sit on the bed and cry. Weep and shake. Gasp and choke. Clench my fists. Punch things. I start drawing in my sketch book. Colourful images of bloody colons and a violent self-portrait with the words "certain women *bleed*" scrawled across it. When I calm down I decide that I need to go out and be places where other people are. I get on a tour bus. It's dusk, it takes us all around the city until it is dark and the lights are twinkling.

SCENE 9 – FRIDA'S HOUSE

The next day is my pilgrimage to Frida. So it's Sunday. The day is bright and warm. I take the public transit out to Coyoacan and walk to her house. I don't anticipate how right I am to take this trip until I am standing there … in the courtyard of the Blue House. I take out my sketchbook and sit there drawing for hours. I go through the house where the paintings are hung, lingering at each one … I stand in her bedroom. Looking at the clock stopped above her bed. It's twenty-two minutes past nine in Frida's room. I think the point of travel is less about the moment I inhabit a space and more about creating different rooms in my head. The more places I visit physically, the more places there are to escape mentally. I want to feel Frida's room so I can go back whenever I want to … co-opting real places to form imaginary spaces in my body, like a giant mansion I can wander through at leisure.

SCENE 10 – REVOLUTIONARY ARMY

The next night I meet an Australian couple and we decide to go out for dinner. It is the first time I actually indulge in Mexican cuisine, but seeing as it's my last night I am daring enough to stray from my bread and bottled water digestive-safety diet. We order several dishes to share and giant Sangrias. The food is bliss. We leave and they walk me back to my hotel. It is pouring rain so I suggest that we go to a nearby café until it lets up. When we get inside we realize that it is actually a giant, ancient-looking courtyard. The environment is dream-like, sitting in an ancient place in the middle of Mexico City where the staff is playing the new Radiohead album. I start drifting away with Thom Yorke's ethereal voice. In the corner I see Frida sitting with her sister Christina and Diego. She looks at me, eyes twinkling, and invites me over. I have to push and elbow my way through a crowd of art student ghosts who even in the metaphysical world are trying to get close to her.

We sit and drink and watch the rain let up. A thick fog descends, and I suddenly feel lighter, more transparent, as if I could float. I turn to Frida,

"You know I always imagine you in my revolutionary army. When I can't bear the thought of going into a situation alone, I pretend that you're there with all the people I know would have my back, marching en masse behind me."

She smiles, "I know."

I want to issue a formal invitation,

"Frida, will you really be in my army?"

She cups her hand under my chin, her fingers on my cheek,

"Jules, you know I'm already there."

Her smile lights me through to my core. As I walk out into the fog and back to my hotel I realize that neither of us had accents and I can't really even remember the words we said. I guess that's what happens when souls speak.

Back in my hotel room I don't mind the all-night trips back and forth to the washroom from the spicy Mexican food and alcohol. Deking out the cockroaches isn't really a problem either. The advantage to tropical bugs is that you can hear them coming … giant scuttling things. The mosquitos focus on my inflamed joints, they have clever little noses, with the power to sense where all the hot rushing blood has collected. I fly back to Toronto the next morning.

SCENE 11 –THE TRILLIUM WELFARE QUEEN

Then all I have to do is wait. I am frustrated, terrified, but continually being told by everyone how well I am dealing with it all. The truth is I don't know how to *not* cope … there's just so many details. I am dealing with the government drug program, "Trillium." They need a letter from the Insurance Company. So they're not returning my calls, totally avoiding me, and when I finally speak to a human being she speaks to me like I'm the Trillium Drug Plan Welfare Queen. As if I have some kind of secret recreational purpose for colitis treatments. Her undertone betrays a certain pride in having caught me red-handed in my attempts to defraud the system. Right, cuz steroid enemas are street, yo.

So I lay out the situation for her. She tells me,

"The computer wouldn't lie"

So I read her the number from their own records, she types it into the computer and aggressively replies,

"Well, I don't know why it did that."

She agrees to write the letter.

But it's such a pathetic victory, begging for money for agonizing treatments I didn't even want to take and which completely failed to work. With every encroachment from the cold bureaucracies of everyday life the warmth of the Mexican sun fades from my skin.

SCENE 12 – THE SCOPE

Julie puts hospital gown back on and gets on bed.

When I arrive for the scope they take me into the room with all the gurneys. A nurse starts my IV and wheels me into the room with the machines. The surgeon comes in to see me,

"So we've got your surgery scheduled for next week."

I notice the smell of the Body Shop perfume, White Musk. I ask the nurse if that's what she's wearing. It is. I appreciate the comfort of pleasant fragrance instead of the usual hospital fare. Then Dr. Leonard, the resident who I met at my "education" appointment, starts talking to me and administering my meds in such a way that I realize that *he* is going to perform the scope. The resident. Not the famous and gentle surgeon … But I feel too weak and helpless to argue.

"Do you have your period?" The nurse motions towards the string attached to my tampon, dangling between my legs.

I want to say, "Nope, I just think tampons are fun," but I answer honestly,

"Yes, why, should I not be wearing a tampon?"

It did occur to me that it might be a problem but I wanted to be clean and smell nice so I put it in before I bathed in lavender bath salts that morning.

"Well, it would be better if you weren't, it could make it more difficult to scope you, but that's okay."

"I'll just take it out then." I reach down between my legs.

Julie pulls out tampon.

The nurse looks shocked. Dr. Leonard quickly averts his eyes as if to give me privacy, and frankly, looks somewhat horrified. The nurse rushes to find me something sterile to put it in, and padding to put underneath me in case I bleed. Apparently I should be more squeamish about admitting that I menstruate when I lie naked in front of a room of medical professionals. I do not claim to understand their reasoning.

I am still puzzling over this when he starts.

"The medication is not working. It's really hurting!"

The White Musk Nurse says,

"But he's not doing anything right now."

As if I have some kind of investment in lying about the fact that the camera with the hose jammed into my body still hurts, whether or not he is actively pushing it at that exact moment.

Athena the surgeon comes back and tells him to stop.

He protests, "But we hardly got anywhere."

He looks at me accusingly and says with disappointment,

"There's hardly anything there."

Meaning disease, I presume. I am frustrated. Obviously because of steroids I am taking, the symptoms are *masked*. We know this. And then Athena looks at me. She shrugs and smiles,

"I just needed to see how bad the disease was."

And she leaves.

Medical science has methods and orders that may have some kind of general rationale but when they don't logic is ultimately subsumed by the importance of rigid traditions. And Education. So the resident learned something. I'm not entirely clear on what … I just know it wasn't what I would have taught him. A lesson on scoping the body—as if I were a land mass to be explored, mapped out, by cartographers of human flesh.

What I learned was even more profound. The surgical resident was scared of my vagina. The idea of an actively menstruating woman replacing the disembodied anus, rectum and colon he's focused on is terrifying.

SCENE 13 – THE GRAND CUTTING

There are two Julie's: one sitting here talking to you right now and one still sitting on her stretcher, four years ago. I'm reaching through time right now to tell her that we're still here, we're alright.

They're pushing me into the OR on a stretcher and I say,

"This is weird, this is so weird."

And the nurse says, "What's so weird about it?"

And I wonder if she can see that it's weirder than the spaceship on the *X-Files* where Scully had her chip inserted—with shining bright spot lights and TV cameras and screens and men in masks and I tell the man, the doctor, the anesthesiologist that he's not going to find a vein in my dehydrated hand after two days of not eating, of shitting liquid for the surgery prep to clean the intestine that they're about to hack out. And Blair's adage, never break a clean dish, occurs to me, but I guess dishwasher laws don't apply to surgeons.

So I tell him,

"Here … in the crook of the elbow. You can't see the vein but it's a good one, go straight, go deep."

But he ignores me … as he steadfastly digs into my wrist bone with his needle and to distract myself I turn my head and concentrate on the conversation happening between the intern and the doctor four feet away about the colon. And what they're going to do with *it* and I turn back in surprise as I feel the needle finally give up on the wrist and dig in deep in the crook of the elbow, good and straight, into the vein and tell me that we're in luck and I lose my temper and yell,

"*Lucky*? Who's *lucky*?"

And he says, "Us. Lucky that we found any vein in YOU that we could put an IV in," and if I was still Catholic I would pray for his fragile ego, so weak that he needs to lie when we both know he's lying and the angel nurse leans in and says her name and says,

"I have colitis. I know how you're feeling."

And Needle guy starts yelling about antibiotics and something and finally says,

"Well fine, I won't give her any then!"

And I look up at Angel Nurse and say,

"I'm not going into this surgery without antibiotics."

And she says, "No, you're not. He's grumpy, he's venting, you're going to get antibiotics" and she's livid.

"It's uncalled for! Nobody should be speaking like this while you're awake" and she looks up at him and says, "while the patient's awake!"

As he injects my *lucky* IV line with sedatives I feel my mouth open and I hear words I might have repressed coming out with rage, saying,

"And you know what else is uncalled for? People talking about my colon like I'm not even here and saying 'it' and 'the' like it's no big deal but it's my *colon* and it's a really big deal."

And angel nurse says, "It is. It is a really big deal."

And I like to think that at this point the frog-faced mask, hat, scrub-wearing doctors moved slightly backwards but I can't be sure if they recoiled at even the vague realization of how horrific they were being with this human butcher project lying like a slab on narrow metal almost naked because angel nurse and tantrum doctor were leaning over me and saying,

"Okay Julie, you're going under, keep your eyes open, your eyes open" and I tried and tried and then I was gone.

I dream of a world where healthcare is funded … and governments can't unilaterally over-ride collective agreements to make the state of healthcare even worse…

Where Med Students are taught manners…

I dream of a world where sick people are comforted, our feet are massaged with lavender oil as trays of sweet-smelling organic foods are brought to us in bed.

I dream of healthcare that's about *healing*. And of healers who acknowledge and respect me as a whole—as an intellectual, emotional, sexual, spiritual woman.

I dream of hospital pajamas that cover our entire bodies in comfortable fabrics and pleasant colours. And slippers. I dream of slippers.

SCENE 14 – PUT THE BAG ON

The next morning, the stoma nurse is at my bedside. It is now the day after the grand cutting. She wants me to learn how to change it and use it but I can't look. She does it and cleanses it and talks to me. And don't you know that there's no nerve endings in a stoma? But I can feel every touch, every movement, the inside of my body is now on the outside and I want to throw up.

Two days later it's full to overflowing. Gaseous and painful. The nurse is young. Very young and pretty with lots of eyeliner. She promises to come back and help but she doesn't and it's heavy and it hurts. Blair goes to the nurses' station,

"Where's her nurse? She needs a nurse."

And they say, "she's on her lunch it'll be half an hour" and no one is covering for her.

But I can't wait.

"Ask him," I tell Blair. I point at Odysseus, the nurse my evil Tory roommate from hell has running back and forth at her beck and call and Odysseus *yells* impatiently from across the room,

"What can I help you with?"

And I say, "Can you just come here when you have a minute?" So he comes and I say, "I need help, I don't know how to change it. It hurts."

He looks at me like I'm disgusting. Definitely not sexy.

And says, "Okay, okay, I'll come back."

And he doesn't.

Another nurse comes and says,

"Okay, let's go to the bathroom."

Julie walks over to toilet.

And she says, "Okay, sit down."

And I say, "On the toilet? with my pants down?"

And she looks at me and says, "Yes."

So I do it. With my belly and smelly bag hanging. She's thin but at least she's not pretty. And the bag falls. Splats on the floor and liquid shit and green bile are everywhere and she says, "It's okay" but it's not. She hands me toilet paper and tells me to hold the stoma. It's the first time I've seen it. It's red and bloody and violently sputtering and protruding from my perfect, smooth, cream belly and I cry. I cry and I cry and I tell her that I can't look and she rhythmically responds as she wipes and cleans, wipes and cleans, and says that's normal and that everything I'm feeling and all the emotions are normal and fine and she rinses and deodorizes the smelly plastic bag to the rhythm of my tears but it's not normal.

I'm sitting on a toilet with my legs wide open with a red piece of my small intestine hanging and did I mention sputtering? Nothing is normal. I want to throw up.

SCENE 15 – THE SHOWER

I desperately want a shower. I am not allowed and not physically able to go by myself but I do not want to ask a nurse. So I ask Blair to take me. I am feeling very ambivalent about this. The idea of being naked alone with my partner and washing the hospital film off of my skin is very appealing. It is also terrifying. I wonder if he will be disgusted with the illeostomy bag (which is in hospital-regulation clear plastic so that my "output" is visible for professional monitoring). I am frightened that he will find me sexually repellent. As we stand in the hospital shower I tell him my fears.

He looks at me very intently and says, *"The bag is just something on you. It's not you. You're still sexy, you're still Julie."*

We later joke that I should alter the educational brochure to reflect that my desire for sexual contact was dampened for about three or four hours after surgery rather than three or four months.

SCENE 16 – WASTELAND I

The next scene begins in the Recovery Room. It's 2004; two years, eleven emergency rooms, five specialists, and two surgeries down. Six months since my last operation. On my stretcher I discover the April of T. S. Eliot's *Waste Land*,

> "… the cruelest month, breeding
> Lilacs out of the dead land, mixing
> Memory and desire, stirring
> Dull roots with spring rain." (Eliot 51)

I can't feel my body but feel very present in my mind so I ask the nurse, "Is the bag still there? Can you look?"
She lifts my gown,
"Yes, it is."
I don't believe her so I ask another nurse. I need a second opinion.
"Can you please look?"
So she looks and agrees.
But I'm still not sure if I believe them. I ask what happened, why the surgery didn't go as planned, where the doctor is and why no one is explaining what happened to me. They don't know.
Then I'm alone again. So I start crying. Loudly and unashamedly.

> "There is shadow under this red rock,
> (Come in under the shadow of this red rock)." (Eliot 52)

Gasping and shaking, I'm fading in and out of consciousness but I sense that a lot of time is passing. Patients move on either side of me but I'm still lying here. Every time I wake up I'm still crying and

107

I don't know if I've stopped crying even in my sleep. This moment is immortalized in my chart notes with the words, *"Patient weepy."* They encourage me to push the button on my pain pump. It's making me feel really woozy and not changing the fact that no one has explained to me why there is still a bag on my abdomen following five hours of surgery that was supposed to reverse it.

One of the nurses asks another nurse over my head,

"What's the matter with *her?*"

"Oh, she's just embarrassed because she still has a bag."

"No, I'm not!"

The ghost of Julie has a megaphone in hand. When on the outside I am calmly and dispassionately addressing medical professionals the ghost inside screams and curses … the bell of her megaphone full on in their faces.

Now, on the stretcher in the recovery room I am possessed by my own ghost.

> "And I will show you something different from either
> Your shadow at morning striding behind you
> Or your shadow at evening rising to meet you." (Eliot 52)

In this moment I accept myself and everything about me without question. It really is the rest of the world that is irreconcilably flawed.

"That's not it at all! I've been in and out of hospitals for two years. I'm 24! This is supposed to be over, and all I know is that it isn't but no one has come to tell me why, or what happens next, or anything!"

"I will show you fear in a handful of dust." (Eliot 52)

The nurse looks contrite.

"Yes, okay, we'll find someone to talk to you."

I'm still fading in and out and sobbing. The nurses intermittently come back and apologize that they don't know what's going on and they've put in lots of calls to the doctors but no one is responding.

A nurse comes to tell me that my respiration is a "2." I don't know what this means but apparently the value of my breathing is inadequate. I suggest that maybe if I had some information about the state of my body I could start breathing normally.

She asks me to rate my pain between 1 and 10.

"8.5"

Impatiently, she repeats the same rote I've heard a thousand times before.

"A '10' is the worst pain you've ever had. How much pain are you in?"

"8.5."

"There's no way your pain could be that high!"

Julie rolls eyes, addresses the audience:

Because I just faked five hours of bowel surgery.

"Well we can't move you out of the recovery room until you rate your pain lower."

"How low does it need to be?"

"I don't know, 3 or 4 maybe."

"Okay, it's 3 or 4, can I go to my room now?"

Finally recognizing the absurdity of the situation she softens, agreeing that I must be in a lot of pain and encouraging me to push the button on the morphine pump.

She returns a little while later,

"How are you feeling?"

As my ghost finally leaves my body she whispers, *"Like I was pinned down, knocked out, sliced up, and stapled back together. Like I was lied to. Beaten and bruised into submission."*

But the spirit leaves me before my mouth opens to respond, so I just say, "Fine."

SCENE 17 – BROWN EYES

So it is now 24 hours after the surgery, and a doctor finally deigns to come and speak to me personally about what happened. The doctor, the fellow, with the round, round brown watery eyes, appears by my bed the next morning. Scared. Hollow. Alone. No team of students with clipboards.

She's not an Exhibit anymore folks. This, this is serious.

"You were disintegrating,"

His eyes search mine, as if for a sign.

What does the soul of a Disintegrating Woman look like?

I was invisible on the gurney.

Then when I yelled in the Recovery Room, I was a Basket Case.

He searches my eyes, the eyes of the Disintegrating Woman.

The Doctor with the brown eyes has seen pieces of me that I have not ... that hopefully I never will. Yet, I was unconscious while he voyeuristically observed the cutting, the reconstruction. When I am simply a mass of cells, a Body, there is no need for clarity on the notion that The Disease is the threat, the enemy to be eradicated. Dealing with The Person is a much more complex challenge.

I look back coldly, directly and push out words, like lightbulb shards into his warm, brown eyes.

He begs,

"It was just so, so diseased."

"I know."

"It was almost disintegrating."

"I know."

We both wish he could be the Hero. He wants to save me. I want to be saved.

But we are both drowning. Clutching, gasping. He in impotence, me in fear. And so he goes away. *Nothing to learn here kids.*

SCENE 18 – DAWN ESCAPE

I go home and a week passes. And then a night where nothing passes. I phone the ward, the nurse tells me to come into Emergency and that Kathy and Nicole, the specialist therapy nurses, will come down and meet me when their shift starts at 6:30 am. Being driven down Yonge Street in the pre-dawn dark I am exhausted from not sleeping, nauseated from pain-killers ... my senses are threadbare.

In the meantime, somewhere, in the gallows of the hospital a team of surgical residents are using their supersonic senses to detect that I am coming. I no sooner arrive than I hear their thundering steps in rhythm and see their white coats billowing towards my booth in the ER. The senior resident is wearing loud clicking high heels and a brisk, clipped smile. It's not her fault that she has the same name as a woman in Vancouver that I hate, but the shoes are definitely her fault.

She immediately starts hammering me with question after question in a booming Gym Teacher voice, flanked by messy-haired just-woke-up med students on either side. Without actually listening to the answers she orders a battery of tests and admits me to stay until the next day.

When the nurse comes back I tell her,

"I don't need these tests, I just need to see Kathy and Nicole."

Clearly sharing my opinion, she looks gleeful when she responds,

"Well, you can refuse."

Kathy and Nicole arrive and gently and sweetly fix what they describe as a "mechanical problem." As they work technologists arrive with orders to take me to various places for various tests. I apologize to each one, explaining that I don't think the tests are necessary, so I'm not going.

The ER nurses page the residents again so I can talk to them and ask them to discharge me but they don't come this time. Hospital pages are apparently less compelling than supersonic senses. The nurses bring me a form to sign that I am leaving against the doctors' orders. I feel powerful, and considering what has transpired this feeling is somewhat remarkable. The sheer force of my illness made everything solid in my life melt into air. Now, everything that disintegrated suddenly becomes solid.

Julie puts on her clothes.

Dawn happened while we were in the dank and faceless ER. The space that exists beyond geographical borders. The land of latex and disinfectant. It happened sometime between my first "refusal" of "treatment" and the moment I discharged myself from the ER "against medical advice." In that place furiously buried between my brows. Between fear and defiance, in my simple act of resistance. But I didn't know that morning had broken until we were in the car, driving home. And then I finally fell asleep.

REFERENCES

Eliot, T. S. "Waste Land." *Selected Poems.* 1922. London: Faber and Faber, 1954.

Minh-Ha, T. T. "'Write Your Body' and 'The Body in Theory'." *Feminist Theory and the Body: A Reader.* 1989. Ed. J. Price and M. Shildrick. New York: Routledge, 1999.

Shildrick, M. *Embodying the Monster: Encounters with the Vulnerable Self.* London: Sage Publications, 2002.

TANIS DOE AND BARBARA LADOUCEUR

TO BE OR NOT TO BE?
WHOSE QUESTION IS IT, ANYWAY?

Two Women With Disabilities
Discuss the Right to Assisted Suicide

WOMEN WITH DISABILITIES HAVE been assaulted not only by individuals in their lives but also by a legal system and mass media that claims authority over their physical bodies as well as their minds. Women with disabilities of all types have had their bodies measured, altered, and judged by medical professionals, policy makers, and the general public. The question of whether to live or die must come back to the individual woman with a disability. The following dialogue is one that not only takes place in faculty rooms or at conferences, but also in living rooms, bedrooms, and sometimes hospitals. *To be or not to be. Whose choice is it anyway?*

Tanis: I wanted to die. I know I wanted to die. I wanted life to end as much as I wanted suffering to stop. I was not terminally ill. I was not even severely disabled in a medical sense. I was chronically ill and felt that my own depression was worse than any possible disease or disability. But I am alive to talk about it and glad that I am alive. I can honestly say that I am happy to have survived depression and that others like me are still alive. Some of us were rescued by friends or crisis lines and others just didn't succeed at getting dead. But we are only one side of the story. How can we ask the women who were actually able to die? Why do we assume that all the women who failed at suicide are the successful ones? I do not want to debate the afterlife or the ethics of dying. I want women to enjoy living, and to participate in a satisfying life, but I also want to ensure that suicide is a choice for us.

Barbara: You say you wanted to die because you were chronically ill and depressed; I can relate to your situation because twenty years ago

112

I was depressed and deeply dissatisfied with myself as a mother shortly after my daughter was born—it was probably tied in with post-partum depression. I remember how real my feeling was that everybody, including my daughter, would be better off if I was dead. But I'm glad I didn't "succeed." My failure at suicide felt like a "success" because afterwards I saw my attempt as a cry for help which I couldn't overtly articulate at the time. Fortunately, I did receive counselling which helped me build up the self-esteem and confidence that I needed in order to regard my life as worthwhile and fulfilling. Since then, whenever I contemplate others' failed or successful suicide attempts, I think of them as desperate cries for help, and thus if the woman fails at suicide I do think of her situation as more positive or successful than if she dies. I do think there is a reality that there are many people who killed themselves who could have gone on to live out their natural lives if their suicide had failed and intervention had taken place. I do think of people who are in a suicidal frame of mind as being emotionally disabled. In your case, did you actually attempt suicide or did you seek help beforehand?

Tanis: For me it was actually both. I did ask for help, and [I did] get some help before I tried. I attempted suicide by over-dosing on medication given to me by a doctor, combined with alcohol. I remember waking up thinking I was once again a failure and couldn't even kill myself properly, but that seems to be common. It is actually difficult to know how to die safely. By "safely," I mean finding a way that will end your life rather than result in permanent brain damage or further disability. Women tend to attempt suicide more often than men, although men are more likely to actually die during their attempts. I think many women are medically treated or restricted during their expression of suicidal thoughts, which makes it very difficult for them to complete their wishes.

Barbara: You make an interesting point in saying that women are more medically treated or restricted, and thus less successful in their suicide attempts. The two most famous cases in the Canadian "right-to-die" movement were initiated by women with disabilities, Nancy B. and Sue Rodriguez. I don't think either of them thought of their legal battles as gender-based. However, if we acknowledge that women in general and women with disabilities in particular tend to have less control over their lives than their male counterparts, it does seem most appropriate that it is women leading the fight for the ultimate choice: to be or not to be.

Tanis: I feel very strongly about the right to commit suicide because I know that it was a choice for me. When I hear that for some people it is not a choice because of disability, it scares me. Women with disabilities are not able to make their choices because society legally takes away their rights. Does this mean that as women, we are devalued by society, labelled by medical professionals and marginalized from the mainstream, and yet refused this final dignity of choice? They try very hard to prevent fetuses with disabilities from being born, yet once we are alive they won't let us take our own lives? It has a rather paradoxical ring to it: we don't really want you here but we won't let you leave either. And this is important because there are many ways to address the issue of wanting to die.

Barbara: I agree with you that women with disabilities are especially devalued and marginalized by mainstream society, including the health care professionals to whom they go for service. When you point to the issue of choice, it seems to come down to the ongoing issue of women's control over their bodies, again. I see parallels with the abortion issue—anti-abortion groups wish to deny all women the choice to terminate pregnancy, yet they do not on the other hand support every child's welfare after birth. There are not large-scale efforts by society in general to show that we value the lives of all children, or to alleviate their problems. So the message seems to be that all children are valued until they are born, when they have to contend with mainstream society's hierarchy of rights and privileges. Children are certainly not born equal when there is still such deeply entrenched sexism, classism, racism, and ableism in society.

Tanis: If everyone wanted us to be part of society, if all access questions were already dealt with, and perhaps integration was commonplace, would some women with disabilities still want to die? Yes.

We still might want to die the same way thousands of non-disabled women want to die, and their situations are often very different from the lives of women with disabilities. The complexity and diversity of motivations must be considered because disability is not the only "justifable reason" for wanting to die. Should it matter if you want to die because of Alzheimer's or because of a personal crisis? In fact, it is silly that if someone is not fatally ill but physically able enough to end her own life we allow this, but if the person is so ill or incapacitated that she requires assistance, then we don't allow it.

Barbara: You are saying that we should separate the issue of disability as the motivation for a woman committing suicide. We are getting into another paradox because the right-to-die movement is based on the person having a "justifiable reason" for ending their life. It is argued that if a person is terminally ill and/or permanently and severely disabled, they have the right to end their lives because their suffering has become unbearable or the quality of their lives is non-existent. Women with disabilities understandably feel devalued when the degree of physical disability is put forward as justification for suicide. When I follow your line of thinking to put aside motivation and focus solely on the concept of every person having the right to decide when and how they will die, I feel comfortable in saying that I agree with this idea. If a woman kills herself then she has successfully exercised this right. But I am still haunted by the possibility that she was in a temporary state of mind—suffering an emotional disability that could have been alleviated by intervention.

Tanis: Intervention that might be drugs? Or maybe electroshock therapy or restraints and isolation? It is difficult to condemn women's choices when their alternatives seem so poor. So there are two questions about women with disabilities choosing death that need to be thought through—one is their motivation and the other is their ability to follow through with their ideas.

Barbara: You are so right. Given the reality of women's lack of self-esteem and/or lack of "success" in life being rooted in concrete prescribed codes of behaviour according to gender which already restrict their life choices, how can others tell us that we are mentally incompetent if we want to die? Perhaps the opposite is true.

Tanis: Motivation for death is not always due to one specific issue. Some older women want to die to avoid wasting away or suffering unnecessary and intrusive medical procedures. Some people feel that pain is unbearable and prefer the shelter of death over drugs to resolve their pain. Other women may want to die because life has become so emotionally and spiritually empty that life is of no value. The discussion about suicide usually ends up with the issue of disability not being considered worth dying over. In fact, it is not always their disability that motivates women to want to die. In any event, the reasons women choose to die should not affect the judgement of others in power.

Barbara: When I contemplate the overwhelming problems of our world— hunger, war, environmental devastation—and when I visualize the huge number of people, especially women and children, trapped in oppressive and violent situations, it seems clear that a right-minded person would certainly be justified in wanting to make a final exit. I would still prefer to achieve more options and control over our lives for all women, so that less lives are "emotionally and spiritually empty," but such a revolution is not likely to be achieved in the near future.

The right to die is such a complex issue, I have conflicting ideas within me. Yes, I can agree that all women should have total control over their lives including whether to end them but if it was my daughter or friend who successfully committed suicide, I'd be devastated and definitely regret that I hadn't been able to intervene. I guess you could say that sometimes the political conflicts with the personal. So let's move on to the second issue.

Tanis: The second issue is being able to carry through wishes. Searching out and being able to administer a method of death is problematic for women with disabilities. Often the difficulty is finding one that is fatal enough that one can be sure of death and not another version of existence which could possibly be worse than the current situation. But women with severe physical disabilities who need assistance with daily chores and personal care may be dependent on others for several types of assistance.

In fact it is the issue of assistance that is almost more contentious than that of choice. Once a woman with a disability who is dependent on others has made the choice to die, who will help her? Can she ask her friends or doctors to do this? If she asks and they refuse, what action can she take? It seems almost cruel to deny a person who normally receives assistance without question this final assistance. Can I have a glass of water please? Can you move my left arm onto my lap? If an assistant ignored these requests and continually denied the woman food or comfort it would be criminal. In fact, it would be considered abuse and neglect if it continued.

Barbara: Yes, it may be that relatives of caregivers are just not emotionally or morally capable of enabling a woman with a disability to end her life. Perhaps our society will have to support more doctors like Kevorkian who are physically and emotionally removed from such situations. They are perhaps in a better position to "objectively" and non-exploitively agree to assist people to die. If we put aside the potential for exploitation and the issue of motivation in order to morally and legally recognize the right to die, then maybe we need "death doctors" just as there are abortion doctors and still others who won't participate.

Otherwise we run into another tragic paradox. I can agree with a woman's right to choose death, but I also think whoever is requested to assist her death has the right to say no for whatever moral or emotional reasons they may have. Following this logic, it is unfortunately quite possible that although women with disabilities may have the legal right to die, there will be no one in her life who can or will assist her to die. Because no one should be forced to help someone die, we are possibly moving towards the ultimate conflict of interests.

Tanis: But women with disabilities who are asking not to be fed, or not to be connected to machines or even to be given medication that would result in death, are not being helped. The helpers themselves are not necessarily making these judgements. There are countless situations that have never been publicized in the media in which women had their friends help them make the final exit without much attention. However, once the public sphere is involved, once there are media, courts, and politicians, death no longer becomes a choice. Death becomes a legal debate, an ethical question, and a political issue.

In many cases women with disabilities have had their rights taken away by the medical system which labels them as incompetent. An insidious legal technique is to institutionalize and medicate her; this process also dehumanizes the woman. Judges look favourably on a medical doctor's opinion regarding the mental competency of a patient, particularly suicidal ones.

In fact, even a layperson would agree that no one in their right mind would want to die. Ergo, suicidal women are mentally incompetent, with legal and medical procedures to support this. But the politicians have a hand in this too.

Barbara: I like your point that it is only when the issue of suicide becomes public that choice is eliminated and suddenly strangers are given the right to tell us whether or not we can choose to die. But I do think it is more a question of the final and irreversible consequences of assisted suicide rather than the apparent inequality of rights we see when we acknowledge the ability of an able-bodied woman to kill herself versus the inability of a woman with a disability to kill herself due to a lack of assistance. If a person assists a suicide, then they may wonder if the suicidal person might have later changed their minds about wanting to die. They may question themselves as to whether they made a correct assessment as to whether the assisted suicide was actually in the suicidal person's best interests. In any other "helping" situation, you can still see and communicate with the assisted person and evaluate how they are doing in order to adjust or change strategies accordingly.

At an abstract level, I agree with the right-to-die concept, but when I visualize concrete situations, I start having doubts because once the person has died, they can't come back and assure you that the right decision was made. It's one thing to decriminalize suicide when a person commits the act on their own, but when other people become involved, the issue becomes much more complicated with a wider range of circumstances and variables to be assessed.

Tanis: Suicide has been decriminalized as an act, and yet assisting or encouraging suicide is still against the law. It seems quite discriminatory that this law about suicide was made by able-bodied people who would be able to take their own lives without assistance if need be. However, if a woman with a disability makes the choice to die on her own, and needs help to carry it out, is she a criminal? More specifically is her assistant a criminal? The injustice is obvious: there are two types of equality—equality for those who are able-bodied, and equality for those who are different. Women are already subject to many kinds of violence and control over their bodies. Women are raped, assaulted, battered, stalked, and robbed by people who have power over them. Suicide is a way for women to have control over their own lives.

Barbara: Yes, women with disabilities must have the right to refuse care or treatment. However, the ending of life-support efforts does appear more feasible in terms of merely requiring the cessation of intervention by health-care professionals. But actually taking action to kill a person, even when the person has requested death, is more problematic. There is always the legitimate concern that caregivers who are already powerful forces in the lives of women with disabilities could exploit a woman's right to die in the interests of the caregiver and not the woman. So I can only agree that on the one hand women with disabilities must have their choice to die respected and, if necessary, assisted, but as long as society builds in safeguards to assure that the woman with a disability herself has decided to die and that no one coerced her into her decision in order to exploit her.

Tanis: The question of abortion, of fetal testing, or genetic manipulation is not being debated in this case. It is adult women, not science, that is being discussed. Some women have become disabled, and generally feel it is tragic that their lives have changed. Some women have had disabilities throughout their lives and continue to lead happy productive lives. Regardless of their status in life, all women must have death as an option. Not because society wants them to die, but because it is a legal and moral obligation of society to allow the dignity and security of the person. Choice.

Choosing death over life is not a decision made hastily. In fact, there are probably many women who have regretted attempted suicides and are now leading fulfilling lives after treatment or life situation changes. But there will always be women who do want to die and do need help in order to kill themselves. If you are so physically dependent on others for assistance that you need to ask to eat, then you should also have the right to not eat. Forced tube feedings and intrusive operations against personal wishes seem far more criminal than the issue of assisting a choice of a woman.

Questions are raised about abuse, or rather overuse, of this process should it be legalized. Too many people would "help"others die, and there would be ulterior motives in assisting suicides, issues of living wills, estate, inheritance, and burden would come up. There are equally large numbers of violent crimes that now occur, particularly against women, which are not being adequately addressed by the existing laws. In fact, there may eventually be a long list of situations which allow for assistance and others which preclude it. Yet this again avoids the question of choice.

Barbara: Just as outside parties such as police, lawyers, and judges often have to enter an abused woman's life situation in order to assess the appropriate action to protect her against her abuser (such as issuing a restraint order) which guarantees her right to life, so too there should be outside parties involved in the process of facilitating a woman's right to die and to assure that it is in her own best interests and not someone else's.

Women with disabilities are not supported in their choices to die, to live or to procreate, because a system of legal and medical procedures is in place to make decisions for women. But non-disabled women, and to an even greater degree, able-bodied men, are given better choices because of the lack of restraints in their lives. If they choose to die, it is a private matter and their decision. Women with disabilities lack this freedom of choice in death.

Remember that women with disabilities are not asking only for the right to die. Women with disabilities want to live, and live happily and with positive results, but they cannot do that without control over their bodies. It does come back to the role of women's bodies in society. Women in general are seen as baby-makers, life givers, and service providers. But women with disabilities challenge that role and confuse the everyday assumptions about the role of women. As a result, there are endless possibilities for debate: Can women with disabilities reproduce normal healthy babies and do we want these women to be mothers? Should we allow a fetus with an obvious disability to be brought to term? Which disabilities are considered severe enough to terminate pregnancy and which disabilities in adult women should preclude her from being allowed to have children? Can a child or woman with a disability experience any quality of life beyond that of mere existence? If she wants to die should we let her? Should we help her? Who are we to decide for her, whether she is to be or not to be? Whose question is it anyway?

Tanis: Lawyers and medical professionals are paid well for their work but women with disabilities, for the most part, are poor, and they are not able to spend their last dollars on hiring specialists to defend or evaluate them, and often would be unwilling to use their time and money for this. The issue of choice must be a personal one, and that choice should be legalized so that no procedures are initiated once the choice is made.

The trouble that some disabled women have with this issue relates to quality of life. Women with disabilities suffer higher rates of sexual and physical abuse, live with psychological abuse, and generally are mistreated by society. Some women with disabilities advocate for better education, safety, and employment while others work for better personal assistance, transportation, and housing. Regardless of the status of women with disabilities in general, a woman with a disability can personally make a choice to die. The issue of birth and death is also tied in with the issue of choice—thousands of women have taken their own lives because of inaccessible abortions. Thousands of women have died because of illegal and unsafe abortions. Choice is a matter of life and death for all women. But even if the situation for all women with disabilities was horrible and painful, each woman would still have to make the personal choice. There is no general rule or procedure because it is a matter of choice. If everything in this complicated world was perfect and accessible to women with all disabilities, some women as individuals would still need the right to make the choice to live or die. It is my life, and my choice to make.

Originally published in CWS/cf's issue on "Women and Disability," 13 (4) (1993): 88-92. Reprinted with permission.

NANCY E. HANSEN

A DELICATE BALANCE

Chronic Conditions and Workspace

T HIS IS A PORTION of a qualitative critical disability survey examining the timing and spacing realities in the lives women with physical disabilities. The women in this chapter identify as having a chronic condition or illness (Hansen), and each of the women chose their own pseudonym to disguise their identity. The social context of disability in public/private space is examined from their perspectives. Moving beyond individual incapacity in the workplace, this study explores wider social perceptions and attitudes. Through a series of in-depth interviews developed in conjunction with and involving women in Scotland and Canada, the interconnection of a community and workspaces is explored.

The amount of "work" required for many to "go to work" and "do the job" in "regular" inflexible workplaces is overwhelming. Constantly working against physical, social, and emotional barriers exacts a heavy personal toll, particularly when fatigue and impairment issues are a daily reality. Nonetheless, these women have devised complex and creative methods to work within and around the non-disabled parameters to make their own way on their own terms in the workplace.

WORKSPACE AND IMPAIRMENT: SOCIAL JUXTAPOSITION

Assumptions about the nature of employment are often at odds with social perceptions of the incapacity that is commonly associated with disability and chronic illness. Parallels can be drawn with the presence of non-disabled women in the workplace: "the embodied woman appears as an inferior 'other'" (McDowell and Court 734).

Fear of job loss, or misperceptions of inability stemming from negative social attitudes and stereotypes, lead many women to minimize or to conceal the reality of their condition in the workplace. Passing and resisting can be both physically and psychologically demanding:

> Social and physical environments are designed and built to exclude particular mind/body differences ... histories of able-ism, medical categorisation and surveillance can enlighten us, and how people collectively and individually resist embodied and social limitations that mind/body differences can bring.... (Butler and Parr 10)

Consequently, these individuals take great pains to "fit" into the non-disabled workplace with as little disruption as possible. McDowell and Court's study of women in banking noted that many of the women they interviewed: "[S]uggested that their workplace persona was unreal. They talked about 'building up a shell,' of 'adopting a different sense of myself'" (746).

Some women feel the need to justify the right to be present in the working environment. Kim's experience is typical:

> I'm in a chair, and they knew that from my application but they also knew, because where you state you have a disability, I always say that it's not progressive and that I'm fit and healthy enough, because really, I mean it means nothing, but yeah, it's good, it's hard work. (Kim, 48, Scotland)

Camryn sees advantages in an invisible condition (arthritis) as she is able to maintain some privacy. She is not on "display" to the same degree as those with visible markers of chronic illness, like wheelchairs. Her experience shows the level of energy required to maintain appearances:

> I'm lucky I guess in that way because I can pretty much hide it.... Some bosses I haven't told either ... and I wouldn't because I don't think they would be accepting ... after a while you forget who knows and who doesn't know! ... So somebody asks ... what happened, have I hurt my leg ...

or … if my feet are sore because of the shoes I'm wearing, and I can't remember if that person knows the real reason or not, so you tend to get into a bit of a mess…. (Camryn, 39, Canada)

Mitzi relates her experience:

It wasn't something that anybody knew about [Mitzi has arthritis]. The only thing that bothered me was stairs…. Everybody knew I didn't like going up stairs. If there was a lift in the building, I'd use that; if I had to go upstairs, then I would, but other than that, no, I didn't go upstairs. That was really the only thing…. I was always able to work and able to do things myself … so it never really disabled me enough to stop me working. My knees used to be sore all the time, but I mean, no, it never bothered me. (Mitzi, 46, Scotland)

Others told of their conditions being discounted by their employers because the impairment was not readily identifiable and therefore "all in the head." Molly relates her experience prior to her diagnosis with multiple sclerosis (MS):

I think everybody was very concerned, I got lots of help actually, and I saw lots of different neurologists and I had everyone telling me it was probably a psychological problem, and so we couldn't imagine quite why that would be. I even went to the extent of going to see a psychiatrist who told me that I seemed to be a very level-headed type of person. (Molly, 63, Canada)

The same thing happened to Chris:

My director said, "There's nothing wrong with you, Chris [Chris has repetitive strain injury], it's all in your head," and I've had comments like that because people can't see anything wrong with me, and I think sometimes people with visible disabilities have a better chance at things than people with invisible ones [disabilities]…. (Chris, 42, Canada)

Babette refers to "tricks of the trade" to "pass" as a sighted person in the more "public" spaces of her job setting when she held the position of university lecturer. (She has limited vision resulting from a stroke.) She did this in order to be seen as competent and professional by students and colleagues:

> I taught three courses a year and I always got really good ratings, but I used to go into the classroom before I would actually teach in it and get the lay of the land, so that I'd know where the steps were and if there were stairs that went up into the classroom, or how the ledge was for the board, and I used to write on the board, and I used to memorize my overheads and point to them as though I could see it. Then I'd stand back—you know the tricks of the trade—you'd stand back, and somebody would say what's the fourth word and I'd say, "Oh, I haven't got my glasses on, what word are you talking about?" … so no one ever knew I was vision impaired. (Babette, 47, Canada)

Women expressed real fear that their employers would discover their conditions. Barbie felt that employer knowledge would compound an already difficult working environment:

> I didn't tell them…. That was when I worked in the Department and it was really very hard going because … I had to put up with a lot of jokes because I was the only girl. (Barbie, 38, Scotland)

Olive did not want to change her work activity for as long as possible (visiting clients) and adopted a label to help explain her condition in a manner that she felt would be more palatable to her supervisors:

> I still continued the job I was doing, but not telling anybody that I had MS…. I was frightened, I think, because the group of people I used to go round [Olive was a community nurse] and see it was in the evening…. I did a round where there were quite a few people with MS, really bad MS, and I felt that if I told … the people I was working for, the health board, that they might stop me from going to these people, so I didn't

tell them. I didn't want a lighter load, so I didn't tell them. I did get support from my GP, who used to write out "post-viral debility" instead of saying she's got MS, so that was quite useful. (Olive, 52, Scotland)

Alfie shares the experience of different levels of disclosure arising because some impairments are considered more socially acceptable than others. She believes her bodily scars resulting from burns are more acceptable than the less visible chronic depression. She speaks about the possible detriment to her career should her depression be discovered. Alfie relates the conditional nature of the level of acceptance of impairment in her workplace and the reality of the "public" and "private" nature of her condition:

... a couple of people at work know I'm on medication, that I see a shrink once a week, so it's possible that they knew and if they do then they're okay about it.... With the appearance thing, I'm fairly upfront with people once I get to know them a little bit and can assume that they want to know what's different or wrong with me, and so I'm fairly forthcoming about that. I guess the fear is that if people actually knew—if my boss or senior people in the department who may in the future be looking at hiring me or promoting me—were aware of my psychiatric disability, that could ... would ... impede my chances of climbing the ladder, even though I really don't want to climb all that much higher than where I am now. I want to at least maintain the flexibility, and if they knew, if it was known that I have problems of chronic depression.... (Alfie, 34, Canada)

SUPERWOMAN: PROVING WORTH

Many of the women felt that they had to prove their worth as employees by performing at an exceptional level in order to justify their presence to supervisors and other workers. They felt that they were always "on approval," and because of that had to work to a much higher standard than the "average" non-disabled worker to be perceived as competent as Mary Lou relates:

I feel at times I'm having to always sort of make up for that and put in maybe a 150 percent, but I'm getting better in that regard. I do my job as best I can and don't have the same sense that I'm always having to really prove that I can in fact do with my training what I'm trained to do. (Mary Lou, 45, Canada)

Part-time work is a necessity for some workers in this study in order to manage levels of fatigue or discomfort associated with certain types of impairment. Chris expressed sentiments common to many women working part-time:

I think that even though I work part-time, I still feel as if I should be doing the work of a full-time employee and I still fit five days' worth of work into four days. I often take work home with me to compensate for the fact that I'm not in the other day, but then I do all that toward time off.... But I feel like I do have to work that bit harder because I'm only here part time. (Chris, 42, Canada)

Camryn speaks of feeling compelled to perform while dealing with energy restrictions:

Some days I don't find ... I have the energy levels I used to, so I do feel I'm underperforming, but that's not really anything that's said to me, that's just me. I do feel pressure, the bosses ... I can't even put it into words. (Camryn, 39, Canada)

However, a supportive workplace environment can substantively enable chronically ill employees to work to the fullest, as Mary Lou explains:

The years prior coming to my current job site was at a rehabilitation hospital and actually they were very accommodating there. I really had the opposite experience—things were in place for me immediately. Certainly one example comes to mind—that I had trouble holding the phone to dictate reports into a central word-processing centre—so within a few days of mentioning that to my supervisor, I had a hands-free Dictaphone system on my desk, which I used with a foot pedal, and I could simply just sit and dictate my reports and it was terrific. Also, just in terms of shelving and things that were adapted in my own office, they were done very quickly, sometimes even before me pointing them out. I just had a really exceptional supervisor who just seemed to be willing to have everything in place to enable me to do my job. (Mary Lou, 45, Canada)

BUILDING COMFORT LEVELS

Many women spent their energy trying to create and to maintain their physical space in the workplace. These women work hard at trying to accommodate their conditions in addition to meeting the requirements of their position. Indeed, these requirements must be addressed before dealing with employment duties.

Performance and ability remain bound up in physicality (McDowell). Lack of creativity and the inflexibility of some employers restrict workplace opportunities for many women. Barbie's experience is typical:

I mean they said things to me like, "Well, you can't get training anyway because you won't be able to stand and you can't use your arm." (Barbie, 38, Scotland)

Workplace accommodations are frequently done grudgingly and women often feel that their need for adaptation disrupts the "natural" functioning or flow and order of the workspace as Mary Lou explains:

I'm just feeling that I have to continually advocate to make sure the accommodations are in place.... It really has taken a toll because your energy is being channelled in that area instead of ... being able to ... do my work. (Mary Lou, 45, Canada)

Chris discusses the experience of seeking necessary accommodations:

It's very stressful, especially as disabled employees are, well, obviously if you're disabled enough, that helps to start off with, but you're not as strong, you're weaker, not necessarily weaker, but you don't have the energies often to fight with, and I think they use that, knowing that you're more apt to back down, and a lot of disabled people I know that feel uncomfortable asking for special things or something different, not necessarily special, but something they need. (Chris, 42, Canada)

Requests for employment accommodation are often avoided by the women for fear of questions relating to work competency, as Camryn relates:

I just don't even go there and I should, right? So that would make it easier, and most of that might just be me too, right? But I'm not willing to step out of that one and say, "I need this, I want this." It would make life easier, I think, being able to order ergonomic equipment … like I would want something better for my arm to rest on. Right now I have something, but it's not that great, but asking for something better or different [makes] you feel kind of like you're asking [for] something unreasonable. (Camryn, 39, Canada)

High levels of stress and anxiety resulting from struggling for accommodation is a common issue. For individuals with compromised energy levels, this is taxing, as Mary Lou conveys:

I certainly have sensed from early on that it probably isn't a level playing field in terms of some of the accommodations I've needed. I often have to really persist, certainly in terms of getting a wheelchair-accessible washroom. It took about eight years for that to be completed. In terms of my office set-up too, it's just a constant struggle…. (Mary Lou, 45, Canada)

The "workings" of the workplace entail more than the job. The social-cultural intricacies are often quite complex. There are micro-social relationships, some of which bear directly on advancement or salary increases. Accessing these elements can be difficult for chronically ill employees because of fear on the part of non-disabled people. It is usually left to the employee to address the situation, as Alfie explains:

> I've developed more of a sense of humour about it, and I try and kid around a bit, or if they're opening a conversation and I'm comfortable with the person or the people there, I'll use the opportunity to explain and they're usually quite surprised. Well, not surprised because they all usually wonder what the scars are about … (Alfie, 34, Canada)

Employees can be supported and accommodated within the work-space when the information they share is met with creativity and empathy. In many instances this holistic approach to the workplace has been instrumental in building self-esteem and a positive self-image, as Barbie's experience illustrates:

> The agency … offered me the job.… It completely changed my life in a fantastic way, and I just felt so valued and useful and I felt like I was creative for the first time in my life, and I felt I was innovative for the first time in my life and I felt I had good ideas. It was just a fantastic job for me and I was working from home and I had incredible flexibility and if I had to travel, which I had to do quite a bit of travelling, they were happy to pay me travel expenses because they knew I couldn't drive far … so it was just a great job. It was really sort of putting me back together again. I was kind of like a remodelled person! (Barbie, 38, Scotland)

Employers can be ill at ease with a worker with a newly diagnosed chronic illness returning to the job, as Barbie illustrates in an experience with her previous employer:

> [T]hey just said, "You know, this isn't working," and if I went back to work, I wouldn't be allowed to stay on as an assistant manager and they wouldn't let me keep that grade because I was trying to maybe reduce my hours and go back part-time, but they said, well, I couldn't do the job … and that was it. (Barbie, 38, Scotland)

Alternatively, Joanne's employers showed what can happen when teamwork and creative thinking come together to facilitate accommodation of a newly diagnosed condition:

> They've been fantastic ... really good. They've tried to keep me on, much longer than they need to. I don't just mean legally, they kept me on even more than they had to within the local authority. They've been very, very supportive, given me equipment at home, computers, comfortable chairs, you know, worked with me to decide what little bits and pieces I could work with them, even though I was still off work. (Joanne, 48, Scotland)

TIMING AND SPACING

Time use is a pivotal factor for individuals with restricted levels of mobility, agility, dexterity, and energy. Maintaining time, speed, and personal energy levels is a constant, delicate balancing exercise for chronically ill women. This level of time management is largely unknown to the non-disabled. As Chouinard explains:

> For women with disabilities, negotiating spaces of everyday life, such as the home and workplace, is often difficult, contradictory and oppressive. This is because experiencing spaces through a disabled body not only involves significant physical and mental challenges, dealing with significant limits to one's ability to act, but also encountering and responding to complex, often social rules and cultural codes which mark the disabled body. (142)

Chronically ill women are using and battling with space and environments in order to present themselves as competent workers, as Kim and Dolly relate:

> [I] have it organized so that most of my teaching is in the morning.... I've more energy in the morning. I've said to them, "Look, if I can do my teaching in the morning, then I can go home and crawl into bed in the afternoon.... There's been lots of times when I work at home. (Kim, 48, Scotland)

I have to empty my bladder every couple of hours, and I also have to make sure that I'm not sitting or standing for long periods of time … I tire easily. (Dolly, 34, Canada)

Time-space demands are an integral part of the job for any employee. There are those that apply specifically to chronically ill women managing their own time and space to allow them to be seen as competent employees before, as it were, any of the specific requirements of the job are taken into consideration. For example, Olive speaks of extreme fatigue experienced at the end of a workday and how it impacts heavily on her domestic life:

Sometimes it's quite hard because I have to go in maybe at lunchtime, and then I'm not getting home until after 8 p.m., which is very tiring. It is very long, but I usually have somebody waiting in here so that when I come back, they can sort of help me get to bed and maybe make me something to eat if I'm not past it by that time, so that's quite a hard day. (Olive, 52, Scotland)

Maureen has ME, or Chronic Fatigue Syndrome. Her positive experience shows how, with a bit of creative thinking and flexibility, employers and employees are able to develop approaches to timing and spacing:

One of the ways that we managed to accommodate my needs to work in this environment was to have a seven-day week and flexible hours with the ability to work from home as needed and not scheduled…. I was given taxi chits to go to courses, whereas most employees would have to travel by local transport system, so again in a confidential and privileged manner, I was allowed to spare energy by the gov- ernment paying for my transportation costs [and avoid fatigue by taking taxis instead of public transportation]. (Maureen, 49, Canada)

DOMESTIC TIME/WORKSPACE

Traditionally, the "public" environment of the workplace is viewed as separate from the "private" environment of the home, reflecting socially ascribed beliefs. Convention dictates "private" domestic activity does not impact on the "public" domain of the workplace. But as Davies (2001) explains, the time/space demands lack demarcation for women:

> Space and time are thereby not individual resources as such; rather they must be understood in a relational manner. Put in simple terms, where women find themselves and when they find themselves and when they find themselves where they are, are importantly determined by the needs of others. (137)

The "home" environment has a profound impact on individual ability to access workspace. Personal care and domestic activities are generally treated as both "personal" and "private," yet, for chronically ill women, they connect.

Fawcett (2000) showed that respondents with impairments often spent significantly more time and energy on household and personal care responsibilities than they did on employment-related duties. Fawcett (1996) drew strong links between support in the household and the person's availability for employment. Organization and timing at home can often play a pivotal role in workplace success. "Activities cannot be neatly scheduled; the unexpected repeatedly rears its head and demands flexibility and a process relation to time" (Davies 143).

There is a complex "science" of timings, spacings, and organization enabling these women to manage in non-disabled space and gain the "approval" of colleagues and society. It is as if these private activities are remote. Often these "taken for granted" and "private" activities have a profound individual and social impact, so obvious but "invisible." Little conscious awareness from these women of the time, effort, or importance involved does not suggest insignificance. Lilly and Vicki explain:

> It's a science. I've been working on this for the past four years, just because I have difficulty getting up early, so in order to catch my 7:30 a.m. bus, I need to be very organized and structured the night before, [and] do all the prep the night before, otherwise I would not have enough time in the morning. (Lilly, 34, Canada)

It's planned to the minute. Well, I get up as late as possible. I hate getting up, and I just shower or wash, get dressed. If I'm really organized, I'll have planned what I'm going to wear the night before. I'll have it all out, even down to jewellery. (Vicki, 29, Scotland)

Frequently a difficult balance is sustained between fixed amounts of time and limited energy levels (Fawcett 1996). It may take longer to complete personal care or domestic tasks. These women begin their mornings at a very early hour in order for their medication to take effect, thereby enabling them to function effectively on the job, as Barbie illustrates:

I'm managing really by ... [going] to bed really early. I have to rest as much as I can. I have to get up really early to get myself dressed and ready in time, and to be able to drive in the morning is quite difficult, as it's really painful driving in the morning, so I have to get up really early and get medicated really early and I do that. I wake up about 6:30 a.m. and take all the medication and I eat at 6:30 a.m., and then I get up at 7:00 a.m. (Barbie, 38, Scotland)

The time and effort required for personal care, such as bathing or housework and meals, is often overlooked, but it is the real "work" that begins the working day for many women. Kim's experience is common:

I'm up about 6:30 a.m. and 6:45 a.m., shower, breakfast, unlock the door because I hate sitting in traffic, and my first class is at 9:15 a.m. I like that quiet hour. If I'm in at 8 a.m., I can have a coffee ... organize myself for the day a bit ... up and out after a healthy breakfast, just my usual shower, and then I'm out the door.... (Kim, 48, Scotland)

Links between employment and domestic assistance must be understood: Employment should not preclude the need for domestic help, which may assist work performance. Domestic assistance would be cost-effective, thus enabling more women to enter paid work. Audrey and Babette discuss this need:

> We tend not to get home help because you're working.... Well, ... they seem to think that because you're working, if you're able to work, you're able to do housework. (Audrey, 55, Scotland)

> I would really benefit from a couple of hours of home support where someone could chop vegetables for me, or whatever, and I could make a chili, but I don't have that.... You have to be incapable of standing for a certain amount of time, and I am sometimes, but other times I'm perfectly capable of doing it, so it's the variability of my symptoms that prevents me from accessing anything, and it's also—and I say this with some caution, but it's true—I don't like to say it, but it's true. It's also because my physicians don't want to see me as needing home support so that when I broach it with them, it's ... "Oh, you're young and you're okay." (Babette, 47, Canada)

Wider community space in relation to work is an important factor in a chronically ill woman's ability to function in and access workspace. Many do not drive or have their own means of transport and therefore utilize other mechanisms. Proximity takes on greater significance when speed, fatigue, and distance are complicating factors. Hence, centrally located housing, shopping, and medical services enable these women to schedule numerous activities.

Working-life experiences are markedly different. Babette has more control over her workspace (she is a psychologist). Her experience in this respect is very different from many of the women I interviewed.

> Recently I've closed an office that was out of my building because I was travelling by [disability transport] and it was taking me roughly an hour and a half to get to work in the morning, so I now have a practice where my office is one apartment away from my own home, so getting to the office is no longer an issue, it's just basically walking to an office. (Babette, 47, Canada)

Yet, despite a different educational experience, Wendy has been able to adapt her work in the home around a changing impairment:

I did bed and breakfast, just two rooms, when I found out I couldn't work. I wanted to do something, and bed and breakfast is fine when you have a young family. What I did when I was running the B&B is, I'd rest in between each activity, like after making beds I'd rest for an hour; after cleaning I'd rest for another hour. I really had to measure what I did. I never hurried. It's hard because I was always a fast person. Now I do everything in sections. (Wendy, 56, Scotland)

CONCLUSION

The effort required to work (paid or unpaid) begins long before chronically ill women enter the working environment. Revolutionary changes are needed in order to achieve substantive results. In order to facilitate this process, the depth, texture, and complexity of chronic illness in a relational context must be fully understood. If real progress is to be made, a grounded sensitivity to the timings and spacings of everyday life for women with chronic illness is needed. Imagine if the majority world thought beyond established boundaries and recognized the potential of these women on their terms.

This article was previous published in Dissonant Disabilities: Women with Chronic Illnesses Explore Their Lives, *D. Driedger and M. Owen (Eds.), CSPI/Women's Press, pg. 131–145, 2008. Reprinted with permission of Canadian Scholars' Press Inc. and/or Women's Press.*

REFERENCES

Butler, R. and H. Parr. *Mind and Body Spaces: Geographies of Illness, Impairment and Disability*. London: Routledge, 1999.

Chouinard, V. "Life at the Margins: Dïsabled Women's Explorations of Ableist Spaces." *Embodied Geographies Spaces, Bodies and Rites of Passage*. Ed. E. Kenworthy Teather. London: Routledge, London. 1999. 142-156.

Davies, K. "Responsibility and Daily Life Reflections Over Timespace." *Timespace: Geographies of Temporality*. Eds. J. May and N. J. Thrift. London: Routledge, 2001. 133-148.

Fawcett, G. *Living With Disability in Canada: An Economic Portrait.* Ottawa: Human Resources Development Canada, Office for Disability Issues, 1996.

Fawcett, G. *Bringing Down the Barriers: The Labour Market and Women With Disabilities in Ontario.* Ottawa Canadian Council on Social Development, 2000.

Hansen, N. *"Passing" Through Other Peoples' Spaces: Disabled Women Geography, and Work.* Unpublished Ph.D. dissertation, University of Glasgow, Glasgow, Scotland, 2002.

McDowell, L. and G. Court. "Performing Work: Bodily Representations in Merchant Banks." *Environment and Planning D: Society and Space* 12.6 (1994): 727-750.

McDowell, L. *Gender, Identity and Place: Understanding Feminist Geographies.* Oxford: Polity Press, 1999.

SALLY A. KIMPSON

LIVING POORLY

Disabled Women on Income Support

ISABLED WOMEN ARE AMONG the poorest Canadian citizens, and those disabled women who are single, single-parenting, Aboriginal, immigrants or refugees live in the deepest poverty. Women with disabilities are more likely to be lone parenting than their non-disabled counterparts, to be separated, divorced or widowed, and to remain single. Perhaps not surprisingly, disabled women are also more likely than disabled men to assume more responsibility for household chores and, even when living with others, are more likely than disabled men to perform household chores without assistance (Fawcett 163, 165).

Clearly, many factors influence a disabled woman's chances of living well or living poorly, but the single most important factor is her source of income. Income sources available to disabled women vary and, for some, include earnings from paid employment. However, labour force participation for disabled women is no guarantee of adequate income as they are more likely to be underemployed, underpaid and/or temporarily employed. Because of this they are more likely to live in poverty and less likely to be eligible for more generous (employer-sponsored) disability income support programs, or Workers' Compensation programs. Disabled women often have insufficient labour force participation to be eligible for CPP/QPP Disability Benefits,[1] or if eligible, receive minimal benefits because support amounts are tied to (low) pay levels while working.

For those disabled women without employment earnings, those ineligible for income support programs because of compromised labour force participation, and those who are unable to rely on social networks, such as family and friends for income support, their only recourse is to apply for provincial social assistance programs, or "last resort" benefits. Women receiving this type of assistance are among the most disadvantaged in Canadian society, and "face the greatest likelihood of living in poverty" (Fawcett 147). Women receiving provincially-administered disability income support, in particular those living with mental impairments, like chronic depression or bipolar conditions, are also more likely to be stigmatized by society, and increasingly, constructed as the "unworthy" poor (Bach and Rioux 318).

This article presents short narratives, accompanied by verbatim accounts from the lives of two disabled women living on provincially-administered income support in the province of British Columbia, drawn from current doctoral research on the effects of provincial income support policy in the everyday lives of disabled women. (See Doe and Kimpson for a description of the lives of disabled women living on CPP/QPP Disability).

The everyday lives of disabled women receiving provincially-administered income support are constructed in relation to government policy and programs in unsettling ways.

My intention here is to show how difficult, and even impossible, it is for these disabled women to live well. The women whose lives (and difficulties) are revealed here live with physical and/or mental impairments experienced as a result of acquired chronic illnesses, one as an adult, the other a woman who developed juvenile rheumatoid arthritis before five years of age. Both live alone. One woman single-parented a mentally-impaired child into young adulthood; he is limited in his ability to provide support to his disabled mother. The other woman did not have children.

WHAT DO I MEAN BY POVERTY, AND BY EXTENSION, LIVING POORLY (OR LIVING WELL)?

Canada has no firmly established or commonly understood "poverty line," below which people are considered to be living in poverty in this country. More commonly, social policy researchers, social groups and the media use Statistics Canada's low income cut-offs, referred to as LICOs, to define poverty as "the income level at which families or persons not in economic families[2] spend 20 percent more than average of their before tax income on food, shelter and clothing" ("Low

Income Before Tax Cut-Offs"). Those spending this additional twenty percent—average families spend approximately 50 percent—are not considered to be "poor" but rather in "straitened circumstances" ("Low Income Before Tax Cut-Offs"). However, I consider these Canadians to be living in poverty or poor. The most recent (2008) low income cut-off for single persons living in an urban centre the size of that in which the disabled women discussed here live (100,000 to 499,999 people), is $19,094 (before taxes) per annum ("Low Income Cut-Offs for 2008").

In all Canadian provinces social assistance rates, including income support for disabled people, fall well below the low-income cut-offs. For single disabled women in British Columbia the monthly assistance rate is set at $531.42, with an additional $375.00 maximum shelter allowance, regardless of the cost of living in the region where a woman lives in the province ("Employment and Assistance Rate Tables"). This benefit amounts to $10, 877.04 per annum, about $9000 yearly below the low-income cut-off for the region in question. Basic benefit rates in B.C. have not changed in eight years, despite the increasingly high cost of living. Even though disabled women are potentially eligible for various kinds of subsidies and services, these are constantly under threat as the neo-liberal economic and political regime of the B.C. government seeks to reduce deficits by either cutting programming or changing policies in ways that make access to these programs and services increasingly difficult or impossible.

The stated concern of Western democratic governments is the well-being or welfare of their citizens. The British Columbia government is no exception. In its strategic plan, vision statements, and Ministry of Housing and Social Development (MHSD)[3] service plans, the government has set vague but lofty goals for the well-being of its disabled citizens, which is one of this particular Ministry's direct concerns. In particular, the Minister has stated, "we want to ensure low income earners and people dealing with addictions, mental illnesses and disabilities have access to supports when and where they need them most so they can become independent and participate more fully in their communities" (Coleman 3).[4]

Disabled women in B.C. want to live well in many of the ways the government articulates: they want to be as independent and participate as fully as possible in communities; they want to live full and rewarding lives and be able to pursue and fulfil their personal aspirations; and, they want to have timely and uncomplicated access to the kinds of supports and services they need to do so. Unfortunately, the structural poverty within which they live, combined with the need for enhanced supports because of disability, intersect with the difficulties they have accessing the very supports they need to live well. The effect is to position them on the margins of society, further disabling them and deepening their social and economic inequality. Simply put, for the most part, they are living poorly. In these women's lives, like so many impoverished people worldwide, "The poor are those whose greatest task is to try to survive" (Farmer 6).

For the women whose stories are narrated briefly here, the struggle to survive is relentless and multifaceted. Narratives from two women's lives are presented to make visible the lives of disabled women living poorly on "last resort" benefits.

BEING CAUGHT: A FAUSTIAN BARGAIN?

Galya[5] is a refugee from a former Soviet bloc country, who is well-educated and was completing a second master's degree at a western Canadian university at the time of the onset of her mental impairment, chronic depression. As a student, employed seasonally and part-time as a research assistant, she had no access to employer-sponsored disability benefits or CPP. In fact at the time of disablement she had a large student loan, on which she and her son lived. Galya continues to pay the Ministry of Housing and Social Development $10 monthly for paying off the student loan whose large monthly payments she could not afford when she withdrew from her program and became eligible for disability benefits. She also lives with high blood pressure and chronic bronchitis, chronic physical conditions that significantly limit her energy and what can be done physically in a day.

Galya requires ongoing psychotherapy to help her deal with the effects of depression. In part because of the poverty in which she lives, and her doctor's referral practices, she seeks therapy offered by psychiatrists who are subsidized through the B.C. Medical Services Plan. Ironically, despite being a trained psychologist (and a thesis short of a graduate degree in counselling), Galya cannot utilize the services of either psychologists or therapists because their practices are largely unsubsidized in B.C., unless they work in institutional settings. Their services are beyond the means of disabled women like Galya: living in community, receiving provincial disability benefits, but not connected to the few institutions providing free psychological services beyond psychiatry.

Galya has a level of self-awareness commensurate with her education and knows what it means professionally to be helpful. Despite seeing a number of psychiatrists, she does not receive the compassionate, non-judgemental, respectful care she needs and expects. In her experience none of them were helpful:

> I found all of them—and my doctor referred me to all possible people who could take new patients—I found them so absolutely not empathic, but even worse. I found them almost using me and my time to talk about how they became psychiatrists, or how they can help me, or what their life looks like. It's unbelievable. I even said to one person, "you know the medical plan is paying to you to talk about yourself." So they were just patronizing, classifying and just making all kind of judgements. It was just totally insane.

In frustration she even speaks back to one of the psychiatrists who is wasting her time. Despite the fact that the services of psychiatrists are affordable, that is, covered by the provincial health care plan, Galya opts not to further expose herself to the "insanity" of their treatment of her.

Not only do the psychiatric services she tries fail her, Prozac®, the conventional anti-depressant she is prescribed, has unintended adverse effects; she becomes extremely depressed physically and mentally, and aggressive in interactions with others. These are side effects she is not willing to live with. Contrary to her doctor's recommendation, and the fact that she is forfeiting a subsidized medication, she discontinues it, risking the possibility of the return of more debilitating depression, which would significantly immobilize her. She seeks out and finds a physician who approaches her condition with megavitamin therapy. Of the supplements he recommends, niacin and folic acid are subsidized by the Ministry of Housing and Development via a $40 monthly nutritional supplement allowance for vitamins and minerals.

Procuring this nutritional supplement is no mean feat. Galya has to engage in the energy and time-consuming work necessary to find out what she needs to know, plan and then execute that plan to secure the allowance. Despite seriously compromised energy, and shortness of breath associated with chronic bronchitis, Galya has to travel via public transit (for her, two buses) to Ministry offices to get the form for this request (she has no computer), make an appointment with her doctor, travel to and from the appointment via public transit, and make sure the required forms are completed and delivered. Once the forms (completed by the doctor) reach the Ministry the applicant must then wait for approval according to detailed regulations. Despite this, receiving financial help with this expense is worth Galya's effort, and presumably continues to be worth it because she must reapply to the Ministry on an annual basis to ensure she remains eligible for this nutritional allowance. Recent changes to supplement policy may affect her eligibility for this allowance in the future, but she will not know that until she applies, because the Ministry is not forthcoming with this kind of information. As for the remainder of the vitamins and minerals she is prescribed that are not subsidized, Galya must either forfeit some aspect of her daily life, such as going without food or eating less nutritional food, or she may be forced to expend more energy in order to purchase these products. This would entail researching where she can purchase these supplements cheapest, often at discount or big box stores typically located two or three exhausting bus rides away.

But she also needs prescription medications for her bronchitis; for example, one antibiotic in particular that the government Pharmacare program delisted (removed from the provincial subsidized medications list), costs $78 for a course of treatment. In this case, Galya must make a critical decision. Either she can reduce her income substantially by purchasing this medication, and do without things she needs to live on (or work harder to get them for free through community-based agencies, like the food bank or St. Vincent de Paul), or she can do without the antibiotic (or take a subsidized one) and run the risk of continuing to be ill with bronchitis, and perhaps even getting worse.

This is not unlike the dilemma she faces with respect to either taking the Prozac® or treating her depression nutritionally. For Galya, getting the most appropriate treatment for bronchitis is infinitely more expensive than she can afford, but she is willing to make substantial sacrifices in order to have it. What might she be going without or doing more of to do so? With her monthly income decreased by $78, she might choose not to purchase any fresh food for a while, or she might have to make extra trips (despite compromised energy) to the food bank and other charitable organizations to obtain donated goods. She would also have to intensify her efforts to find cheaper products and household goods she needs—toilet paper, cleaning products, toothpaste, shampoo—which she cannot buy in bulk to save money because the transit system is the only form of transportation she can afford. Galya tells me:

> So how does it affect my health? It's scary. I have anxiety that it will be less and less and less available things. I have anger that, for example, I love theatre, I love music. I'm not able to go to even to the museum. The gap between someone who has money and someone who is on disability benefits—yes, it's enough not to die out of hunger *if* we have subsidized housing. If I didn't have subsidized housing I probably would have less than $200 for everything, like a hundred something. So using food banks one can just survive. All my clothes are from people's donations or St. Vincent de Paul. Of course because I'm depressed it doesn't really bother me, but sometimes it does. Because as I said when I go to the bank, and if it is not my bank where people know me and they feel like I'm a neighbour, if it's a different bank, I see the difference in treatment. I feel anxiety so I'm sure that it is unsettling emotionally and mentally.

"Unsettling" is an understatement. Despite her own efforts to get better, Galya lives in constant fear that she will either get worse and perish, or get better and lose her meagre benefits. Like many disabled women with chronic illnesses, she wishes for stability in terms of her health, at least enough to fulfill aspirations, in her case to complete her degree, but fears the consequences of this stability, i.e., the potential loss of benefits. She describes it this way:

> There is this sense of being caught between getting well and losing the benefits. This is the very main thing, this desire to

get better and fear to lose it if I get better, although I meditate every day on enhancing my health, in the morning. But there is part of my psyche that is caught in that old—"Don't. Stay where you are. Otherwise you will be on the street, under the bridge."

Galya engages in spiritual (self-care) practices that reflect a strong desire to improve physically and mentally in the face of strong doubts about the possible consequences—losing her benefit, becoming a street person, living under the bridge where local homeless people congregate. In comparison, maintaining her current health status (but not getting better), and continuing to receive benefits while subject to the constraints of income support policy seems a less risky option than increasing her efforts to get better, and losing her benefits—a kind of Faustian bargain. Galya's fears demoralize her, as does living with relentless difficulty; these undermine her will and her spirit, conditions directly counter to becoming better, or even living well.

It is entirely possible that she will never be able to regain her health for a variety of reasons, including the chronic nature of her medical conditions, along with the constraints and difficulty she faces just surviving. But, regaining her health is Galya's aspiration, as is retaining her eligibility for benefits or being able, however restricted, to support herself. She is caught between these competing aspirations because efforts to regain her health are thwarted by the structural poverty in which she lives and the way programs are administered by the Ministry. But also regaining health is a double-edged sword, because if she were to do so Galya runs the risk of losing her benefits, which would cast her into even deeper poverty. This she can ill afford.

LIMITING CHANGES, JUGGLING LIMITS

Marion developed rheumatoid arthritis as a young child and lived at home with her parents until her late twenties, while she completed an undergraduate degree. Unlike the others I interviewed for my doctoral research she receives regular home support services (120 hours monthly) because of impairments that affect her mobility and ability to perform activities of daily living (bathing, dressing, cooking, housework). Like Galya, she is "fortunate" to live in subsidized housing, and unlike many other disabled women does not spend the bulk of her disability benefit on housing. She has seen many changes with respect to income support programs in the twenty years she has been receiving benefits, particularly changes to subsidized allied health services such as physiotherapy and massage, that enable her to participate in paid work while continuing to receive her disability benefit. Like Galya, Marion also directly experiences changes in Pharmacare policy, in particular the delisting of many common proprietary (brand name) medications, replacing them with their generic counterparts. This change does not result in the intended effect in her case, that is, the simple matter of being prescribed the generic drug, which she then would take regularly.

> I've seen a lot of changes in the benefits and also in the offices and the staff. The biggest change with the benefits, which is really, really hard on people like myself and other people with disabilities are the changes to the medical. Because for a long time there they would cover so many of each, and extra appointments [with physio and massage, naturopathy and chiropractic]. Now they only cover ten. And even the cutbacks to medication now—like for example I take Entrophen but I can't take the generic kind of Entrophen. If I could take the generic they would cover it. If I can't take the generic, which I can't, I have to every six months, regardless of the fact that I've been on this pill for like 18 bloody years, I have to go through my specialist, get a special form filled out—a special authorization form—to get them to approve the Entrophen, which I have been on since I was seven years old—to get them to approve it every year. Because they don't really like to do that because they like you to take the cheapie brands. That's been the most hurtful is those—and also changes in cutting out pills specifically. Like some pills are just totally not covered at all.

These changes and cutbacks directly affect Marion's ability to be independent and to participate in paid employment, contrary to the government's stated intention of fostering disabled people's independence. Marion works part-time as a trained disability advocate with a non-profit society, and every cent she earns goes towards the health services and products she needs which are no longer subsidized, or require extra effort to ensure subsidy. Other policies also affect her efforts to live well. Currently, people receiving provincial disability benefits in B.C. can earn up to $500 monthly and retain their benefits. At the time of the interviews (2003/4) the allowable monthly earnings were $400. I wondered if Marion felt any pressure from government around these earnings.

> I'm still leery right now about making the extra income per month, because I would like to make more. But I know for a fact that if you make $400 a month, which I could frankly use for paying for these medical things that they're not paying for now—you know like physio and massage and podiatry and everything else. The reality of it is that if you start making that money every month I think they are going to lean on you hard to be doing that more often, getting off the benefits. And there's no way I could do that and live you know with my expenses. I mean I don't even know how you would pay rent. I could not live in my own place if I was not living here in subsidized housing because the rent alone, never mind groceries would be what?—it would be more than my cheque a month, which is $700 and change. Well you try finding a place to rent for that kind of money. And that's not groceries. Or gas payments or car insurance. So there is just no way.

Unlike most people with disabilities who use wheelchairs, Marion has her own vehicle, which she is able to drive herself but needs help to transfer in and out of, and with managing her chair once in. The privilege of owning a vehicle is not without additional costs that, should she lose her benefit, she would not be able to afford. Having a vehicle enables her many of the things Galya is unable to do. She can travel to several destinations in one outing, according to her own schedule and pace, purchase large or bulk items, thereby saving money, and travel in relative safety in terms of being exposed to violence on public transit. Having a vehicle also reduces any isolation she might experience, and enables her to participate in her community as an advocate and to work part time.

Marion's part-time work, which is very flexible, accommodates the conditions with which she lives, in particular, chronic pain.

> I can change the nature of what I do on any day depending on how I feel. But the flip side of that is that pain is part of my life. So if I didn't have the physio and I didn't have the massage, there would be a lot less computer work I could do. There would be a lot less going out-and-about making contacts that I could do because without physio I just wouldn't be able to move. So I've got to have it. One facilitates the other.

Like most people with disabilities, Marion wants to engage in some kind of paid employment, and unlike many has found the kind of work that enables her to participate in paid employment in ways that do not compromise her health (or ability to work). Yet she wants to work more, in part so she can increase her income enough to pay for the health services and products she needs to participate in employment, now no longer subsidized by the B.C. government. This is a vicious circle for Marion.

Despite her desire (and ability) to work more and regardless of the advantages it would provide her, Marion limits herself with respect to paid employment using the earnings exemption as a kind of bellwether, indicating what limits she has to set on her earnings. She believes that if she were to earn the monthly maximum allowable earnings exemption ($400), this would send a signal to the Ministry triggering a campaign to "encourage" her to keep earning that amount in a more consistent way, which would present considerable difficulty for Marion who experiences unpredictable fluctuations in her abilities because of the chronic illness she lives with. Marion fears what would be for her a logical outcome of this kind of campaign—having her benefits disallowed—forcing her to rely solely on earned income to live, with the resulting domino effect in terms of her ability to live independently and to participate in paid employment. Her fears are not imagined; her contacts at the province's most prominent disability advocacy group urge caution with respect to the earnings exemptions, as she points out in this passage:

> I make $200 extra a month. And potentially I'd like to make more. Like I would like to go out and sort of find the same

kind of thing with another non-profit. But the tough part is—my advocacy group is already saying to people, "Be careful" because they [the Ministry] are already leaning on people who have done this. But as an advocate I told people candidly that I wouldn't be going out and making $400 a month. Because I could then see them turning around and saying "Well if you can make $400, then you can make $600 or $800 and why do you need to be on [disability benefits] anymore?" And I could see that really happening. So I've told people to be very, very cautious about that. Quite honestly earning $200 extra a month, over and above the $200 I am earning, meaning I would have an extra $400 total monthly, would give me a lot more freedom in terms of medical stuff, but if it's going to cost me in terms of just having the income I need to live here, I can't do that.

Marion does not trust the government to accommodate her (or others') needs with respect to allowable earnings. In her mind, pressure from the Ministry to force those earning the full exemption to earn more and/or to go off benefits is real, and she acts on this understanding in her own life but also in her role as an advocate, cautioning others to be careful about earnings from employment. Marion deeply senses how precarious her situation is and responds accordingly: her hard-won independence is not worth jeopardizing. So she limits herself, a difficult choice considering her desire to work more.

CONCLUSION

Disabled women living poorly is made visible through these brief accounts. So much of what is necessary to live well is economically and physically beyond their reach; they must struggle to secure even the most basic of life's necessities. These disabled women, like so many on provincial benefits, live with a high degree of uncertainty, in part because of their chronic physical and mental conditions, but more importantly because of the capricious nature of government policy. Mistrust of government is a hallmark of their lives, and the ways government structures dependency are evident as disabled women exercise self-restraint for fear of losing the (precarious) security of their disability benefits. This is in direct conflict with their desire to actively pursue and fulfill personal aspirations, something they are unable to do freely. Their lives reflect a striking contradiction to the stated intentions of government with respect to supporting disabled citizens to participate and thrive in communities, and to lead full, rewarding lives.

Living poorly means to live in ways that reflect the substantial disadvantage disabled women experience with respect to access to basic income, goods, and services, inequalities in health status, barriers to education and the paid labour market, enjoyment of human rights and fundamental freedoms, and cultural representation (Hay, Rutman, Rioux, Drover and Kerans 100-106). Making visible the poverty and struggles of disabled women living with "last resort" benefits challenges our beliefs and values as citizens about supporting disadvantaged Canadians. In particular, these disabled women's lives provoke questions about the thresholds we set (or permit governments to set), below which we will not tolerate income inequality, the primary basis for living poorly.

[1]The Canada Pension Plan Disability Benefit (or CPP-D) is administered by the Canadian federal government, and the Quebec Pension Plan Disability Benefit (QPP) by the province of Quebec. They are both self-supporting, contributory, earnings-based social insurance programs designed for all working Canadians in the event of disability. Most working Canadians contribute to either the CPP or QPP through their employer, and are potentially eligible for benefits should they be unable to work due to disability. Eligible beneficiaries receive a taxable monthly pension, which is adjusted yearly (in January) to cost of living increases as measured by the Consumer Price Index. To qualify for benefits, an individual must have contributed to the CPP for four of the previous six years, be considered disabled according to CPP legislation, and be between the ages of 18 and 65. To reduce discrimination against women who leave the work force or reduce employment to raise small children (under age seven), low earning years are dropped from the calculation.

Disabled according to Canada Pension Plan legislation refers to a definition of disability created by the CPP to delineate both medical and employment criteria used to establish eligibility for disability benefits.

A person can have a condition which is either physical or mental, and which is "severe" and "prolonged." "Severe" means the condition prevents a person from working regularly at any job, and "prolonged" means the condition is long term or may result in the person's death (Doe and Kimpson 3). In B.C., disabled persons applying for provincial disability benefits with previous engagement in the workforce are required to apply for CPP benefits. Successful applicants have their provincial benefit reduced by the monthly CPP amount.

[2]According to Statistics Canada an "[e]conomic family refers to a group of two or more persons living in the same dwelling and are related to each other by blood, marriage, common-law or adoption. A couple may be of opposite or same sex. Foster children are included."

[3]At the time of the interviews, the Ministry was known as the Ministry of Human Resources. It was subsequently renamed the Ministry of Employment and Assistance, and then recently the current name, Ministry of Housing and Social Development, was given. In this article, to simplify, I refer to it using the current name.

[4]In 2006 the British Columbia government articulated "Five Great Goals" as part of its strategic plan for its forthcoming four year mandate, including to "Build the best system of support in Canada for persons with disabilities, those with special needs, children at risk, and seniors." The context for this goal was articulated as follows:

> Everyone deserves the opportunity to live a full, rewarding life, to pursue their goals and dreams, and to participate and thrive in all aspects of society. Government has an important role to play in supporting such opportunities for the most vulnerable members of society, including people with disabilities, those with special needs, children and youth at risk, and seniors. ("Five Great Goals")

[5]Names have been changed to protect participants' identities.

REFERENCES

Bach, Michael, and Marcia H. Rioux. "Social Policy, Devolution, and Disability: Back to Notions of the Worthy Poor?" *Remaking Canadian Social Policy: Social Security in the Late 1990s*. Eds. Jane Pulkingham and Gordon Ternowetsky. Halifax: Fernwood Publishing, 1996. 317-326.

"B.C. Employment and Assistance Rate Tables." *Ministry of Housing and Social Development.* 2007. Online: <http://www.mhr.gov.bc.ca/mhr/da.htm>. Accessed 8 June 2010.

Coleman, Rich. *2009/10-2011/12 B.C. Ministry of Housing and Social Development Service Plan Update.* 2009. Ministry of Housing and Social Development. Online: <http://www.bcbudget.gov.bc.ca/2009_Sept_Update/sp/pdf/ministry/hsd.pdf>. Accessed 8 June 2010.

Doe, Tanis and Sally Kimpson. *Enabling Income: CPP Disability Benefits and Women With Disabilities.* Ottawa: Status of Women Canada, 1999.

Farmer, Paul. *Pathologies of Power: Health, Human Rights, and the New War On the Poor.* Berkeley: University of California Press, 2005.

Fawcett, Gail. *Living with Disability in Canada.* Ottawa: Human Resources Development Canada, 1996.

"Five Great Goals." *Strategic Plan 2006/7-2008/9.* B.C. Government. 2006. Online: <http://www.bcbudget.gov.bc.ca/2006/stplan/>. Accessed 8 June, 2010.

Hay, David, Deborah Rutman, Marcia Rioux, Glenn Drover, and Patrick Kerans. *Well-Being: A Conceptual Framework and Three Literature Reviews.* Vancouver: Social Planning and Research Council of British Columbia, 1993.

"Low Income Before Tax Cut-Offs (LICO-BT)." *Statistics Canada.* 2006. Online: <http://www12.statcan.ca/census-recensement/2006/ref/dict/fam020-eng.cfm>. Accessed 8 June 2010.

"Low Income Cut-Offs for 2008 and Low Income Measures for 2007." *Research Paper Series.* Statistics Canada. 2008. Online: <http://www.statcan.gc.ca/pub/75f0002m/75f0002m2009002-eng.pdf>. Accessed 8 June. 2010.

Statistics Canada. "Economic Families." 2010. Online: <http://www.statcan.gc.ca/concepts/definitions/economic_family-familles_economiques-eng.htm>. Accessed 30 September 2010.

MARIE ANNHARTE BAKER

DISABILITY DISS AWAY

downsized disease
as usual not under
down quilt cuddle
& bed bug bites

cool so damn cool
might get off cool down
all the time down
feather fluffy on inseam
more let down
down & out every day
down the tubes
down river without
proverbial paddle

keep one oar pull
in swirling rapids
or else flip out
drift down river
no return salmon
spawn origin
outdoors door slam
welcome except
greeting door mat
revolves intolerable
unnatural practice

broke down broken
press firm brake even
easy on day break
soon get the breaks
eventually give out
soon after alarm buzz
breakfast then let go
pacification flow in cup
java drowns depression
upper fix downward
lip corner curl composure
pictures no micro details
economic disparity jokefest
flat broke ndn tee shirt FBI
wear out me laugh me funny
onset episode spasms me

me nervous breakdown obvious
recite if nervous keep calm relax
you can do it you can do it words
discomfort leaves me disturbed
sly do not disturb oblivious me
suffering potential exposure
stressors whoever I induce
matrix of me being prophetic
just lay off stop networking
because you chum friend not so
trusting girl granny person trigger

feel unsafe in family influence
glare eyes do not see larger insidious
Indigenous down pressure endgame
odious economic differential self
wounded knee get over classed-based
mutilation no more amputations
mind muscle medication fussy
fixation down get down on it
stare eye red eye black eye whitey

de-stigmatize my wealth condition

internalized ableism racism classism
original mood swing not aboriginal
post-colonial syndrome failure
to remediate trajectory
F bomb exhortation
emergency endemic
betrayal ending
collective decision to deconstruct
realities dislocation loss of tropes

racism under dominant translation
internal gab no discernable accent
settler of colour alienation is often
de-skilled vulnerability lodged de-
attachment enclave ambivalence
tolerance toward expulsion okay
visit ethnic cleansed asylum but
double chocolate cake prizes
awards no surprise ndn resistance
surrounded with other dark skins
dark hand pushing tongue depressor
dark eyes grateful for occupation

resettlement yet somatic repression
lateral torture vicarious violins tune
apparatuses trafficked resilience non
virtual imprisonment friendly
cautious fear consents to therapy
modality fluent incongruous
those mandated report abuses
risk at-risk competence custom
sensitivity selective knowledge
ripples through flashbacks
accidental compassionates
me disease you cure all curator
make self-meaning cultural

make sense atonement grievous
casual truncated just a sec spew

increased caregiver connection
encompasses spiritual reconfigurations
be brief cogent counseling referral
intensified meaning fermented since
resemble reassemble remnant
historical trauma iteration ongoing
internecine conflict pauses to reflex
ignorant with-in wars scars coalition
group channeled metaphor mythology
makeover must be opinionated self
me witness divine diatribe diss-cention

JOY ASHAM

THE GEOGRAPHY OF OPPRESSION

I DON'T REALLY LOOK that extraordinary when I see my reflection in the mirror. About the only thing truly of note is that my lips are moving: once more, it appears I am talking to myself.

I scan my head from the top down and then begin to realize how very strange I truly am. My hair is dyed kind of purple: I like a burgundy cast to my dark brown hair (which is actually grey). Moving down my face, I stop at my eyes and perhaps it is only I who knows this, but I have artificial lens implants from cataract surgeries in both eyes. Every time I fall down (which is fairly often these days) I break my face. This means that my nose has a plastic septum.

At the sides of my head exist my ears: they have now reached that state in life where I need hearing aids in order to follow even loud conversations. Back to centre, lower face: False teeth. Not all of them, I have six of my own that hold down my lower plate.

All of a sudden I realize the truth of me: I have a bionic head! And this is only the head. I also have a shunt in my neck, catheters coming out of my chest, a pacemaker, and exist, for several hours three times a week, strictly by the help of dialysis. Most of these spare parts are somewhat invisible, which creates a whole new set of problems.

AGING AND SUCH

I am actually more spare parts than real as, with my back also broken in three places, I get around in a scooter or wheelchair. Getting hit by a Greyhound bus is not recommended.

I have just turned 63. But I have a really good start on very Old Age. In fact, I am the sole survivor of nine babies born in a remote hospital in Hodgson, Manitoba, in the same week: seven died that week, only one other than me survived and he passed away about fifteen years ago. We lived seventeen miles north of Hodgson and the road was actually Red River oxcart ruts. I was almost born on the road! My longevity is famous in my family.

DIABETES AND DIALYSIS

You have probably guessed by now that I am a person with diabetes, type II. It was diagnosed thirty-one years ago and I have been following one strict regimen after another from that point on. I've given up smoking for seventeen years, and well, warmth, if you know what I mean, for five years.

When my kidneys began to fail two years ago, I went on yet another regimen and this became very complicated: my diabetes diet and my kidney meal plan conflict with one another. For example, rule out dairy, beans of any kind, anything from the Nightshade family (like tomatoes—which are in everything!), dairy, brown and dark breads, whole grains, and squash family items for the kidneys. For diabetes rule out anything white, pretty much, i.e.: potatoes, white bread, pasta, etc. and of course, anything that contains or converts to sugar (this is pretty much everything).

I scoot aimlessly through grocery stores these days, finding few things to eat that either won't kill me or send me along the way. I *can* eat salmon, fish, seafood, skinless chicken breasts, and an occasional small piece of red meat. Problem is, these days, so can everybody else, and with the expense of top-line food, my budget falls way short.

VISIBLE DISABILITIES AND DARWINIAN SOCIALISM

The only things about me that are visible other than the scooter, in terms of disabilities, are my age, my race and my gender. I list all of these things as disabilities because dominant Canadian society is built on the Pyramid Principle. Sometimes this is also known as Darwinian Socialism: survival of the fittest.

In our western world this means strongest, not smartest, not most experienced, not even most knowledgeable. Just who got to first base, well, first.

IT'S NOT GOOD TO BE LOWEST ON THE PYRAMID

So when you happen to be a woman, you already have an uphill struggle and add to that being Aboriginal as I am (obviously so) and old, well, forget even common courtesy in this society. Most oversights are just thoughtless but some are downright mean.

By thoughtless I can list a bunch of things that happened over the last while: going to the store that has only one narrow ramp way and finding it blocked by parked bicycles. Another problem resulted from the lack of funds these days devoted to such things as clearing pedestrian sidewalks. With a scooter, the sidewalk is the place for it; even though it is often a rougher ride than the road (the road doesn't have cracks every six feet).

It seems that in the climate here in Thunder Bay, Ontario, while it is so rapidly changing, we have severe freeze-ups then thaws all winter. The sidewalks are not plowed so huge ruts begin to appear made up of frozen bumps of ice. Snow-clearing (removal of snow banks) is no longer done, so frozen drifts also line the streets, often very high.

I came out of a rehab hospital where I had gone for an audio appointment and began to travel to my next stop. Before I knew it, my scooter wheels had gotten trapped in a deep rut and pulled my steering to one side. My timing is magnificent: at the same time my battery surged and I couldn't stop the scooter.

Up and over this huge frozen mass the scooter went, finally tipping and throwing me fiercely to the ground. I heard the snap and felt surging hot pain and knew my arm had broken. But the scooter had not yet finished with me: it then fell on me and my wrist broke as well.

I lay there behind this frozen snow bank that blocked the sightline from the street. I realized that there were no pedestrians and no one could see me from their cars. I began to yell my head off and finally a car stopped. The female driver was a wonder and quickly organized others to tip me back up and make sure I was okay. I wasn't of course, but I decided that I had too much to do that day to let a small thing like a broken shoulder and wrist to stop me.

I did not realize my scooter was broken and off went everyone, quite happy they had helped me with me expressing extreme gratitude. Then I tried to start the darn thing! Finally someone actually pushed me and my scooter to my next appointment, at the end of which I finally said: Take me to the hospital.

When I got there, they x-rayed my arm and gave me morphine for the pain. I had never had morphine before and sure enough, it collapsed my blood pressure. I ended up in hospital for twelve days. Finally, on the third day, when I kept complaining of pain and swelling there, they actually x-rayed my wrist, and discovered it was broken as well.

Now comes a more intentional type of abuse by medical staff. I never received care when I was in hospital, couldn't even get a nurse to tighten my sling. My doctor would come every day, but that was for five minutes. The rest of the time, other than in dialysis, I was subjected to such terrible rudeness that all I could think of was going home and hiding, pain, sickness, or not.

One example of the kinds of treatment I received was this: I had been laying there for a few days; my blood pressure did not go back up for five days. By then I had a sling, a cast, and was more than a bit dead. A nurse came in and demanded: "Comb your hair right now!! If it isn't combed by the time I get back, I will take my scissors and cut it all off!"

BEING ABORIGINAL: A "VISIBLE DISABILITY" IN THIS SOCIETY

It is definitely a visible disability being Aboriginal and sick to boot. That is unless you are in dialysis. What always surprises me is this same hospital has the most cooperative and helpful/supportive dialysis unit one could ever hope for. Perhaps different areas have different management styles or hiring practices.

We also all know that workplaces are cultures in themselves and people act accordingly. Somehow the dialysis unit seems to have maintained a fair and equitable working environment and this gets passed down, just like bad practices, to the person at the bottom: in dialysis this is the one hooked up to the machine. They have avoided this "kick-down" there, possibly by the kick not being present at the top.

TEACHING/LEARNING METHODS

My dad, a very wise man, long since passed, used to say: "You can train a dog with cruelty or with love, really doesn't matter, you will get the same result—till you turn your back." My dad was one of the most loving and respectful people I ever knew, with humans and four-leggeds alike.

Another dad-digression: He and I were watching a movie on TV one day. The setting was a sheep farm and I was fascinated at watching how the dogs rounded up the sheep, looked for, found and returned strays, and basically worked together: very smart indeed.

I said to dad: wow, would I ever like to meet the person who trained those dogs, s/he must be very smart. Dad gave a short answer that was truly precious philosophy: "It is the dogs that train the dogs."

I guess I am coming back full circle to the issue of race: I have found in my life that we (whatever downtrodden group, whether that be race, gender, creed, etc.) can do many things to change image and political will: we can "clean up our act" if necessary, we can learn to use the right fork (while others use a spoon—rules are different for different people), we can become experienced, educated and be full of boundless positive energy. We can work cooperatively or we can confront. In most cases the movement is not only small but very likely to become a pendulum as we have seen since the sixties till now.

PEOPLE ONLY CHANGE WHEN THEY WANT TO? HOW CAN WE HELP THEM WANT TO?

But, the only way people will really change is when they feel peer pressure from their very own peers. I once heard that people do not have rights if they have to ask for them: large "P" political activity is basically that, whether it is done with request or threat.

As a teacher I learned some basic things. We all know about the Bell Curve: when something is first learned it is easily retrievable and then it slides down to marginal if retrievable at all. The rapidity of this slide has been measured: if the learner is coerced the retention time is very short. If the student likes the teacher and wants to learn because of it, the retention time and the retrievability greatly improve.

I have had a column in the *Thunder Bay Chronicle Journal* every second Sunday for fifteen years. I have built up a wide readership. Even though the column is called Anishnawbeg Scene (Aboriginal) my readership is very wide. I know this as I get letters and emails from people in every walk of life. I get recognized almost every time I go out (not because of how I look—the picture of me on the column is thirteen years old) but because people see the Red Scooter, who I call Babe, coming from a far distance. I am the only nut that is out there, regardless of weather, treating the darn thing like it is my own personal ATV (hence a few scrape-ups).

COME TO MY KITCHEN AND DRINK TEA OUT OF PEANUT BUTTER JARS

My style with the column I best can describe is as you and I sitting at a kitchen table drinking tea out of peanut butter jars. Yes, we have trauma, we have negative things happen, we even have extreme personal challenges. But I really believe that we are in this together, and that is also what society should be about. There have been times when I have helped others who cannot speak for themselves. In turn there are times when I need a hand, and hence we build a strong community.

LAUGHING ALL THE WAY

So when I try to do remedial anti-oppression work, number one, I try to get people laughing (now this is a bit of a trick—humour cannot be at the cost of others, cannot be racial, cannot be belittling in any way). I was raised in a culture that always had one old uncle or grandmother sitting in the corner saying really corny things. I never wanted to become either, however.... What can I say, what happens happens and I am glad that occasionally my very droll and corny humour can set up a bridge between people. It is hard to frown and be cranky when you are laughing. It then becomes possible to open the door and find some common ground.

SEXUAL HARRASSMENT EXAMPLE

For years I was the "sexual harassment" specialist in Northern Ontario. Not that I harassed anyone, but I was often asked by public institutions and unions to run many workshops on the subject. Back in the mid-'80s, a lot of people were unaware that sexual harassment was basically unacceptable. I talked about what constitutes sexual harassment and possible remedies.

I always used to ask a group about its composition before I went. If it was a totally female group I delivered the workshop in one way; if it was a mixture of male and female I'd deliver it another way. So, in one instance, I asked about group numbers and composition: "How many and is it mixed?" I was told the group would be mixed so I prepared different handouts and examples than if it had been a more "progressive" female only group. When I got there I realized: "Oops," it was the staff of a seniors' home. I had no idea that they considered "mixed" to mean old and young. ALL of the attendees were men! I was befuddled for a minute, then I realized that they had sisters and mothers and wives and daughters and girl-friends. That gave me the "hook" I needed to enter into a valid exchange with them.

Why the "hook?" When I work with women, I can be direct with this issue. Most have either experienced it first-hand or know someone who has had to leave a job or submit to unwanted advances. Men, on the other hand, sometimes do not realize what their wives/daughters/sisters/mothers go through; in fact, men sometimes cannot understand why women complain, rather than be flattered by, unwanted attention. So, in dealing with this subject with men, it requires tact and discretion to encourage discussion, rather than creating an atmosphere that puts them on the defensive. I learned early in my life that to learn and maintain information, it helps if the learner likes the teacher.

PEERS ARE NEEDED TO CHANGE THINGS

Around this time, a past boss of mine asked me to help him shop for his wife's Christmas gift. They were both really good friends and he wanted to get her a new diamond ring as they had just passed their tenth anniversary. He had suffered some face paralysis from a small ocular surgery and he needed to be blindfolded to allow his eyes to rest.

So, Gary asked me to go with him and be his eyes. I was to pick him up at a private house where a woman friend of his family was having a Christmas Tea. At that time, I was, I guess, a "professional" and dressed as such: high heels, a dress, hair immaculate. I went to the door to let them know I was there.

My boss's friend who was hosting the tea answered the door and I asked for Gary. She said to me: "What is someone like *you* doing here?!' and I immediately realized that she was negatively referring to my race: you can dress me up but I still look Cree.

Gary stood behind her and said, "Come on in, Joy, I am just about ready."

I said I would wait in the car and when he arrived, I discussed this with him. "Well," he said, "she has never been like that around me [a Caucasian man] and she does some very good things in the community. If you didn't like what she said," Gary went on, "why didn't you say something?"

I said to him, "I am standing between a rock and a hard place. If I dispute what she said, then I would be seen as troublesome. If I came into the house, it would be like I was accepting her treatment." Sometimes it is better just to disengage.

PEOPLE WHO STAND ASIDE AND DO NOTHING ARE ALSO AT FAULT

I saw that in the afore-mentioned incident I was almost a spectator/ victim. I felt this silence to be my role, but ideally I saw Gary's role to be different than he did. I felt that it was up to him, as her accepted peer, to tell her that her attitude to me was unacceptable. I still believe that people who stand aside and watch injustice happen are also guilty.

My meander leads me back to say this: it is not just the responsibility of those who are victims to work toward positive change in a culture or work environment. Nor does it rest solely on the shoulders of the perpetrator. It is the job of peers to educate their own, to bring forth the welcoming of voices from the affected masses so that they may be heard. Some may say to leave that to the survivors, but to me, to be part of a community means a sense of responsibility to positive growth.

I know I have talked here about racism. It happens to be a field of experience for me and has had a tremendous impact on my life and opportunities (or lack thereof). I have also worked industriously in the feminist community and am now doing community work with anti-poverty and disability justice groups as a volunteer.

I flip back and forth between these things, not because I am not dedicated to any one in particular, but because I find so many common denominators. Oppression, top-down and lateral violence, economic disadvantage and hyper-surveillance (everyone looking down their noses and NIMBY[1]) happens to us all, even if we are only slightly different. The distribution affects the target, as described in the footnote.

AVERAGE AND UNIQUE AT SAME TIME

I am not JLo, I am not Jessica Simpson. I never aspired to be the "hottest" woman in the world and have my husband run around on me (as it has happened with all the hottest), nor do I need vast riches. A little bit of fame wouldn't hurt … lol.

I do have real and severe concerns about our society. I don't think we two-leggeds were meant to be cookie-cutter people. I think our differences are rich. As for survival of the fittest, I have found one thing to be universally true: privilege is not a good teacher.

We who struggle with everyday life and challenges, we who have no doors open to us (even the automatic ones which often aren't turned on), have learned the skills of survival. I can exist in a northern community with no running water and no hydro, as well as in downtown Toronto.

When I worked for the Ontario Women's Directorate and headed the northern office in Thunder Bay, I found a strange thing: Toronto co-workers could not come here and stay overnight. They seemed to think that the Valhalla Inn had an outhouse. They knew nothing of community etiquette: you don't go in to our local Finnish restaurant and ask for Perrier water. At that time, Thunder Bay had the third best water in the world and it wasn't contaminated like that well-known French brand. But then again, it wasn't Swiss or French, just plain home-grown Ontarian water. How ordinary.

HAVING AN OPEN MIND

There is no better gift in life than an open-mind. We do not realize though, how young we can be when our minds close. I know it took me a long time in my life to sort through what I call my filter-screens. I am a creature of two cultures: my father is Cree, my mother English. The main difference in childrearing was this: When I was told or asked to do something or stop, I would ask why. My dad would always say: well, if you do this, this might happen, but the choice is yours. My Mom would say: because I told you so. My father's techniques opened my mind, my mother's closed it. Now I think my mind is so open it has air-holes.

It took me a long time to look beyond the hierarchy and question authority. What any authority figure said was gold, even when I was told by the Home Economics teacher in grade nine that I would never be attractive because my face was round. It took me until about five years ago to truly deal with that one.

SELF-ACTUALIZATION AT LAST

One final digression: I must tell you how I did it, how I finally managed to shake the burden of lowest rung. I had been divorced for several years and had begun to see this little pointed-headed guy. One night, he showed up at my door with a bag full of laundry. My back was already bad and I had a homemaker who did my laundry as I could hardly walk, never mind carry anything. He asked me if he could use the building's laundry facilities and I said, no, the other tenants watch it like hawks, only tenants are allowed to do clothes there.

I kind of felt bad, because he really needed clean clothes (I could tell, but that is another story). I finally said, put them in the basket of my walker and I will try to do them for you. I did them, after which I cooked him a full vegan dinner. I am not a vegan but he was and I adjusted my own likings accordingly.

We went to bed, fooled around for a while, and then, at 11:00 p.m. we were laying there and he had the remote control to the bedroom television. He began to flip through channel after channel and finally stopped at *The Simpsons*. All of a sudden it dawned on me, that after living for several years alone, I had my own habits. Why aren't I watching *Law and Order*? I thought.

Right then, he turned to me and said: "Joy, this is the most wonderful evening I have had in a really, really long time."

I thought a minute and then said to him: "Dougie, get lost."

This was the latest in a series of self-actualization events that have allowed me to take back my life in the fullest.

DO UNTO OTHERS

And that was that. I no longer need others to tell me I'm okay, but it would be nice once in a while just out of etiquette. It would also be great if that etiquette extended to the simple rule: "do unto others."

People who are mainstream often have no idea what it is like to be a little different. I look a lot different from some, I am unusually able in certain things and not in others. I have also had a culture that has nurtured me in one way, but sent me out into the cruel world in another. For example, within Aboriginal culture if there is a feast (others would call it an all-you-can-eat buffet), elders and those with physical disabilities and/or diabietes are either served or serve themselves first. This means that those on canes and the infirm do not have to wait till the end of the line to eat. I recently went to the annual meeting of a large non-native organization. There were over a hundred people there, only two Aboriginal: myself and a man. He was in a manual wheelchair and I had my walker. They called people up and everyone got to the trough first. Both he and I had diabetes as well and had waited a very long time through endless speeches to eat once we took our insulin.

I know this is the way of dominant society. But sometimes, other people can learn simple etiquette from ours. In this case, it was not etiquette that was needed but simply understanding that physically disabled people occasionally have the need for empathy and kindness. Just like everyone else.

If you spend your life never being able to get there first, never being taller or stronger or cuter, or just plain more acceptable, you learn to step aside for others. Not because they have more power, but because they don't. We usually help the ones who are more disabled, we usually celebrate recovery rather than being lucky enough not to get sick in the first place. People like me spend our lives trying to flatten the pyramid, as we know first hand that that is what is needed to become finally the Just Society of which many dream. It is not here yet.

STOP AND SMELL THE COFFEE

Stopping to smell the coffee on the way can enrich everyone's life. When you reach out your hand, it is yours being clasped. After all, people are merely like those dogs: we can be trained with cruelty and neglect until you turn your back. But, for that Just Society, where we can walk in freedom, or roll through it in our chairs, training with love is the best.

I wish for harmony and humility in high and low places: like water, these graces do not stack themselves up, but seek the lowest possible place. Yet, with time, they can erode away even the strongest rock.

My all-over-the-mappedness has ended. Be well in heart and spirit.

[1]NIMBY: Not In My Back Yard—common phrase used to denote that often people do not want to see such things as poverty close to home, because then they can no longer ignore it. Instead of actually doing something about it, they just want the problem to move elsewhere. An example of this kind of thinking is in communities where there is a high concentration of a cultural grouping that is non-mainstream. There usually is also a smaller group of diverse cultures. Let us say a community has a large Aboriginal presence and a small Afro Canadian presence. Often mainstream people will work hard to foster and support the smaller group while venting on the larger. Depending on which group is the largest cultural "other," the victims change. For example, in a community with a large Black presence, the mainstream will likely support other groups, such as Asians or Aboriginal. After all the smaller group members are Not in My Back Yard.

VIOLENCE ON THE EDGES

MARIA BARILE

AN INTERSECTIONAL PERSPECTIVE ON VIOLENCE

A New Response

HISTORICAL OMISSIONS OF DAILY events experienced by women with two or more marginalised characteristics have placed them in a vulnerable position in all spheres of life, including the social response of their survival of violence. When looking at the experience of violence among women with disabilities, one needs to be aware that women with disabilities experience emotional, physical, and sexual abuse at similar or higher rates than women in the general population. Beyond this, however, women with disabilities may also experience disability-specific forms of abuse for prolonged periods of time and from multiple perpetrators (Hassoune-Phillips and Curry).

By applying the intersectional framework in order to understand how women with disabilities experience violence, we propose universal design as a model that responds to the needs of women with disabilities. Universal design can address both the physical environment and the manner in which services are implemented. The two models can be used to analyze women's experiences related to violence, and to respond to their needs while acknowledging the needs of other survivors of violence.

MULTIPLE DISCRIMINATIONS

In the last few decades, awareness of discrimination toward people from marginalised groups has increased. This awareness was first evident at the academic level; however, it has since transcended the community and is equally evident at a political level. Statistics show that women in all countries experience greater poverty (Moghadam) and violence

(Jaden and Hoennes; Crenshaw) compared to men in their respective countries. What happens when women have additional "marginalised characteristics," such as women with disabilities, women of ethnic, linguistic, racial, religious minority backgrounds, or lesbians? This advancement in human understanding has made it obvious that the life stories of women with two or more "marginalized characteristics" were not being told, therefore, "her-story" was incomplete.

When someone experiences discrimination based on more than one "marginalized characteristic," the discrimination is considered multifaceted. Most models do not account for this multifaceted discrimination; as such there was a need to find models that can recognize and explain these dimensions of discrimination. To put it simply, this facet of human history was new and complex, especially since it was fused into politics and human emotions. In the 1980s we called this form of discrimination "double oppression" (Stuart; Vernon), "triple oppression" (Alma and Garcia), "multiple jeopardy" (King), or "multiple minority" (Barile 1993).

According to M. J. Deegan, a multiple minority group is a group of people who are singled out from others in the society in which they live for differential and unequal treatment. They are defined as members of more than one minority group who therefore regard themselves as objects of this combination of collective discrimination.

Regardless of the name, women with marginalised characteristics find themselves living in inferior positions in all aspects of their lives (Barile). As women from these groups began to tell the stories of their lives, they identified discrimination as subtle, systemic and ingrained in the fabric of existing institutions (Masuda and Ridington; Makkonen).

Consequentially, native women, women with disabilities, women of colour, and women from other minorities have found themselves continuously at the lower end of economic and services provisions. This occurs despite the creation of "specific groups" such as the Black women's associations, and disabled women's groups, which aim at improving their situation as well as changing laws, policies, and organizing and improving programs (Verloo).

Additionally, the United Nations Convention on the Elimination of all Forms of Discrimination Against Women (CEDAW) directly links discrimination to violence: "[g]ender-based violence is a form of discrimination that seriously inhibits women's ability to enjoy rights and freedoms on a basis of equality with men."

A NEW AWARENESS

As women from these groups continued talking about their lives it became clear that it was the intersection of the combined layers of oppression that created a unique disadvantage. This distinct disadvantage places these women in situations where one or more characteristics or minority identities overlap. As such, they find themselves in less advantageous positions including but not limited to employment and education.

Timo Makkonen reports that "intersectional analysis first arose out of the experience of African American feminists in the U.S., who noted that the traditional understanding of *racial* discrimination did not include experiences that were *particular* to African American *women*" (9). Different components of discrimination may interact with each other and produce specific experiences of discrimination—"unique disadvantage." This reflection has also allowed the rest of society to understand that the explanation of discrimination is more complex than originally thought. The Ontario Human Rights commission explicitly recognises that:

> [A] single ground approach has resulted in inappropriate outcomes and the erasure of the complexity of the discrimination in cases involving any combination of grounds including race related grounds, age, and disability, sexual orientation, creed and gender. The need for an intersectional approach is therefore necessary to apply a proper analysis, no matter what the combination of grounds involved.... (12)

Thus, it was important that an analytical tool be developed to respond to this new understanding.

As expressed by the Association for Women's Rights, "Intersectionality is an analytical tool for studying, understanding and responding to the ways in which gender intersects with other identities and how these intersections contribute to unique experiences of oppression and privilege." It is through this analysis that one may begin to understand how the experiences of people who live with dual or multiple disadvantages emerges from the fusing of all of these experiences.

To illustrate the concept of the intersection of multiple minorities, imagine a Venn diagram with three colour circles; the central part is where each different colour overlaps, intersects, and changes into a new colour. This intersection is the fusion of different experiences that become the reality of these women. As eloquently put by the Thai Disabled Developmental Foundation:

> [I]ntersectional discrimination recognises that two or more forms may combine to create new forms of discrimination. For example, a woman, who also is a person with a disability, will face discrimination against both of these characteristics when seeking education, training and employment [and other opportunities].

This is a combined disadvantage experienced by women with disabilities that White women without disabilities and from a heterosexual orientation ("uni-minority women") do not experience. This could explain why, although there seem to be improvements in the lives of White non-disabled women, this does not reproduce itself in the lives of women who hold more than one minority status.

Intersectional discrimination is subtle. No one outright says, "this woman is in a wheelchair, is Black, and has children, so I will not hire her." In most countries there are no segregation laws that dictate segregating practices. Rather, it becomes second nature to government and social groups to assume that equity can be achieved through their understanding of the "uni-minority" concept. One example of this is found in research. When research is conducted on women's issues, at the end one lumps all the categories of women together which forms "the shopping list" concept. Similarly, this occurs when one sets up services and names different groups of women it aims at servicing without considering the specific needs of women with disabilities, racial/ethnic minorities, lesbians etc. In doing so, this ignores that a uni-minority woman will have had privileges in her life that are closer to those experienced by a White non-disabled man.

The focal point of intersectional understanding is that the combined characteristics of daily experiences of women with disabilities, women from ethnic or racial minorities, and/or lesbians, create combined experiences of compounded disadvantages in a personal and social arena. A reason for intersectional discrimination is the social system's services, social contracts and values, which have been designed to respond to the needs of a "political majority." In the past the "political majority" has been allotted to non-disabled White men first, and people from "uni–minority groups" such as other men and white women second. Thus, if we focus on how one defines violence, it goes without saying that the definition is often lagging in the experience of women with disabilities. To be inclusive of violence as a form of discrimination, from a disability-specific perspective, it needs to include removal of technical aids, economic violence, and the use of their disability to make them feel vulnerable, such as speaking without facing the hearing impaired woman and then accusing them of consenting to activities. Furthermore, these also include using complex language, threats, and contradictory messages so that women with cognitive disabilities are made to feel "stupid" or as if it is their fault.

CASES OF VIOLENCE

In cases of violence, one has to remember that historically, "uni–minority" women have most often identified men as being the primary aggressors and sex-based violence as the predominant form of violence. As a result of this understanding, services were organised to deal with and eliminate that specific form of violence. Consequently, the design of the services, in terms of physical space, structure, as well as intervention methods specific to this form of violence, were created to respond to the form of violence identified by the "victims." Thus, factors such as adequate accessible space for women who are older, women with disabilities, and children with disabilities whose mothers may have been abused, were not taken into account. The interventions were also designed to meet the needs of the cultural majority. The resources put into place did not consider the needs of a diverse culture, or subculture such as that of women with disabilities. One example is the period allotted for women to find an alternative place to live. If a woman is nondisabled, and has only one child, apartments are easier to find and less expensive than it is for women who use a wheelchair, or who have more than one child.

Similarly, interventions focus on women separating from the abusive husband or partner. For women with disabilities for whom this person may be the primary service provider, it is more difficult to consider leaving him. Finding alternative accessible living arrangements is harder because there are fewer available options for her and interventions may thus be considered a failure by both the woman with a disability and the worker. In the cases of women who are accepted in shelters, most shelters have specific criterion with which women must comply. One such criteria is that she leaves the aggressor, be it a partner, husband, etc. This is based on the fact that the primary aggressor of violence toward women was thought to be the partner, husband or other male. As stated before, the predominant form of violence was identified as sex-based. Given this perception of who the potential aggressors were, it's natural that services and criterion were developed around that view.

However, as established in the recent literature on violence against women with disabilities (Nixon), the aggressors against women with disabilities are actually most often people in positions of power paid for by the state, such as service providers working in and outside of institutions, hospitals, long term care facilities, as well as family members including but not necessarily the husband (Doe and Sobsey). Another indicator of this question is explored by E. P. Cramer and S. B. Plummer. They utilize the conceptual framework of intersectionality to explore various reasons why women with disabilities and / or from ethnic groups who seek help from abuse have difficulty receiving appropriate assistance, such as the trust issues with "personal assistance services."

In the early 1980s, DisAbled Women's Network (DAWN) Canada started looking at violence against women with disabilities and the perpetrators of violence against them. Most often service providers, who are often women (Masuda and Ridington), analyze and talk about the dual reality. DAWN Canada started to expose the fact that women with disabilities had added jeopardy of physical and sexual abuse, while at the same time experiencing disability-related abuse from multiple sources. This problem was compounded because services were inaccessible to them. At the time, Shirley Masuda did not call this the intersectionality frame of reference. In fact, most of the DAWN

Canada literature from 1987 through the 1990s began identifying the framework of what we now acknowledge as the intersectional framework.

Some issues related to violence are understudied in the feminist literature, while others have perhaps remained taboo in the women's movement. This becomes evident by looking at the dearth of studies and funding allotted to these questions. One area that is underdeveloped in research is the contradictory social messages that women with disabilities receive. On the one hand, women with disabilities are in a system that promotes overprotection, segregation, and trains them to comply with requests from staff. On the other hand, there is an expectation that all women must become self-assured, independent, and defend themselves. This is an important issue to explore because when one lives in a segregated surrounding, seeking help is nearly impossible. Another understudied issue within the feminist perspective is woman-to-woman violence, especially where the perpetrator of violence is a service provider or family member.

Although there is a body of feminist literature and community acknowledgement that violence should not be kept quiet, the issue of violence by service providers who are often female (Balsam and Szymanski) is still a subtle shame to speak out. There is a lack of knowledge, and in some cases "social permission," to allow women in service provision or women with disabilities to tell these stories. One may excuse violence by service providers due to the fact that one believes they are stressed out because of a heavy workload. Some facts are: the majority of the service providers are primarily women, their workload is heavy, they are not well paid, and they get very little recognition.

Presently, very little is known about the reality of women-to-women's violence. What happens when service providers do not have the opportunity or place for recovery from being exhausted and overworked? Despite these valid concerns, these are not reasons to excuse abuse. Studies with an intersectional framework will notably provide useful information in this area.

Thus, when trying to respond to the intersectional discrimination lived by groups such as women with disabilities, one needs to look at historical omissions both socially and politically as they are practiced in mainstream social institutions, communities and alternative agencies, and in individual relationships. One needs to take into account intersectional oppression, the institutional systemic omission that came about due to lack of knowledge about the communities that experience these "combined oppressions." One also needs to take into account the inflexible way in which the system has taught the political majority to respond to the needs of minorities—people are not comfortable in dealing with differences, and the different needs of women experiencing intersectional reality.

We need to create a flexible structure that will allow women with combined minority characteristics to express themselves as well as allow them to try out various ways to tell their stories. By creating these flexible structures, we will avoid forms of discrimination that have been experienced in the past. This means being more flexible with how we define violence; definitions of violence must include all forms of violence that women experience, including violence by other women. It must be recognised, but also respected where women are at a given moment, including their religious beliefs. CEDAW makes reference to the creation of safe and supportive "girl-friendly spaces and environments" as a basic right. This includes girls with disabilities.

The service providers who respond to violence against women need to understand and take into account that the aggressor may be someone other than a husband, lover or partner. The aggressor may be one of many other persons interrelating with the woman with a disability, such as a blood relative, father, son, or brother. However, it might also be another woman. It may even be medical personnel or other service providers. Regardless of whom the aggressor is the services provided must give all women the same refuge. Help women with disabilities fight institutionalised violence in and outside the home or wherever they live.

UNIVERSAL DESIGN AS SERVICE OPTION

Universal Design was first introduced through the architectural and graphic design of products, environments, and communication tools in the late 1980s. Its central tenet is: "the design of products and environments are to be useable by all people, to the greatest extent possible, without the need for adaptation or specialized design [or at extra cost]" (Story, Mueller and Mace). This principle has quickly spread to other areas of scholarship and practice such as teaching and learning. Proponents of this concept hold that if something works well for people with disabilities, it will enhance it for everyone (Weisman 1999).

The basic intent of universal design of instruction is to design environments that can be used by learners with diverse abilities (Burgstahler 2005). The field of universal design can provide a starting point for developing an appropriate model for delivery of services to a diversified population. In areas of services, Sheryl Burgstahler (2009) gives examples for college and university services. All the same criterion can be applied when setting up other services. The following is her checklist:

Planning, Policies, and Evaluation: Consider diversity issues as you plan and evaluate services.

Physical Environments and Products: Ensure physical access, comfort, and safety within an environment that is inclusive of people with a variety of abilities, racial and ethnic backgrounds, genders, and ages.

Staff: Make sure staff are prepared to work with all [participants of services].

Information Resources and Technology: If your services use computers as information resources, ensure these systems employ accessible design, that staff members are aware of accessibility options, and systems are in place to make accommodations.

Outreach: Pictures in your publications and website should include people with diverse characteristics with respect to race, gender, age, and disability.

Events: Ensure that everyone can participate in events.

Universal design is consistent with a frame of reference presented by the intersectional framework, in that it recognises the needs for flexibility in order to accommodate combined and diverse needs. Moreover, universal design takes this idea one step further by stating that all environments need to be useable by the largest number of people with diverse abilities. In social justice language, this denotes concepts of "access for all," human rights, and equitable access to social resources.

In a speech at a National Endowment for the Arts planning meeting in 1999, Leslie Weisman presented universal design as a medium to promote social equality, justice, environmental sustainability, and human health and well-being. She called it the link between "interdependence of humanity, the natural world, and the products of human design, while upholding the imperatives of democracy" (Weisman 1999: 2).

Sheryl Burgstahler states "to be more useful to individual with specific roles in institution, U.D. strategies can be organised according to where they are applied, such as instruction, service…" (2008: 14). Furthermore, Burgstahler recognises that universal design can respond to our ever growing diversified world. She states, " U.D. is a promising approach to integrating all we know about gender, race and ethnicity, disability, and other diversity" (2008: 15).

Thus, if one recognises that persons with combined marginalized characteristics have many diverse needs, it follows that to respond to intersectional reality one will need to organize responses based on an equitable flexible model. As such, I propose the following:

Universal Design for Services as an Option

1. *Equitable space and human ecology:*

Make sure that women with different abilities can use services in an equitable way: physical space that can be used by all. The environment allows all women to feel physically and emotionally healthy.

Equity can be established by respecting a woman's religious beliefs, her perception of her situation, and the choices she makes regardless of the shelter workers' opinion of the women's choice. In this way there is equality of all.

2. *Flexibility in use / intersectional reality:*

Be flexible in accommodating each person and all of the person's identity and or characteristics (i.e., women from Latin American backgrounds, women with disabilities, etc.). The way the events are told by the victim may not reflect the textbook version; this may be because of the diversity of their experiences and the complexity of the way they express it. For example, during interview/investigation of the facts, regarding the incidents of abuse, the victim's memory can be affected (i.e., for persons with certain disabilities whose speech or cognitive abilities are already different). For persons from different cultural backgrounds, their understanding of events and the way they recount these events may be based on their cultural perception or age group.

The police, or others who do the collecting of evidence, need be flexible while collecting evidence, and presenting it in court.

3. *Simple and intuitive:*

Provide the "survivors of violence" with information and skills that are easily transferable to different experiences so that they can pass from victim to survivor. Provide information in different formats (written, tapes, etc.,) in the language of the person's choice.

4. *Perceptible information:*

During intervention and/or counselling: provide information about violence: why it happens, its rationale and consequences. This allows a woman's self-perception to change from victimization to survival.

5. *Tolerance for error:*

Be aware that the victim may have confused memories from previous abuse or other flashbacks. Don't dismiss it. Ask and listen. Do not assume that the person is lying.

6. *Low physical effort:*

Minimize non-essential physical effort to allow for maximum possibility to be accommodated (talk on phone/visit individual), provide alternative formats, use interpreters where necessary.

7. *Feedback:*

Provide effective feedback during counselling. Be aware that some people express themselves differently due to culture and/or type of disability.

8. *Accountability:*

The first priority is to ensure accountability to the person in question (victim/survivor of violence).

CONCLUSION

As mentioned above, the CEDAW directly links violence as a form of discrimination against women. This paper puts forward the idea that, from a human rights perspective, universal design of services can respond to the challenges identified by intersectional frameworks mentioned within this paper. This perspective is inspired by Leslie Weisman, who attests that factors such as gender, race, and occupation intersect to create distinctly different spatial experiences for people, even within the same environmental setting. If such is the case, then indeed, "social equality is informed by spatial consciousness" (Weisman 1994: 37). It follows that universal design will be a positive change for all. One might argue that universality (universal design) may be inconsistent with the intersectional framework. In fact, as argued by Weisman, "universal designers strive to create products and spatial settings that provide the same level of comfort, accessibility, and assistance to multiple users and multiple publics" (37). Consequently, one can expect that by responding to the concerns identified by women living with the overlap of two or more marginalized characteristics, we will be inclusive of the experience of women from "uni-minority" groups. Making use of the universal design model from a basic structural perspective suggests that while the present structure may be creating exclusion for women with disabilities, and other marginalised groups, changing it will be an improvement for all.

REFERENCES

Alma M. and C. García. *Feminist Thought: The Basic Historical Writings.* London: Routledge, Taylor and Francis Group, 1997.

Association for Women's Rights. "Intersectionality: A Tool for Gender and Economic Justice. *Women's Rights and Economic Change,* August 2004. Online: <http://www.awid.org/eng/Issues-and-Analysis/Library/Intersectionality-A-tool-for-Gender-and-Economic-Justice2/(language)/eng-GB>. Accessed 21 February 2009.

Balsam, K. F. and D. M. Szymanski. "Relationship Quality and Domestic Violence in Women's Same-Sex Relationships: The Role of Minority Stress." *Psychology of Women Quarterly* 29.3 (2005): 258-269.

Barile, M. "Women with Disabilities Define System-Based Discrimination." MSW Monograph, McGill University, 1993.

Barile, M. "Disablement and Feminisation of Poverty." *Women in Action* 2 (2001): 49-53.

Burgstahler, S. "Universal Design of Instruction: Definition, Principles, and Examples." DO-IT, University of Washington, 2005. Online: <http://scholar.google.com/scholar?q=Burgstahler++S.+2004+UDI&hl=en&as_sdt=0&as_vis=1&oi=scholart>. Accessed Sept. 2010.

Burgstahler, S. "Universal Design in Higher Education." *Universal Design in Higher Education: From Principles to Practice.* Eds. S. Burgstahler and R. C. Cory. Boston: Harvard Education Press, 2008. 3-20.

Burgstahler, S. "Equal Access: Universal Design of Career Services." Seattle, WA: University of Washington, 2009. Online: <http://www.washington.edu/doit/Brochures/Academics/equal_access_cs.html>. Accessed 19 August 2010.

Convention on the Elimination of all Forms of Discrimination Against Women (CEDAW) (2010). "CEDAW Interactive Benchbook." Posted in Uncategorized by admin on 27 February 2010. Online: <http://www.cedawbenchbook.org/?page_id=247>. Accessed 21 August 2010.

Cramer, E. P. and S. B. Plummer. "People of Color with Disabilities: Intersectionality as a Framework for Analyzing Intimate Partner Violence in Social, Historical, and Political Contexts." *Journal of Aggression, Maltreatment and Trauma* 18.2 (2009): 73-89.

Crenshaw, K. W. "Mapping the Margins: Intersectionality, Identity Politics, and Violence Against Women of Color." *Stanford Law Review* 43.6 (1991): 1241-1299.

Deegan, J. M. "Multiple Minority Groups: A Case Study of Physically Disabled Women." *Journal of Sociology and Social Welfare* 8.2 (1981): 274-295.

Doe, T. and D. Sobsey. "Patterns of Sexual Abuse and Assault." *Sexuality and Disability* 9.3 (1991): 127-131.

Hassoune-Phillips, D. and M.-A. Curry. "Abuse of Women with Disabilities: State of the Science." *Stanford Law Review* 43.6 (1991): 1241-1299.

Jaden, P. and T. Hoennes. "Prevalence and Consequences of Male-to-Female and Female-to-Male Intimate Partner Violence as Measured by the National Violence Against Women Survey." *Violence Against Women* 6.2 (2000):142-161.

King, D. (1989). "Multiple Jeopardy, Multiple Consciousnesses." *Feminist Theory in Practice and Process.* Eds. M. Malson, J. F. O'Barr, S. Wesphal-Wihl, and M. Wyer. Chicago: University of Chicago Press, 1989. 75-105.

Makkonen, T. "Multiple, Compound and Intersectional Discrimination: Bringing the Experiences of the Most Marginalized to the Fore." Institute for Human Right Vaasa, Finland Åbo Akademi University, 2002. Online: <http://www.abo.fi/instut/imr/norfa/timo.pdf>. Accessed 21 March 2009.

Masuda, S. and J. Ridington. *Meeting Our Needs: Access Manual for Transition Houses.* Vancouver: DAWN Canada, 1990.

Nixon, J. "Domestic Violence and Women with Disabilities: Locating the Issue on the Periphery of Social Movements." *Disability and Society* 24.1 (2009): 77 -89.

Ontario Human Rights Commission. "An Intersectional Approach to Discrimination: Addressing Multiple Grounds in Human Rights Claims." Discussion Paper, 2001. Online: <http://www.ohrc.on.ca/en/ resources/ discussion _consultation/DissIntersectionalityFtnts/pdf>. Accessed March 2009.

Story, M. F., J. L. Mueller and L. R. Mace. *The Universal Design File: Designing for People of All Ages and Abilities.* North Carolina State University: The Center for Universal Design, 1998.

Stuart, O. W. "Race and Disability: Just a Double Oppression?" *Disability and Society* 7.2 (1992):177-188.

Thai Disabled Developmental Foundation. "Righting the Wrongs Against Women and Girls with Disabilities." 2009. Online: <http://www.tddf.or.th/tddf/newsroom/detail.php?id=0003727>. Accessed March 2009.

Moghadam, V. M. *The "Feminization of Poverty" and Women's Human Rights.* Paris: UNESCO, 2005.

Verloo, M. "Multiple Inequalities, Intersectionality and the European Union." *European Journal of Women's Studies* 13.3 (2006): 211-228.

Vernon, A. "The Dialectics of Multiple Identities and the Disabled People's Movement." *Disability and Society* 14.3 (1999): 385-398.

Weisman, L. *Discrimination by Design: A Feminist Critique of the Man-Made Environment.* Urbana: University of Illinois Press, 1994.

Weisman, L. *The Social Basis and Role of Universal Design as a Builder of Democracy.* Statement for NEA planning meeting, 1999. Online: <http://www.archvoices.org/downloads/WeismanStatement.doc>. Accessed March 2009.

ALEXANDRA PASIAN

UNDR THE DISLEXIC TREE

ther iks a plaec
whre speling dose not count
wheer thots and imaginatons
   run free
wher we express waht we feel
and no one laghs
ad it is important

there is plase
where eveyrone is equal
wher is not a lukery
where cleen air adounbs
where women are safe
and never alone
and speling dose not cont

I was diagnosed as having dyslexia at age eight. I read my first book when I was twelve. This is how I see the world.

Originally published in CWS/cf's *issue on "Women and Disability," 13 (4) (1993): 46. Reprinted with permission.*

MICHELLE OWEN

"HAVE YOU EXPERIENCED VIOLENCE OR ABUSE?"

Talking with Girls and Young Women with Disabilities

I AM A FEMINIST academic who identifies as a woman with a disability. In 2007, I conducted research with girls and young women with disabilities (GYWWD). It was a privilege to talk to GYWWD about such difficult topics as violence and abuse, and I am grateful to all the participants. In this paper I will present the findings from these discussions.[1] A fuller discussion of my research can be found in an anthology currently in progress entitled *Gender and Beyond: An Intersectional Analysis of Violence in the Lives of Girls.*

Poverty cuts through all of types of abuse, leaving girls and young women with disabilities with few resources or options. Race, ethnicity, sexuality, etc., intersect with gender, age, and class to further marginalize some girls and young women with disabilities. Unfortunately, different forms of abuse can and do overlap (Renooy), and multiple disabilities make GYWWD even more vulnerable (Ridington).

Girls and young women with disabilities confront violence at all times of the day and night in a variety of settings including home, school, work, institutions, medical facilities, and public transportation (DAWN Ontario). Many kinds of people abuse GYWWD, including relatives, caregivers, friends, peers, neighbours, doctors, teachers, and strangers. In Lorna Renooy's opinion: "Violence and abuse can happen when someone has power and control over a girl with a disability. You experience empowerment when you make your own choices or decisions." The main types of violence and abuse experienced by GYWWD are sexual, physical, and psychological violence, and neglect.

It is a myth that GYWWD are asexual—just because they may not fit the near impossible ideals of femininity does not mean that GYWWD do not have sexual desires and sexual lives. They are sexual beings and, unfortunately, targets of sexual violence. Regardless of ability, girls are more likely to be sexually abused than boys. By the age of sixteen, one quarter of Canadian females have experienced some form of sexual abuse (NCFV 1993). Joanne Doucette found that women with disabilities were 1.3 times as likely to have been sexually abused as children as non-disabled women were (qtd. in Randall, Parrila and Sobsey 3).

The Canadian Association for Community Living cites that 83 percent of women with disabilities will be sexually abused at some point, and 40 percent to 70 percent of girls with an intellectual disability will be sexually abused before they reach eighteen years of age (8). Several factors make people with intellectual disabilities particularly vulnerable to abuse and increased stress, including negative stereotypes, lack of support, poverty, and isolation (8). As Miriam Ticoll and Melanie Panitch state: "Without options, people may continue to live with caregivers or in service settings where they are abused" (85). Violence, including sexual abuse, can also cause or aggravate disability (McPherson 50). For instance, one of the young women in my study describes how being gang raped worsened her physical condition and resulted in a disability.

While the statistics are alarming, the vast majority of sexual offences against children with disabilities are not reported (Sobsey and Varnhagen 2). Charlene Senn argues: "Ironically, society appears to offer less protection to children with disabilities than to other children because it does not view children with disabilities as likely targets for sexual abuse" (qtd. in Sobsey 1994: 68). This is ironic because children with disabilities are even more vulnerable than children without disabilities. Dick Sobsey and Connie Varnhagen also found that children with disabilities are most often sexually abused by relatives, in a location known to the victim (10).

Girls and young women with disabilities (GYWWD) are at greater risk of physical abuse than their non-disabled peers (Sobsey and Varnhagen 4). The physical abuse of GYWWD exists on a continuum and includes "assault, rough or inappropriate handling, inappropriate personal or medical care, over-use of restraint, inappropriate behaviour modification, over-medication, and confinement" (NCFV 4). While physical abuse is often obvious, sometimes there are no signs of external injury, making the abuse hard to identify (Sobsey 1994: 17). For example, someone may take away something a girl with a disability needs such as a "cane, dog guide, or bliss board" (Renooy).

Some GYWWD, especially those who live in institutions, are also subjected to medical abuse, which includes over-medication, inappropriate care, and behaviour modification programs. Certain drugs can produce a lack of awareness, which can leave the person more open to abuse, especially sexual abuse (Mansell, Sobsey and Wilgosh; The Roeher Institute 1995: 50). Drugs are sometimes used as an inexpensive alternative to behaviour programs, or to make "human warehousing" or storing people with little care, easier for institutions (Sobsey 1994: 136). Other methods of control, such as sensory deprivation, electric shock, and restraint, "make it difficult to separate behavior management from abuse" (137).

The most extreme form of physical abuse is homicide. As of 2000, the University of Alberta Violence and Disability Project database on homicides included 208 women and adolescent girls with developmental disabilities who were victims of murder or attempted murder (Sobsey 2000). While the murder of children by strangers receives more attention in the media, children with disabilities are more apt to be killed by caregivers (Sobsey 1994: 18). On October 24, 1993, Robert Latimer, a Saskatchewan farmer, killed his twelve-year-old daughter, Tracy, who had cerebral palsy, by using a hose to feed carbon monoxide from his truck's exhaust pipe into the cab where he had placed her. The Canadian public overwhelmingly sided with the father rather than the daughter, agreeing with Judge Ted Noble that this was a "compassionate homicide" (CBC News).

According to Sobsey, "psychological abuse is the most complex form of abuse to objectively define or detect" (1994: 33). Included under this category are: "verbal abuse, intimidation, social isolation, emotional deprivation, denial of the right to make personal decisions, and the threat of having children taken away" (NCFV 4). Psychological abuse can also include "lack of love and affection, threats, verbal attacks, taunting and shouting that leads to the victim's loss of confidence and self-esteem" (Wescott qtd. in The Roeher Institute 1994: 12).

Power and control play a large part in this type of abuse. The way children feel about themselves is influenced by people in positions of authority such as parents and teachers. Some children are taught they are worthless. Also, when children are abused, their opinions of others are affected; sometimes they learn to expect the worst of others

MICHELLE OWEN

(Sobsey 1994: 34). Peers can also subject GYWWD to psychological and verbal abuse.

In the words of NCFV (1993), "Neglect includes the failure to provide the necessities of life, the withholding of the necessities of life, emotional neglect, and the failure to seek needed medical attention" (3). For example, a a girl with a disability may not be fed or get the help she needs to bathe (Renooy). In its most extreme form, neglectful behaviour is passive euthanasia, defined as "the failure to provide the necessities required to sustain life (e.g., withholding medical care or food)" (Sobsey 1994: 123).

RESEARCH FINDINGS

The types of violence most often cited by the participants in this study were psychological abuse and neglect. This trend fits with the existing research. Covert and subtle forms of violence against GYWWD are all too common: name calling, bullying, belittling, lack of care, disempowerment. Moreover, the participants in this study reported rates of sexual and physical abuse in keeping with the current literature, with over two-thirds of women with disabilities experiencing physical or sexual assault when they are young. What this study adds to the small body of work that has been done is to gather in-depth narratives from GYWWD. Previous research has relied more on surveys with, and reflections by, older women with disabilities.

Before I provide an analysis of the findings of this research, I will say a few words about the methodology. After I had written a background paper for the Alliance of Five Research Centres on Violence (AFRCV) on intersecting sites of violence in the lives of GYWWD, it was apparent that more research needed to be conducted. I was fortunate to receive further support from the Intersecting Sites of Violence in the Lives of Girls and Young Women project, funded by Status of Women Canada, for this purpose, and thus I set out to speak to GYWWD about their experiences.

I decided to start by interviewing young women with disabilities eighteen years of age and older. After months of recruitment efforts, I ultimately managed to interview nine young women with disabilities in Winnipeg, Manitoba. This number may seem low, but this type of research is not an easy sell. Moreover, the population I was drawing

190

on is relatively small. Participants had to identify as a girl or young woman, be between eighteen years and early thirties, consider themselves disabled, have experienced some sort of violence or abuse that they were willing and able to talk about, and be able to participate in an interview.

Fortunately Mirlande Demers, herself a young woman with disabilities, was able to work as a research assistant on this project.[2] She conducted one interview, and organized and facilitated a focus group in French, with girls with disabilities under the age of 18 in Québec City. She also assisted the translator and provided analysis of the data. Similar to my experience in Winnipeg, Mirlande found the recruitment process challenging and time-consuming.

Ultimately we spoke with eighteen GYWWD ranging in age from fourteen to thirty-one years old. Most of the participants identified as white, middle class, and heterosexual. Seven participants had Cerebral Palsy (CP), four were wheelchair users, one of which was quadriplegic, two had Attention Deficit Disorder (ADD), two were blind or visually impaired, two had hearing impairments, one had a severe panic disorder, one had a learning disability, one was diagnosed as bipolar, one person had spina bifida, one had left hemiplegia, three people identified as having depression.

Experience of Violence or Abuse

In response to the first research question, "Have you experienced violence or abuse?" all GYWWD the participants replied in the affirmative. And, as already mentioned, the most often reported types of violence were psychological/emotional and neglect/acts of omission. School and family were the most common sites of abuse, with classmates and parents named as the most frequent perpetrators of violence. Intimate partners, teachers, and siblings were also referenced in this regard. GYWWD also reported being subjected to violent behaviour at work, in public, on buses, and in medical facilities. Abusers included friends, acquaintances, on-line contacts, supervisors, strangers, caregivers, nurses, and doctors. Societal attitudes were also highlighted as violent by some of the participants. Kendra,[3] who is twenty-seven and uses a motorized wheelchair, and has CP as well as a severe panic disorder, summed up what many of the participants expressed in this research:

… personally I have never been physically abused as of yet but there have been a very few close calls when people have lost their temper with me, either due to my physical or emotional disability, and the tension level between us … has gotten very high. I am however a victim of subtle abuse rather frequently.

Note that she articulates she has not been "physically abused as of yet," leaving room for this possibility. Kendra also stresses that there have been a "very few close calls" when people have become frustrated because of her disabilities. Finally she states that "I am however a victim of subtle abuse rather frequently." So the spectre of physical abuse hovers close by, while GYWWD navigate tense situations and inappropriate remarks and actions.

Kendra cited, by way of example, strangers who she considers well-intentioned but can be "pretty mean, condescending, patronizing and demeaning, etc., at times." She also talked about her mother, who is her closest caregiver. While Kendra emphasized that her mother never meant to hurt her, sometimes her mother would pull her clothes a little harder than usual when she was impatient, or run the toothbrush or hairbrush a bit roughly when they were having an argument.

Other participants spoke about their families. According to Ruth, who describes herself as visually impaired and has a guide dog named Juno, when she started to lose her vision, neither her parents nor her doctor believed her. And then her parents "wanted so much for me to be independent that they took it too far." For example, they drove her brother to a job interview but made her find her own way. (At the same time Ruth's brother thought she got special privileges because she was visually impaired.) While she believes this probably did make her stronger in the long run, Ruth sometimes felt neglected. And despite her fierce independence, she stated:

It's scary, being a woman with a disability, and the fact that you never know when somebody's going to think, whew, vulnerable person. I'm always worried, like when I take a cab, especially when all of a sudden they get interested, "oh, you can't see anything at all."

For some of the young women with disabilities I spoke with, both their families of origin and the families they formed as adults were highly problematic and fraught with violence. Jennifer, who has Cerebral Palsy, stated that "...I feel that growing up my parents had a really hard time with my disability. They didn't want to acknowledge it or have anything to do with it"—except when her mom would refer to her as "her handicapped daughter." Jennifer often felt that she was an "embarrassment" or "inconvenient because of her walking," and would get sent to her room for drooling. She told me about a painful incident: her parents planned a family trip to Calgary without her. "They gave me the reason that it would be easier without me, I would slow them down."

Jennifer continued to live with her parents until she was seventeen, and then she was put into first a foster home and then independent living. Fortunately she had a good experience with her foster parents, and still maintains a connection with them despite the fact that they live outside of the city. Living on her own before she turned 18 was more difficult. This was when Jennifer met her first husband, who became physically and sexually abusive when she got pregnant. "He gave me bruises, smacked me, raped me, threw things at me and called me names." She left three years later when he threw her against the wall and hit her in front of their son. "That's how it ended," Jennifer told me, "I came from home to this." She definitely makes the link between her abusive family, her lack of self-esteem, her need to be loved, and her two abusive marriages. Today Jennifer has two children, a new partner, remains estranged from her father, is in touch with her mother, and her first husband (who was himself abused as a child) is now her best friend.

Lucinda has lived with a violent common-law partner for five years, since she was twenty. She attributes her vulnerability to abuse, and her current abusive living situation, to her isolation as a woman who has been diagnosed as bipolar. Lucinda expressed this sentiment to me in a few different ways:

> ... I leave him who the hell else is going to put up with me when I'm right out of whack? Like no one probably, I mean, and that scares me, being alone for the rest of my life because I'm too nuts. That scares the crap out of me.

So someone is better than no one, even when they're abusive, and in this case, "…drunk most of the time and gone half the time." Lucinda was certainly not the only young woman in this research to make this point. She told me that she finds the physical abuse a lot easier to deal with than emotional or mental abuse. But she also stated that "I can take a beating but one of these days I'll find a guy that likes knives or guns and I'd wind up dead and that scares me."

Lucinda also ended up in a complicated relationship with a local gang that became an important source of support. However, she was gang raped at sixteen by some of the members, and hospitalized with internal injuries. People she confided in blamed it on her and her depression, and she internalized the blame. In many ways, Lucinda regards the diagnosis of bipolar as the hardest thing to deal with, saying that it "would honestly be better not to have a name on it." She would rather be thought of as "fucked up" than having a "disease." The effects of labelling are subtle, and Lucinda wasn't sure she could call it abuse, but the stigma has led to many of her actions being interpreted in the context of mental illness.

Xena, who is twenty-one, often uses a wheelchair, and has CP, ADD, and depression, has certainly noticed the assumption that because she's physically disabled she must be mentally incompetent. She points out that "there've been instances where I've gone into stores or restaurants and I've noticed that people are quick to try and cheat me on change…" Xena's parents also didn't understand her or her disabilities, although they took care of her physical needs. Her mother questioned why she wanted to go to university, and did not respond well when Xena told her she might be gay. Her father was generally unsupportive and made her feel like a burden. He said things that hurt her and were psychologically abusive. For instance, he would put Xena down, saying, "what are you, crippled?" She finally had to move out on her own: "I don't have to worry about their put downs or, you know, saying you can't do this, you can't do that, anymore…"

Jenny, who is fifteen years old, has been belittled by both her father and her boyfriend because she has a learning disability. She said that her father has threatened her "physically and verbally." She continues, "It was no fun at all when he was making threats when I went to his house and now, I don't feel like going there anymore." For example, her father called her "stupid" and said "I'll kill you." He has also threatened her with a knife. Jenny said that she also argues sometimes with her boyfriend because he talks to her friends on MSN (Microsoft Network Messenger) and they say things that aren't true like that she smokes and takes drugs. "'Do you believe my friends or do you believe me?' That's what I said to him."

At school many participants encountered abuse from their peers, and indifference or lack of support from their teachers. Jennifer, who has CP, recounts that "Between grade six and nine it was just hell. I hated school." Sometimes the violence from her classmates got "a little bit physical," but mainly it was verbal. Jennifer was called "retard," and she once heard a kid say, "Look, that retard has tits." Unfortunately she didn't find the teachers helpful, and she had no support at home.

Melissa, who has mild CP and a slight limp, describes how she was particularly vulnerable to physical abuse in junior high and early high school. For example, she would be tripped in the hallway on purpose by other students, who would say things such as "look at the gimp" and "we just wanted to see the gimp fall."

Melissa also encountered violence when she wanted to work in the school system as a young adult. Although university was overall a better experience for her, she found "the cooperating teachers out in the field emotionally abusive." Originally enrolled in Education, Melissa was sent out to schools to teach. She was told to stand on a chair to reach the top of the wall, even though this was dangerous, and told to draw a calendar and criticized for not being able to draw straight lines. Melissa was also reprimanded for being late when it was the fault of Handi-Transit. These experiences damaged her self-esteem, and Melissa changed departments. She went on to achieve both a B.A. and an M.A.

Renee, a twenty-six-year-old mother of a two-year-old child, had her right eye removed when she was eight because of cancerous tumours and is considered legally blind. Her daughter has the same condition, Bilateral Retina Blastoma, and had an eye removed when she was one. When Renee had her baby she recounts that "the nurses were quite insistent that I couldn't look after my child by myself..." She was given the strong message that "...you don't have the right to have a child." One of the doctors, for instance, told her that if she got pregnant again she "...should get an amniocentesis at sixteen weeks, which is right before the deadline for abortion. She didn't even have to say what her intentions were."

Renee stated that elementary school and junior high were the worst for her. Renee experienced a lot of psychological abuse: "the more different you are the more likely you're going to get picked on." In gym class other students would hit her with as many balls as possible before the teachers noticed. Renee was also called names. Ruth, who is visually impaired, also endured a lot of abuse at school between the ages of twelve and eighteen, with an increase in violence during high school. She was called names (until she started to be able to identify voices and went to the principal), and students coloured in her lock so she couldn't read it, which she described as "mentally exhausting." In grade seven and eight Ruth remembers:

> I was already straining my eyes a lot because nobody believed me… and I was getting a lot of headaches, and one of my fellow classmates decided that whacking me over the head with an encyclopaedia was a good way to, you know, relieve my headaches… things escalated from there.

In high school she was pushed in front of a bus. Although the bus was going to stop, Ruth had no way of knowing that. "…So I technically wasn't in any physical danger, but the mental stress…."

Xena also remembers a lot of bullying in public school. She was the only kid with physical disabilities (she has CP and uses a wheelchair), and there were no services or resources for her. Xena wasn't allowed to join the basketball team and when she was twelve, was not allowed to go on a school-wide ski trip. When asked by people at school why she wanted to go, she told them "…it's an inclusive thing, I can still watch…. I ended up sitting in the library by myself all day." She was also excluded from social events like birthday parties when she'd be the only person in the class not invited. In high school, Xena was initially placed into Special Education, even though she didn't need to be there. She states that it was "kind of a weird blow" when the students were told that "the program is not designed to allow you to go to college or university and that, you know, you'd be lucky to get an entry level job."

Heather, who is twenty-two, uses a wheelchair, and has some speech difficulties, also remembers not being invited to birthday parties or asked over to classmates' houses because they assumed she wouldn't be able to get in. However, her experience of elementary school was that it was fairly inclusive—she wasn't the only student with physical disabilities and there were accommodations and the building was accessible. In first year university she had a friend who stole money from her by getting her PIN number to her bank card. Heather is not sure if she was targeted because of her disability which she finds a "scary thought." As she explained: "…that's what I've had to learn, especially with people taking care of me, like I have to feel the trust right away.… "

Jenny, who is fifteen, and has a learning disability, says: "There are a lot of people who manipulate me at school and I don't do anything about it. Talking about it won't change anything." She told the interviewer that her classmates lie about her taking drugs, "…but if I talk back, it'll just give me more trouble.… " Jenny also gets called names like "stupid," "whore," and "slut" on the school bus. One time Jenny was punched by two girls on the bus and the driver had to intervene.

In the focus group the participants recounted the violence and abuse they have experienced at school. According to Julia, who is fifteen and has left hemiplegia, "…sometimes, you get strange looks from people." Stacey, who is seventeen and has spina bifida, said: "I mostly experience rejection; people don't want to team up with me and don't want to talk with me." Claudia, who is seventeen and has CP, and Julia, added that people at school ignore them. When they try to interact, classmates pretend to accept them, and then disappear because they don't want to be seen with someone with a disability. Claudia said: "In my case, it's mostly isolation, at school, mostly during teamwork. Then, I have a lot of trouble." She continues: "I'm often alone during breaks. You know, I can see that people notice it… there they are, staring at me…."

Julia remembers in grade seven befriending a girl who was pretty and, "…then I realized that she was ashamed of me." She wanted Julia to stop limping, which was impossible, and she was "freaked out" by Julia's hand. "She used to say 'Yuck! You're gross! You're gross!'"

Three participants who experienced name-calling recounted the terms that were used. Stacey "was called 'fat cripple'… 'good-for-nothing'… 'you can't do anything.'" Barbara, who is fifteen and has

CP, remembers the term "freaking cripple." Tania, who is seventeen and has CP, was called: "You fucking ugly cripple." Karin, a 14-year-old with an attention deficit disorder, said that she faced similar comments from students at her school. "They often call me a drug addict because… my head is often in the clouds. They also think I'm mentally retarded." Jane (sixteen) and Rosie (seventeen), both with hearing impairments, said they experience verbal violence from their peers disguised as jokes. As Jane put it, "…they say a joke or something else… and they don't repeat what they said but they laugh because I didn't hear what they said." Barbara added that: "What often hurts the most is the subtle stuff because they think this won't affect us." According to Tania: "I think it's mostly the things that people say…. Sometimes, it's not always that obvious but it hurts. Sometimes, they make weird jokes … sometimes, people are uncomfortable because of differences … but, sometimes, these jokes are not funny at all!"

All the focus group participants agreed that negative comments hurt them even though some of them try not to show it. As Tania stated: "But it hurts a lot inside. We try to harden ourselves but sometimes… It's tough … what did I do wrong?… Maybe it would be better if I wasn't here at all." Karin added that "this really sucks." Julia said: "This is hard to take…." Jane said "It hurts me every time it happens." Rosie agreed: "It hurts me every time it happens … at first, it was even worse. I was just bawling my eyes out."

Stacey said, "I try to be indifferent to all this but I always end up crying in a corner." Moreover, people often think or say, "Anyway, she's retarded; she doesn't even understand what's going on." Stacey thinks this helps them to feel less guilty.

Barbara added: "But sometimes, it's impossible to take it all in." Claudia admitted that "it will really hurt me."

Sometimes the verbal and psychological abuse became physical. "When I was a little girl," Julia stated, "I was a bit weaker and another girl tried to strangle me." The participant was in kindergarten at the time, and the other girl was in grade six. Julia didn't realize the significance of this event until she was older:

> … she was taking advantage of the power she had over me….
> She tried to strangle me with a scarf and I fell on the floor.

Someone loosened the scarf, well, in fact, saved my life. And then, for four years, I had bad dreams every night because of this…. Last year, I realized that it was because of this that I had nightmares. This is hard to take. And, to top it all up, I saw that girl again…. She said "Hi!" and I said "I don't want to talk to you."

Claudia remembers how a classmate would help her with writing her assignments. She noticed the other girl doing something behind her back. But then "she started giving me flicks with her fingers and she laughed… I tried to defend myself but it didn't change anything. Someone had to notice that she was doing this for her to get a warning."

Relation of Violence/Abuse to Disability:

When answering the second research question, "Was the violence or abuse you experienced related to your disability?" most participants indicated that they believed this was the case. Some also added that other aspects of their identities, such as gender, race, and sexuality, were contributing factors. Many simply answered "yes" because they felt that they had provided adequate explanation in their response to the first question. (While a few participants cited examples not related to disability I did not include them in the last section.) Others, however, added new information at this point. Nathalie and Xena, for example, both revealed that they had experienced sexual violence related to their disabilities.

Nathalie, who is twenty-six years old and now uses a wheelchair, was gang raped while working overseas. At that time she was not disabled as she is now, but was very ill. She was having a hard time moving and "…after the rape it kind of got worse." The violence that Nathalie experienced both caused her disability and has led to further violence. She was forced to move back in with her mother when she found that the local women's centre and rape crisis centre were not accessible. She describes her relationship at that time (Nathalie was twenty-two) with her mother as violent, although she didn't recognize this at first. Nathalie's mother didn't like her to use the wheelchair in the house, would leave her on the couch all day, and yelled at her regularly. She also didn't want adaptations or homecare workers in her house. As Nathalie describes it, this situation "was really hurtful and depressing and I had like trauma shock from the rape." Nathalie remembers that "...at some point I didn't want to stay alive, I just wanted to die."

Unfortunately Nathalie didn't receive any more support from her father, who she describes as someone who "dislikes people with disabilities," nor from her siblings and extended family. Nathalie felt estranged from them because, in addition to her disability and rape, she is Black while they are white. Moreover, it took her over three months to access any kind of community services. Nathalie has also experienced abuse from an adaptive transport driver who has made sexist, racist, and sexual comments to her. She was afraid to complain because she feared retaliation. Nathalie also admits that she didn't even realize how inappropriate the driver's actions were until somebody else emphasized it. "I guess at some point you're hearing so many things against women and against people with disabilities, against Blacks, that you kind of, not get used to it... maybe don't take it as seriously as it should be."

Xena, who is twenty-one and sometimes uses a wheelchair (she has CP, ADD, and depression) is currently exploring her sexuality. Once when she was intoxicated at a bar, another young woman took advantage of the situation:

> ...a girl followed me into the bathroom [accessible stall], and you know I thought she was there to help me get up, and then all of a sudden she was taking my clothes off and she's touching me, and I, you know, can't stop her, and I don't know what she's doing, and I mean that's my mistake...

Xena admitted that she thought this was funny at first, and didn't recognize it as abusive until her friends pointed it out. Further on Xena added that she's "not sure if gay women are actually accepting of me being there [lesbian bars] or they just think I'm easy to have sex with because I'm in a wheelchair." She feels vulnerable bringing people home from a bar, and says "...it's easier to have sex with disabled people because you don't feel like you can get abused or hurt or beaten." Xena has developed a strategy for feeling safe: "...when I go out after dark I purposely dress like a male so I don't have to feel scared as a woman with a disability going up to the corner store you know just to buy a pack of smokes or milk or bread."

When Xena was in high school she was called names like "cripple" and "gimp." One time she was knocked over in her wheelchair and nobody offered to help her up. Xena punched the guy who pushed her over: "I was like, and that's one for the Special Ed. Team, you asshole." After that she received more respect from the other students. (She was not the only participant who admitted that she sometimes became violent.)

Kendra, who also has CP and uses a wheelchair, told me that strangers on the street sometimes tell her, "Repent your sins and God will make you whole." At work customers have asked her if she actually gets paid, which Kendra finds "mean, rude, and disrespectful." She also doesn't like it when people offer help without asking her first, or treat her like a child because of her panic disorder.

Jenny, who is fifteen and has a learning disability, explained that she has been intimidated and threatened on MSN because of her disability. Sometimes the people who Jenny chats with online try to get her to meet them, but she always refuses: "I go see my friends but not strangers." The focus group participants said that most of the violence they experience is related to their disability because people target their differences. Barbara, who is also fifteen and has CP, put it this way: "This is pretty obvious when people say 'cripple' or 'delinquent' because this is how they see you."

"In fact, many people think we're brainless," Julia (who is 15 and has left hemiplegia) explained. After hearing similar comments from other students, Tania, who is seventeen and has CP, went into a depression and had to take a three-month leave from school.

Two seventeen-year-old participants, Claudia (CP) and Stacey (SB), said they experienced violence while they were at summer camps as children. Claudia explained that the camp she went to did not accommodate people who used wheelchairs, and she was told "Well, you just can't do it. Watch what the other kids are doing." Claudia also experienced difficulty when she needed to use the toilet and the staff wouldn't take her, sometimes all day, and she would wet her pants.

Stacey had a similar experience: "I said that I had to go to the toilet and the camp instructor kept on telling me that she didn't have time to take me there … and that, well, it grossed her out to take me to the toilet." Stacey is prone to urinary tract infections when she can't use the toilet regularly and had to secretly call her mother. Julia and Tania relayed similar stories about not being taken to the bathroom when they needed to go in the hospital.

Some of the girls in the focus group spoke about harming themselves. Karin, who is fourteen and has ADD, said that "...sometimes, when it gets too much, I switch to self-mutilation." By way of clarification she added: "Well, I slash my wrists."

Julia said she was doing the same thing, "Because it hurts and then it brings relief." She has since stopped because she "...realized that it had no real purpose."

Tania revealed that, "...I used to hit my wheelchair..." She would swear: "Shit! I'm a cripple! There's no point in being here!'" When Tania was depressed, she wanted "...to get out of my house and get hit by a car."

Barbara, who is fifteen and has CP, said "Often, I used to hit my legs." She would also speak to them: "You're crooked. You don't want to be straight."

Stacey stated: "Yeah, I also used to hit my legs... And sometimes, I swore and said to myself 'Come on! Why won't you work?'"

WITNESSING VIOLENCE

In addition to experiencing violence themselves, many of the girls and young women with disabilities had either witnessed or heard about violence against other GYWWD. Heather and Kendra both cited Tracy Latimer's murder by her father in this regard. Kendra also has a female relative, who she refers to as mentally handicapped, who was set on fire when she was ten, and had poison put into her food at a restaurant. Ruth knows a visually impaired woman who was so badly abused by her parents when she was young that she has a split personality. Jennifer has a friend with a physical disability who has been in two abusive relationships over the last decade. Nathalie knows a young woman with a mental disability who was raped by her father, but her testimony was discounted. Xena has friends with disabilities who have been abused by boyfriends and personal care workers. Jenny knows other girls with learning disabilities and has seen them being picked on by boys. Rosie has a friend who is also hard of hearing, and a guy she met put a gun to her head and made death threats. On another occasion he tried to beat her up with a baseball bat.

RECOMMENDATIONS

When asked what they thought caused violence against girls and young women with disabilities, the participants listed such things as societal ignorance, emotional abuse, lack of understanding, stereoptypes, inaccessibility, poverty, rejection, and insensitivity. In addition, they articulated their own feelings of dependence, difference, vulnerability, needing to be loved, lack of self-esteem, lack of knowledge, lack of power, isolation, feeling like "damaged goods," their desire to feel "normal," desperation, and feeling like a victim. And they clearly understood the implications of intersectionality in their lives, especially in regards to age, gender, and disability.

Many of the participants concurred that, in order to end or reduce violence against GYWWD, education is key. There is an urgent need, as Jillian Ridington points out, for clear sexual education directed at girls and young women with disabilities. The girls and young women with disabilities featured in the DisAbled Women's Network (DAWN) 2002 video echo this sentiment. The material should include information about unwanted contact and be made available in multiple formats (e.g., tape, electronic, Braille, large print, simple graphics) (Ridington).

At the same time, girls and young women with disabilities need to know that they have a right to feel sexual and express their sexuality. This reality has been denied too often in the past, and accompanied by forced sterilization or Depo-Provera to control reproduction (Ridington).

The non-disabled public needs to be educated by people with disabilities about disability, and this process needs to begin early and be on-going. GYWWD also need to be educated about violence, and given opportunities to speak about it. Teachers and principals need to take an active role in preventing bullying. Self-defence courses for women, such as Wen-Do, should be adapted and offered to GYWWD so they can protect themselves. GYWWD need to know that they can be confident and that they have the right to say "no."

In addition to education, more services and better public policy are necessary. The existing literature, as well as my research, highlight that violence against GYWWD is a widespread and enduring problem. GYWWD need places to seek refuge from violence and governments that take their safety seriously. Reflecting on the murder of Tracy Latimer, Ruth Enns concludes that, "The greatest disability [she] faced was the attitude of her parents and other key people in her life" (123). She elaborates, shifting the focus from attitudinal change to a broader national context:

> [Tracy Latimer's] cognitive abilities were indeed less than most children her age. However, in Canada we profess to value our citizens on the basis of citizenship alone, not on IQ scores, physical beauty or strength and we do not determine citizenship on the basis of productivity or any other marketplace values. Otherwise most Canadians would fail the acceptability test at one time or another. (123)

[1]In the spirit of participatory action research everyone we spoke with was given the opportunity to review the research and offer feedback.
[2]Thanks to Julie Sanfaçon who provided the translation and transcription services, as well as note-taking.
[3]Pseudonyms have been used to protect confidentiality.

REFERENCES

Canadian Association for Community Living. *The Right to be Safe: A Resource Guide Addressing Violence against People with Intellectual Disabilities in your Community.* 1986. Online: <http://www.cacl.ca/english/documents/Safety-Audit_Nov09-2006.pdf>.

Canadian Broadcasting Corporation (CBC) News In Depth. "'Compassionate Homicide:' The Law and Robert Latimer." 2008. Online: <http://www.cbc.ca/news/background/latimer>.

DisAbled Women's Network (DAWN) Ontario. *You Deserve To Be Safe: Advice To a Girl, An Educational Video.* 2002.

Enns, R. *A Voice Unheard: The Latimer Case and People with Disabilities.* Halifax: Fernwood Publishing, 1999.

Mansell, S., D. Sobsey and L. Wilgosh. "Sexual Abuse of Children with Disabilities: Patterns, Prevention, Intervention, and Treatment." *International Journal of Special Education* 12.2 (1997): 1-11.

McPherson, C. "Violence Against Women With Disabilities: Out Of Sight, Out Of Mind." *Canadian Woman Studies/les cahiers de la femme* 11.4 (1991): 49-50, 77.

The National Clearinghouse on Family Violence (NCFV), Family Violence Prevention Division. *Family Violence Against Women With Disabilities.* Ottawa: Health and Welfare Canada, 1993. Online: <http://www.phac-aspc.gc.ca/ncfv-cnivf/familyviolence/pdfs/fvawd.pdf>.

Randall, W., R. Parrila and D. Sobsey. "Gender, Disability Status and Risk for Sexual Abuse in Children." *Journal on Developmental Disabilities* 7.1 (2000):1-15.

Renooy, L. *You Deserve to Be Safe: A Guide for Girls with Disabilities.* North Bay: DAWN Ontario, 2002. Online: <http://dawn.thot.net/safe.html>.

Ridington, J. *Beating the Odds: Violence and Women with Disabilities.* Vancouver: DAWN Canada, 1989. Online: <http://www.dawncanada.net/odds.htm>.

The Roeher Institute. *Harm's Way: The Many Faces of Violence and Abuse Against Persons With Disabilities in Canada.* North York: The Roeher Institute, 1995.

The Roeher Institute. *Violence and People with Disabilities: A Review of the Literature.* North York, ON: The Roeher Institute, for the National Clearinghouse on Family Violence, 1994.

Sobsey, D. "Faces of violence against women with developmental disabilities." *Impact* 13.3 (2000): 2-3, 25.

Sobsey, D. *Violence and Abuse in the Lives of People with Disabilities: The End of Silent Acceptance.* Baltimore: Paul H. Brookes Publishing Company, 1994.

Sobsey, D. and C. Varnhagen. *Sexual Abuse and Exploitation of People with Disabilities: Final Report.* Edmonton: University of Alberta Developmental Disabilities Centre, 1988.

Ticoll, M. and M. Panitch. "Opening the Doors: Addressing the Sexual Abuse of Women with an Intellectual Disability." *Canadian Woman Studies/les cahiers de la femme* 13.4 (1993): 84-87.

WHEN BAD THINGS HAPPEN

Violence, Abuse, Neglect and Other Mistreatments Against Manitoba Women with Intellectual Disabilities

T HIS RESEARCH GAVE VOICE to Manitoba women with intellectual disabilities who shared their experiences and fears with regards to the harms that they encounter in their lives. As far as we know, it is the first study of its kind that focuses specifically on this vulnerable population.

The primary challenge in its methodology was gaining access to women who are protected and segregated by either families or services. This level of isolation from community and non-paid relationships is one of the key factors leading to the ongoing vulnerability of this population. It is well known that vulnerable people are more at risk when surrounded only by paid service providers. Sadly, much of the neglect and abuse, either intentional or not, comes from those that are paid to provide care and support. It is the connectedness, advocacy and visibility within a community that ensures that people are taken care of, watched over and missed when not around.

INTRODUCTION

Violence, abuse, neglect and other mistreatments against people with disabilities are significant and longstanding problems (Roeher Institute). Women with disabilities are particularly susceptible (Brownridge; Martin, Ray, Sotres-Alvarez, Kupper, Moracco, Dickens, Scandlin and Gizlice; Young, Nosek, Howland, Chanpong and Rintala; Rodgers). Through anecdotal reports, many people involved with disability issues have come to the view that women with intellectual disabilities are that much more susceptible to a range of harms.

The terms "intellectual" disability or disabilities and "developmental" disability or disabilities are used widely in Canada as equivalent notions. *The Vulnerable Persons' Act* (VPA) uses the term "mental disability" to describe the same population. As used in the present report the terms "intellectual disability" and "intellectual disabilities" are used interchangeably.

Research on violence and abuse against women with intellectual disabilities is scant but tends to back up the general impression that they are particularly vulnerable. For instance, Dick Sobsey reported the results of an analysis of a sample of sexual assault cases of women and adolescent girls fifteen years and older with intellectual disabilities. The analysis found that most of these women experienced repeated assaults. The offenders were generally known to the victims, were virtually always males and included: special service providers; generic service providers; transportation providers; neighbours, family, friends, and other acquaintances; other people with disabilities; and dates. While more than half of the women sustained physical injuries, social, emotional, and behavioural harm were virtually universal. Only a minority received counselling or treatment services that met their needs. Fewer than a quarter were able to access any services, and more than half of those who did access services were not provided with necessary service accommodations or were provided with inadequate accommodations to meet their needs.

Many of these cases went unreported to authorities. Of those that were reported, only about a third resulted in formal charges, and only half of those charged were convicted. Overall, this meant that convictions occurred in just eleven percent of the 100 cases analyzed (Sobsey).

For those concerned about legislation, public policy and social programs, and the safeguards these afford or fail to afford to women with intellectual disabilities in a given province or territory, there is little in the way of empirical research and "hard" data to inform policy and program development. For that matter, there is little research at the provincial/territorial level on violence against *any* women, regardless of disability (Thurston, Patten and Lagendyk). The present research was intended to help close the knowledge gap with a view to the situation in Manitoba in particular.

Use of Individual Stories of Women Who Have Disclosed Incidents

The experiences of five courageous women were documented through personal interviews with them. All these women have previously disclosed to people in authority the harms that have happened to them. They have either read the interview transcripts or have had the transcripts read to them and in all cases agree with the details and have agreed to make their experiences available to the public. To ensure confidentiality, however, their names have been changed in the present report. Excerpts from these narratives are featured throughout the present report.

Focus Groups for "Non-identifying" Information and Insight

Four focus groups were convened, one in the summer and three in the Fall of 2006. Together these comprised 14 family members, seven service providers, six advocates, eight self-advocates (women), and five government officials. Consistent with the general approach that was originally planned, the focus groups explored the kinds of harms women with intellectual disabilities experience, risk factors, issues in disclosure and response, and measures needed to make women safer.

The discussion with five government officials was conducted in the fall of 2006. It was a "high level" discussion in which participants also discussed the kinds of barriers, harms and other difficulties that women (and men) with intellectual disabilities experience, risk factors and measures needed to address these issues.

Two-day Think Tank

A two-day "think tank" was convened in Winnipeg in November 2006 that brought together 34 people with a range of experience on issues of woman abuse and disability. These people included women with intellectual disabilities, police, family members, service providers, advocates, university students, two university professors, victim assistants, police officers, Community Living-Manitoba (CL-M) Board members, CL-M senior staff, a representative of a Winnipeg disability organization with a focus on independent living, and staff persons from two national disability organizations.

The process used a combination of breakout and plenary discussion groups. The first day utilized a "think-tank" approach and focused on identifying and exploring. Participants examined the situations of harm in which women live and work; various factors that place women at risk and silence them; and lessons learned based on reported abuses and responses to those abuses, as well as lessons learned from research and history.

The second day built on the experiences and data captured on the first day and moved toward the design of a comprehensive strategy, targeting ways in which harms against women with intellectual disabilities can begin to be addressed, e.g., through training and empowerment sessions for women and their families, measures needed in law and government, etc.

KEY FINDINGS

General Dimensions of the Problem

Women who related their experiences, focus group participants, and participants in the think tank for the present research identified a range of harms that women with intellectual disabilities experience. Thematically, many of reported mistreatments fall within the categories of the Criminal Code or *Vulnerable Persons Act*, namely those of a sexual, physical, mental, emotional, and financial nature. Research participants also identified various forms of neglect. In some cases what women experience as mistreatments have occurred at the hands of community services and public agencies with a responsibility to protect vulnerable persons.

However, not all forms of mistreatment reported by participants in this research fall neatly into the categories of the legislation. Nor do the reported harms that may seem to "fit" necessarily meet the threshold of "seriousness" or "significance" specified in law, i.e., that acts or omissions, whether intentional or unintentional, cause or are reasonably likely to cause:

- death;
- serious physical or psychological harm; or
- significant loss to the vulnerable person's property.

There are, then, some in-between "grey areas." Such "grey areas" were flagged by research participants as requiring vigilance and effective counteractive and preventative measures.

SPECIFIC HARMS REPORTED

Sexual Abuse

The sexual abuse of women with intellectual disabilities arose as a major concern in four of the narratives that women provided, in the focus groups, and in the two-day think tank. The sexual abuses that were reported take various forms. Angela's story and one of the incidents related by Veronica involved violent sexual behaviour by the perpetrators. Sarah's narrative tells about how the perpetrator invaded her personal home and, inspiring terror, left her no perceived option but to have sex with him. Jane recalled an incident of unwanted sexual touching, a problem she indicates is occurring to "lots of other women... but they just don't know what to do and there just isn't anyone that they want to tell...." In all these narratives the perpetrators were men.

Research participants' concerns about sexual abuse generally revolved around what men do to women with intellectual disabilities. However, an incident was related about what a mother of a young woman with an intellectual disability perceived as "a girl assaulting a girl," i.e., her daughter was at the receiving end of the aggressive sexual advances of a young woman with a physical disability.

Identifying a "grey zone" between consensual sexual activity and sexual abuse, one participant said,

> [It's] more complicated sometimes because [in] two cases I've known ... [the] young women didn't perceive it [fondling] as being unpleasant.... It begins to seem disrespectful of her feelings if you press it too hard.... How to respect her but let her know that it's actually abusive....

Physical Abuse

In Angela's narrative and one of the incidents related by Veronica the sexual abuses involved physical abuse as well. Other incidents of physical mistreatment were also related for this research, such as program staff hitting women with intellectual disabilities.

In some cases the fear of physical harm is a factor. For example, a woman who participated in the research related how her husband's murderer is now in the community, having been released from jail.

The woman is afraid of this man. "Abusers are still out there," she said. Similarly, out of concern for personal safety Sarah obtained a "personal bond" against the perpetrator of sexual abuse against her.

While not a scientific conclusion, on balance it would seem that sexual rather than physical abuses were of wider concern to the people who took part in this research.

> *It was last summer. I had been out all night and I ran into a friend, or so I thought. We'd gone to school together so I'd known him for a couple of years. We went by my place. The next thing I knew he'd pulled my feet from under me and was on top of me. I'd hit my head pretty hard—I think I got the sense knocked out of me. I was trying to think about what to do next, because my landlord (who lives upstairs) couldn't hear what was going on at 4:00 a.m.... I decided to get the hell out of there. It was getting dangerous.... I didn't think he was capable of doing that to me, but I guess men are capable of doing whatever they want. I guess there was some poor judgement on my behalf because I trusted that he wouldn't hurt me.*
>
> —from Angela's narrative

Emotional and Mental Abuse

Also of key concern to research participants were various forms of emotional and mental mistreatment of women with intellectual disabilities. What seemed to be of greater concern to participants are multiple acts and words over extended periods of time that together have adverse effects, rather than any specific "one time" examples of emotional or mental abuse that individually induced "serious" psychological harm.

More subtle and ongoing concerns include women being subjected to nastiness and meanness, name calling, threats, coerciveness and bullying in service and non-service contexts, and being denied ordinary privileges and freedoms by service providers, e.g., a woman being denied dessert and sent to her bedroom for being "bad."

Jane's narrative relates how a group home staff person made her sit in the bathtub all night because she had soiled her bed, saying she was "very dirty and dirty girls need ... to get clean." The staff person was indifferent to Jane's distress. Other but more pervasive examples of emotional mistreatment were staff who lose their temper and treat women with intellectual disabilities "sharply."

> *I grew up in two foster homes. The second home wasn't so good. When they [social workers] took me out they said I was like a stone statue, unloved.*
>
> —from Veronica's narrative

Financial Abuse

The issue of financial abuse was raised in the research but was not a topic of major discussion. It was acknowledged that "friends," acquaintances, and service staff—both "front line" and supervisory— can be perpetrators of financial abuses and that the amounts of money stolen or manipulated away can be significant.

It was also reported in the research that "merchant abuse" occurs, i.e., where unscrupulous merchants sell products at exorbitantly high prices to people with intellectual disabilities—women included—who are poor to begin with. Essentially the merchants are exploiting women one-by-one.

Neglect

Research participants related several forms of neglect experienced by women with intellectual disabilities as a result of omissions by program staff. These forms of neglect include women being left sitting on the toilet for extended periods of time, not being changed after soiling their clothes, not being welcomed or engaged by day program staff, being subjected to the general indifference of foster care providers and service staff, being required to go for extended periods of time without furnace heat while staff have afghans to keep themselves warm, and being left unattended for hours on end while staff watch movies.

Pervasive and Corrosive "Under the Radar" Harms

Other harms were identified in the research as abusive—or at best, corrosive—for women with intellectual disabilities. These harms do not necessarily fall squarely within the scope of the *Vulnerable Persons' Act* or other legislation or policy.

These harms are reportedly quite pervasive, although they may seem at first somewhat subtle. They include the social and cultural devaluation of women with intellectual disabilities, and prevention by others of women with intellectual disabilities from exercising control over matters that directly affect their lives. As with emotional and mental abuses, it is the cumulative effects of these harms—not necessarily any single incident—that women can experience as abusive.

> *I moved to [the institution] at age ten. The Salvation Army lady told my mother and grandmother to put me there for schooling. But I never learned nothing. I was on a ward. I watched TV, went outside, walked around.... I ran away.*
>
> —from Rachel's narrative

> *Women with disabilities are paying a terrible price for laws and other instruments that seem to take a "black or white," "all or nothing" approach.*
>
> —a research participant

Concerning devaluation, women with intellectual disabilities were portrayed as having to operate in a broad cultural and program environment of belittlement and disrespect. On the one hand it was acknowledged by a research participant that, "Ninety-nine percent of people in ... [the developmental services] field want to do a good job" and that "This needs to be recognized." On the other it was also acknowledged that key messages emanating from the broader policy and service "system" seem to imply that it is acceptable for paid workers to think about and treat women with intellectual disabilities as "less than" others. This general social and cultural devaluation of people with intellectual disabilities has been well documented in the sociological literature by analysts such as Wolf Wolfensberger and is acknowledged by major advocacy organizations in North America and elsewhere.

Denial of personal control translates to women lacking choices

> *... getting away from making decisions for [women], respecting and building their right to make choices, to say "no," etcetera, so they don't have to rely so much on other people. We have to do this from when they are little.*
>
> —a research participant

that square with their needs and aspirations and to women's lack of assistance from support staff and others in making decisions, e.g., such as where to go and what to do today or next week.

Lack of control can also have a bearing on how a woman addresses major issues of harm against herself. Said one research participant about the prospect of reporting bad things that happened to her, "If I report, I will lose control over my own life." Others expressed concern about women who report abuses against themselves potentially losing their homes, e.g., as a result of being taken into "care" by the Public Trustee.

> *I remember for three months I was in the hospital. I was in a crisis stabilization unit. I was on different medications. A psychiatrist put me under the Public Trustee. I had a worker and a lawyer. They looked after my finances and where I lived. For a year and a half I lived at a large group home. I didn't have any control over my money. I didn't have control over where I lived or freedom. I wanted to go on a trip ... and I had to get permission. I was under 24-hour supervision living in the group home. When I was there, one of the cooks took an apple out of my hand. I was ticked off. I was more outspoken. We had group meetings and I would be saying I didn't like certain things that were happening where we were living. Me and another lady wrote a letter to the head people and they had a talking to the cook and then she was a lot better. I got off the Public Trustee. I had to go to a psychologist and pay money out of my own pocket. I had to prove to her that I was competent by proving I could live back on my own again.*
>
> —from Veronica's narrative

Some common forms of "treatment" within the developmental services system, such as behavioural therapy and over-medication, were also reported as abusive. Typically the "treatment" involves a power imbalance between the person administering and the person receiving it, with the receiver being expected to comply with the wishes of the person administrating.

Veronica's narrative relates how her experience of being under the Public Trustee for "crisis stabilization" meant being hospitalized and medicated for months on end. Following those months there was another year and a half in a large group home, in which she experienced the loss of control over her personal finances and living arrangements, and a general lack of personal freedom, within a regime of 24-hour supervision. Ultimately she had to find her own financial resources to "prove" her competence to a psychologist, which was the requirement for living on her own again out from under the control of the Public Trustee.

RISK FACTORS

A variety of risk factors were reported in the focus groups and think tank that render women with intellectual disabilities vulnerable to abuses, neglect and other harms. Some of these risk factors have to do with the women's personal characteristics. Others have to do with their upbringing. Still others have to do with women's social, economic, and service situations.

Personal Characteristics

The cognitive limitations experienced by women with a severe level of intellectual disability can render them unaware that they are in harm's way. That is, they are unable to read the cues in others' behaviours as menacing, exploitative, or as potentially dangerous. Moreover, after the fact they may not be able to appreciate that they have been mistreated.

Due to the stigma attached to "intellectual disability," many women with this condition lack personal self-esteem so may go to extreme lengths to garner approval and acceptance from others, including from people with power and authority. This can involve taking part in activities that are ultimately not in the women's own best interests.

> *It happened in my apartment. I can't remember exactly when. A guy from karaoke that I knew, when I was coming home, he followed me home. I knew him from the hotel I always go to. I like to go there to spend time with friends and talk. When I opened my door to go in, he came in. He wasn't invited. He brought a case of beer. We had one beer each. Then I told him to go home. But he kept saying "no." I opened the couch in the living room into a bed so he would go to bed and leave me alone. But it didn't happen like that. I wanted to sleep in my own bed. And then he told me to sleep with him. I didn't want to but I had no choice. He left the next morning.... I was scared. I didn't know what to say. He didn't want to listen. I was terrified. Sometimes I'm having memories about it. I still wish it never happened in the first place, but it did. Now I can't change it.*
>
> —from Sarah's narrative

The lack of self-confidence of many women with an intellectual disability can result in their not "pushing back" when they suspect they are in harm's way or being mistreated. They may be that much more afraid to disclose actual mistreatment after the fact.

The naturally affectionate demeanour of some women with intellectual disabilities can lead them to spontaneously demonstrate great warmth and good will in relationships, but sometimes with a corresponding naiveté about when people may be taking advantage of that spontaneity, warmth, and good will.

Effects of Upbringing

Some women with intellectual disabilities have not been taught by their family members or the education system to understand the differences between behaviours that are appropriate and inappropriate, safe and unsafe. As a result they may find themselves in compromising situations as adults without clearly understanding that they are in relationships that are abusive or exploitative, or in situations that are dangerous or potentially dangerous.

As well, some women with intellectual disabilities have not been exposed to ordinary information about human sexuality—and may even have been treated as asexual—which can compound any confusion or lack of understanding about behaviours that may not be safe and appropriate. Lack of basic information about human rights, and about what to do and where to go when those rights have been breached, leaves many women with intellectual disabilities without the necessary tools to get others to respond to the mistreatments they have experienced.

Social, Economic and Service Situations

Depending on the social and economic situations of women with intellectual disabilities, they may be more or less vulnerable to various harms and more or less able to remove themselves from harm's way. For instance, a woman with severe disabilities still living with her aging parents may be in a situation where her parents are feeling "stressed," "burned out," and without the time or energy needed to attend to all her needs. That situation may have been ongoing for years. Key issues, here, are insufficient assistance for family members who provide ongoing support and the lack of alternative support arrangements beyond the family home.

It was pointed out by research participants that a woman may be more susceptible to various harms if living in an "affordable" housing complex or neighbourhood that is neither safe nor secure, e.g., one that has more than its fair share of drug and alcohol abusers, dealers, gang members, etc.

> *Not every parent is outgoing. Many are withdrawn, shy, and can become preoccupied with caregiving. They lose capacity to go out and get needed support. My sister didn't build her network so her child has no network. We need to help families with this.*
> —a research participant

A woman without a network of friends has limited opportunities to share stories and learn from peers about the world and its risks. She may not have others "looking into" her life with concern about her safety and well being.

A woman who has not been involved in a respectful and reciprocal intimate relationship may not know "when something isn't right" in a present relationship that may be intimate but not reciprocal. Her felt need for intimacy may take priority over issues of dignity and safety.

In the event of risk or mistreatment, a woman who is verbal and who has quick access to a communication device such as a cell phone has potentially quick access to her personal network for help. A woman without such a device does not have such access to her network.

> *It's scary to know that there are many people who are isolated [in group homes], can't speak, who have no advocates—no one watching out for them. Having more people involved in their lives will increase their visibility and safety. It's important to have a number of people who are witnesses to a person's life. Day programs and residential programs won't report on one another if they're in the same organizations.*
>
> —a research participant

> *Another time a friend of my brother's drove me home and he touched me on my breast and said it was a good idea if we didn't tell anyone but I told Judy. I was very proud that I told her because it was my right to tell. I know lots of other women who have these things going on but they just don't know what to do and there just isn't anyone that they want to tell except me.*
>
> —from Jane's account of her experiences

A woman with an intellectual disability is likely to find herself living in a community where she has limited contact with ordinary community members, where those people labour under various myths and stereotypes about her disability, do not appreciate the risks she faces and would not know what to do and where to go if she has been—or seems to have been—harmed.

A woman who is receiving services from an agency with high staff turnover or from staff untrained on issues of abuse and neglect, will not be in a situation of continuous attentiveness to her well-being, so potential warning signs of abuses against her may go unheeded. A woman who relies on anyone for support—service provider or other

> *[Vulnerability is a result of] isolation in the group home. Depending on the home and the organization, people can be very isolated from the community. They live, work, recreate with the same people. We expect disabled people to do this. Underpaid staff who change [through high job turnover] and who are underpaid are involved in all this. People are not in the community. Building networks and embedding [people] in the community is the hardest thing to do for staff.*
>
> —a research participant

member of the community—may be vulnerable to various forms of mistreatment by that person.

A woman who is receiving services from an agency that has not done appropriate background checks of job applicants and staff may find that she is receiving service from someone with a criminal record for sexual or physical assault. Then again, she may be receiving service from a person without a criminal record who has been disciplined by an employer for sexually exploitive, physically violent or emotionally abusive behaviours. A woman who is poor may have little say about who provides the help she receives and few service alternatives if a helper turns out to be abusive.

Depending on the service context, there may be few or no standards to uphold the safety and security of women with intellectual disabilities. For instance, foster care arrangements can be terminated quickly where there is failure to meet the "necessities of life." Otherwise, the only standards for this sector are reportedly through informal self-regulation. Licensing requirements for residential services afford some protections for women with intellectual disabilities but there are reportedly no such requirements for day services. Concerning standards that are in place for residential services, in the words of one research participant, "The gaps between safety and being in an approved home are large"; living in an approved home is not necessarily a guarantee of personal safety.

The study excerpted here was undertaken by the Association for Community Living–Manitoba and was funded by the Status of Women Canada. The full study is available at <http://aclmb.ca/justice.htm>.

REFERENCES

Brownridge, D. A. "Partner Violence Against Women with Disabilities." *Violence Against Women* 12.9 (2006): 805-822.

Martin, S. L., N. Ray, D. Sotres-Alvarez, D. L. Kupper, K. E. Moracco, P. A. Dickens, D. Scandlin and Z. Gizlice. "Physical and Sexual Assault of Women with Disabilities." *Violence Against Women* 12.9 (2006): 823-837.

Rodgers, K. "Wife Assault: The Findings of a National Survey." *Juristat* 14.9 (1994): 1-21.

The Roeher Institute. *Harm's Way: The Many Faces of Violence and Abuse Against Persons With Disabilities.* North York, ON: The Roeher Institute, 1995.

Sobsey, D. "Faces of Violence Against Women with Intellectual Disabilities." *Impact* 13.3 (2000): 2-3.

Thurston W. E., S. Patten and L. E. Lagendyk. "Prevalence Of Violence Against Women Reported in a Rural Health Region." *Canadian Journal of Rural Medicine* 11.4 (2006): 259-67.

Young, M. E., M. A. Nosek, C. Howland, G. Chanpong, and D. H. Rintala. "Prevalence of Abuse of Women with Physical Disabilities." *Archives of Physical Medicine and Rehabilitation* 78.5 (1997): S34-S38.

ANJALI DOOKFRAN

"Untitled Woodcut"

"Untitled," no date, woodcut.

JOANNA M. WESTON

LIONS

I understand lions:
the way they suck sand
into their skins.
lure festival trees
about their heads
and proclaim orchestra
in the swiftness of kill.
These are my comprehensions
when screams lash
the credibility of sleep
and I am brought down
by claws.

Originally published in CWS/cf's issue on "Women and Disability," 13 (4) (1993): 123. Reprinted with permission.

WITH US ON THE EDGES:
RELATIONSHIPS AND SEXUALITY

MARIA BARILE

NEW REPRODUCTIVE TECHNOLOGY

My Personal and Political Dichotomy

S A WOMAN WITH disabilities, I am aware that what I advocate politically is often quite different from the social and cultural myths I was raised with. One day as I sat in my doctor's waiting room, I came across a letter in a magazine that brought my political ideas into the personal sphere. The letter was written by a woman who expressed joy about having a child of her own through new reproductive technology. I presumed that it was through *in vitro fertilization* (IVF). For just a moment I found myself wondering what my genes would produce. Would I have a girl? What colour eyes and hair would she have? Would she inherit my characteristics? Would she be passionate about women's issues and social justice, like I am? What if...? Then again, what if I had a boy who turned out to have chauvinistic views? These thoughts surfaced aimlessly in my mind, triggered by the letter from this unknown woman. For the first time I came close to understanding, from a personal perspective, those women who want a child of their own at any cost.

Wait a minute! This was my emotional side speaking, not my logic. At once, my political convictions interrupted this rather foreboding day dream. It became clear that if I, with my knowledge of new reproductive genetics technologies (NRGTS) and the multitude of questions that result, can daydream about its possibilities, then undoubtedly most women who do not have the information I do, but who feel a great need to have a child of their own, can be easily seduced into considering IVF as feasible. According to the cultural and socially constructed beliefs I was brought up with, it is non-disabled women's responsibility to reproduce, and I, as a women with disabilities could not, and should not, reproduce. So, where did my daydream come from?

The message generally conveyed to the public creates the impression that the main objective of NRGTS is to give people more positive and progressive options. For example, we hear that NRGTS would allow women who could not otherwise bear children to do so and/or allow people to choose the type of child they want. However, this has negative implications for the human rights of people with disabilities.

How can non-disabled women and men who have constantly been fed misinformation about disability and persuaded to believe that the lives of persons with disabilities are "not worth living," possibly be expected to choose anything but the elimination of a fetus that would develop into a child with disabilities? This view could be assumed especially of women and men who have never had any meaningful encounters with the community of people with disabilities. How can one make choices, let alone an "informed choice," based on myth?

I believe that the choices individuals make will be based on socially-learned negative values with respect to disability. Social dogma dictates that one must be physically able and physically pleasing. These sentiments are subtly reinforced by our economic and social system and promoted by the media. This in turn gives rise to the view that the more one deviates from society's physical and mental norms the more undesirable one is. According to these standards, persons with disabilities are "unwell," and unable to conform to society's strict standards for physical and/or mental ability.

Every economic system in the world has promoted the view that physical desirability and productivity go hand-in-hand. These systems value individuals according to their ability to compete in the reproductive market system. By "reproductive" I mean both the actual physical reproduction of the next "able-bodied" generation, and the production of "able-bodied" replacement workers in the competitive labour market. The so-called "undesirable" often becomes dependent upon the state, and this gives rise to the patronizing notion that "society takes care of disabled persons."

Nowadays, we also hear, if you choose to have a disabled child then you are to be responsible for all his or her needs. Thus, individuals are deemed to be guilty of creating a social problem, a socio-economic burden. One of the main messages that NRGTS is subtly conveying is that it will eliminate this problem for society through a technique known as genetic manipulation, i.e. altering genetic codes to correct imperfections and/or introduce new genetic characteristics (CRIAW).

The fact is that every time a society faces economic difficulties, it tends to blame those in powerless positions, the "undesirables," for wanting more rights and protection, and more of the national wealth. In the case of people with disabilities, the general public has been led to believe that the cost of physical, technical, and human access, as well as financial support, creates an economic burden. In other words, the changes that we in the disabled community demand in order to promote our rights often cost money. The state claims that if it allocates funds to fulfill our needs, it cannot spend that money on other groups. Those in power use this myth to create conflict between equality seeking groups. In fact, by spending money to develop new reproductive technology, funds are being taken away from those of us who require assistance now.

If and when those who hold power—policymakers, state-controlled service providers, etc.—are no longer trespassers in our personal lives, when women with disabilities can make choices that are truly our own, and when our personal is political by choice, then perhaps women with disabilities from future generations can fulfill their personal dreams in areas of reproductive rights.

With respect to my daydream, I quickly realized that I was dealing with a multitude of emotions. On the one hand, I had acquired a new understanding of the personal realities of women who want a child of their own, that very heartfelt, but socially constructed, sentiment most women internalize. On the other hand I am also conscious of the realities that I, along with most women with disabilities of my generation, have internalized, the message that we should not, and do not, want to have children, "for our own good" of course!

However, I am a woman and my disabilities are part of me. Ever since I can remember, I have been aware of the messages conveyed to non-disabled women about childbearing and the social rewards that appear to go with it. As a woman with disabilities, I have always wondered what it meant when pregnant women are told, "as long as the baby is healthy, it doesn't matter whether it's a boy or a girl." What does that say about me and all those like me? It is not without cause that on a personal level I fear the illusory choices that NRGTS and its proponents claim to give women, i.e. that they can have exactly the type of child they want.

Whereas, I regret not having had a child, even a child with disability, today, two decades later, reflecting on the thought of that younger woman, my concern about a Disabelist society and the position about NRGTS remains the same. However, the community of persons with disabilities through "disability culture" is evolving and assisting society to have a change in perspective. Thus, young women with disabilities today have greater opportunities not only in the public sphere but also in the private one.

Originally published in CWS/cf's *issue on "Women and Disability," 13 (4) (1993): 61-62. Reprinted with permission.*

REFERENCES

Canadian Research Institute for the Advancement of Women (CRIAW). *Our Bodies, Our Babies? Women Look at New Reproductive Technologies.* Ottawa: Canadian Research Institute for the Advancement of Women, 1989.

JANCIS M. ANDREWS

DEAF-MUTE?

*"What a pity—that couple can never speak
to each other about their love."*
(Woman talking about a disabled couple).

This dance of fingers
sheds veils of air, reveals
ten times over
the nakedness of my desire.
My palms doubly celebrate you,
inscribe my love
upon the space between us, enclose
tenderness, shape it
like a flower.
And though the world about us roars,
this silence
is our own private universe
wherein I sow a promise: kisses
falling like stars
upon your mouth, each fingertip
a white flame
foreplaying Heaven, igniting us
toward that wordless ceremony
where you and I
will blaze in pas-de-deux
into the profounder silence
that will be our bodies, singing.

*Originally published in CWS/cf's issue on "Women and Disability," 13 (4)
(1993): 58. Reprinted with permission.*

TRACY ODELL

DISABILITY AND RELATIONSHIPS

THERE WAS A LONG time in my life when I thought I'd never have anything to say on either the topic of sexuality or the topic of relationships. I was born with a disability, which wasn't noticeable until I was old enough to walk—and didn't. My life moved forward in every other aspect, such as school and making friends, but relationships—you know, the personal ones, seemed to elude me.

I was a "late bloomer" in that it took a long time for me to develop an intimate relationship. Why would it take longer for me to fully develop as a person as compared to my non-disabled peers?

Common wisdom is that you have to love *yourself* before anyone else can love you. Is it very easy to love yourself if you happen to have a disability? It should be. But it is, in fact, *very* hard for us to love ourselves as we are. At least it was in my day.

I was fascinated to learn that the oldest remains documenting a person with a disability were found in Shanidar Cave, Iraq in 1972. He was a Neanderthal known as Shandy who lived, loved, and died about 50,000 years ago. He may have had spina bifida. His skeletal remains show he had one small arm and some injuries which had well healed over. He was found amid objects from a hearth. Archaeologists and anthropologists can tell us that people who tended the community hearths were valued and respected, even revered. So certainly in 50,000 BC, it was possible for someone who had a disability to be a valued, contributing citizen. I don't know about Shandy's personal life, of course, but his bones tell a wonderful story of how someone with a disability was the hearth, the warm, vital, living heart of his community.

Much later in time, people with disabilities were regarded differently. In nomadic societies, people needed to be quick and agile. The hunter-gatherers were valued, not the hearth-tenders. The Spartans were an example of a society that valued strength and perfection. They're the ones who left their children alone on a hilltop overnight as a test of their strength and worthiness. Children who survived this test were named and joined the Spartan society. I used to wonder: How would I have slowed them down if they had had to carry me everywhere! I guess I would not have been *allowed* to live, if I'd survived the hilltop test.

A quick review of the Bible was hardly comforting either. Biblical references to disability were few, but got a lot of press in my circles. People with disabilities appeared in the Bible to demonstrate the almighty power of God to do as He (She) wished.

Blindness was used so often as a metaphor, I wondered if they were truly talking about people who could not see physically or who would not see spiritually. As a ten-year-old Bible scholar, these metaphors were mixed and confusing. If God didn't have to accept people with disabilities, did anyone?

You need to know that when I was growing up in the mid-sixties to mid-seventies, the popular and accepted mode of treatment for people with disabilities was life in an institution. I met many other kids there who had disabilities. Some could do no more than me, some could do less. I lived in an institution from the time I was seven until I was old enough to sign myself out at eighteen. For the life of me, I couldn't figure out why some of these kids were there. They were so *capable*. At least for my sister and me, our parents had to do quite a bit to look after us. They'd have to help us get up, go to bed, use the washroom, and so on. Kids become increasingly physically independent starting at age two, but someone would always have to help us with everything physical.

I guess the crunch came once mom and dad separated. We were older, we needed wheelchairs and backbraces which my parents couldn't afford, and we were rejected both from the neighbourhood school (too sick) and the segregated school (wrong disability). So off we went to an institution, run by nurses. My mom called it *The School.* This institutional hospital, home, and school was known as "The Home for Incurable Children" when my sister and I went to live there. She says the first time she saw that sign she felt like Oliver Twist.

My life in the institution revolved around rejecting the disabled part of myself by "improving" it through therapy. All of us were taught it was better to use crutches than a wheelchair, better to limp along off-balance than use crutches. The goal was to look as "normal" as possible. Many of us learned later that function was better than appearance. The nurses snubbed my pleas for a motorized wheelchair that would give me effortless mobility, saying it was better to use my arms. Pushing a chair wore me out so much, I was good for little else halfway through the day.

In my day, people with disabilities were rejected on every major front. Many of the kids I met in the institution were abandoned by their parents who could not deal with a child who was not perfect, or who needed more attention. At least our family stuck by us while we were there, but I saw the damage done to other kids literally orphaned at the door. Some families truly thought the child's disability was a punishment for their sins. Oddly, others used us for redemption through charitable activities for our benefit.

Add to this the use of disability to show evil—Captain Hook was more sinister because he had a hook for a hand, villains are disfigured by scars, or missing limbs (Eddie in the *Friday the 13th* series); or the use of disability to draw out pathos—such as the Hunchback of Notre Dame, who was feared, then understood, or Jill in *The Other Side of the Mountain* and other movies like it. As difficult as it was at times to be born with a disability, sent away from home, and raised by strangers, how awful to become disabled when you weren't *supposed to* be that way.

I struggled with all of these messages as I was growing up. Intellectually, I understood what my disability was and how it was genetically introduced. Yet emotionally, I thought people with disabilities were a mistake, or else God wouldn't have been busy curing all those people in the Bible; or that we were just barely tolerated—allowed to live, but not allowed to interfere with anyone else's freedom; or sad but accidental creatures of chance. It's a wonder I emerged with any sense of self-concept at all.

With all this history, literature, and our portrayal in the media, what's going to be in the back of anyone's mind when meeting someone with a disability? What would be going on in the back of a boy's mind that I might meet who was a volunteer at the institution or an able-bodied classmate at high school? Would he imagine me as a potential girlfriend? Wife? Friend? Would he feel sorry for me? Would he only like me if he was weird?

I remember being ten or eleven years old and starting to think about my potential as a complete, adult person. There was a nurse I liked and I remember asking her if I'd ever get married and have children. She was very doubtful. She felt a man wouldn't want the burden of looking after me; he would want a wife who could look after him. Besides, how would I dress my children if I couldn't even dress myself? Now, you need to understand she said all this very kindly. There was no hint of animosity at all. She wanted to help me to learn to accept my circumstances and their realities. She did not wish to pump a child up with false hopes for the future. I think because of all this, I always remembered this little heart-to-heart chat. Because she was so sincere, I not only believed her, but I limited my sights and expectations based on the "facts" laid out for me.

I figured that I probably would never marry, but if I ever did, I'd just let my husband have a mistress so he wouldn't feel deprived. Now, as an adult who still has a disability, but also a career, husband, and family, I can afford to laugh at my naiveté.

Friends teach us what is likable and "cool" about ourselves. Growing up in an institution, we had two categories of friends: 1) kids on the inside, who were not all that important, and 2) kids on the outside who we would live and die for. My whole notion of what a friend was, was totally skewed. These outside friends were volunteers, dropping by once a week or on weeknights to do their good turn for society. This was charity, not natural, freely-given relationships. They weren't paid to be there, but they wore a name-badge. Also, we were friends within an artificial environment—visiting hours were over at 9:00 p.m. I always thought they were as sad to go as we were to see them leave. Our social life came to an abrupt halt at 9:00 p.m. to make way for the institutional routines and rhythms; their social life really began after they left us.

I got to go out to a regular high school, since the institution's school only went as far as grade eight. I was socially inept with non-disabled kids. I finally made a good friend part-way through grade ten, but throughout high school I was never asked on a date. I figured I'd have to wait until university, where I could count on people's maturity to see the real me, through my disability, before I could start dating. But, I never had a date in university either.

It's a wonder that I ever met my husband, David, in the first place. Getting there was anything but smooth. In earlier relationships I probably put up with treatment that other self-respecting people wouldn't have tolerated. My poor self-esteem and low expectations for relationships affected my judgement, and I hung on too long, thinking it was the best I could do.

But as I started working, I gradually developed self-esteem. As I gathered competence and skill at work, my self-esteem increased.

Now, I have two children, with all the accompanying blessings and pains of parenthood. Some days I'd recommend it; some days I wouldn't. Parenthood has been another type of struggle. I have a high degree of acceptance and support of me as a parent from my co-workers, my friends, my daughters' teachers, doctors, and others I have met. My family, on the other hand, was initially very concerned about the physical demands of pregnancy, birth, and raising children. My family also worried that a mere man could never cope in a "mother's role."

By the time I was married with a baby on the way, I had been living outside of the institution for twelve years. It's ironic that it took me the same length of time to throw off all its baggage, year for year.

I lived in an apartment where attendant support was available. Someone who was not a nurse would come and get me up in the morning, help me go to the washroom, go to bed at night, and perform other routine household tasks. My pregnancy met with a low degree of acceptance from the attendants. They assumed the baby would not be looked after properly and that I would put extra demands on them to help me do it. The attendants could not make the transition easily from me as a single person with a disability to being half of a couple with a baby on the way. On top of dealing with my own anxieties about what I was doing and what I was in for, they made my day-to-day life a living hell. I had to move out and search for another setting where I could be accepted as doing a perfectly normal and human thing.

Once I was able to move to another attendant support service setting, where staff got to know us as a family right from the start, I had no further problems with attendants accepting us. When I became pregnant for the second time, the attendants were jubilant. What a change! Since my first pregnancy had gone well, and little Katie survived we novices as parents, my family felt more comfortable about our having a second child as well. My husband, David, has been the primary caregiver for both of our daughters. It is not an option for me to be home, so I continue working.

All these experiences have contributed to my growth and development as a human being. Of course people with disabilities are fully human; we all start out that way! We need families to love us. We need friends to teach us how to care about other people. We need someone special in our lives to share ourselves with and with whom we can be intimate. We need to accept ourselves for all that we are; this helps others to accept us too. We need to be out there in the world, so even our very presence can raise awareness.

In our own unique ways, we need to leave new "bones" which show our own hearths, our hearts, and our "centredness" in our community. Perhaps we have focused too much on *independence*. Human beings are *interdependent*. We always have been.

We always will be.

I've always felt like an explorer—pushing the boundaries of where others said we could go. It's almost as if I had to do the things I have done just to prove the common person wrong. Told I'd never do anything productive for a living, I did. Told I'd never live outside of a hospital, I did. Told I'd never walk, well, who needs to?

What people with disabilities need to work on is protecting our rights to have *choices*. We have not been given many choices in the past. Low public awareness and a poor perception of us has made inadequate service systems acceptable. We've been put on waiting lists rather than offered services which meet our needs with dignity. The people closest to us—our families, medical professionals, and our friends—have betrayed us with limited expectations. And many of us have sold ourselves equally short, believing the shallow possibilities others cast our way.

People with disabilities, more and more, are a powerful force to be reckoned with. We are getting better at making our needs quite clear, whether it's a need for services or uplifting relationships. If we wait for others to do it for us, it will never happen. It's up to us.

Originally published in CWS/cf's issue on "Women and Disability," 13 (4) (1993): 56-58. Reprinted with permission.

LYNDA NANCOO

MARRIAGE-ABLE?

Cultural Perspectives of Women with Disabilities of South Asian Origin

"I WANTED TO RUN away," says Shabana as she discusses how myths surrounding disability within the Pakistani community almost destroyed her self-esteem and confidence when her parents began searching for a suitable marriage partner for her. "My disability was only discussed when for example I would go to Pakistan and would trip over things and they would say things like, 'Oh! you are blind, aren't you, oh'."

Marriage is an important issue in Shabana's culture. Seeking a marriage partner in this community is much different from the western experience. In the Muslim culture, parents from both sides arrange a "meeting" where both families and prospective bride and bridegroom meet for the first time. Prior to this, the parents of both families will research each others' background, religious faith, extended family, education, employment, etc. Although both families are present during the "meeting," the couple is left alone for a while, where they can speak freely to each other. Parents will go to extreme lengths to find suitable partners. Shabana was flown around the world for arranged meetings. She recalls one of these meetings with bitterness because women with disabilities are seen as unmarriageable.

> My parents took me to New York. As far as they were concerned this guy was ideal. He had the qualifications they were looking for, he had an MBA and was working and he had sent his picture. My mother took me shopping like usual [for a dowry].

When alone, Shabana decided to test this perfect partner and told him about her vision disability. "He tried to be sweet about it but I knew that it was going to be a problem."

Two weeks after returning to Eastern Canada she received a phone call from him. He told her he had talked to doctors and friends about her disability. The majority of them told him there was a possibility that their children would have a disability. "I told him that it was the best thing to talk about my disability and if you feel strongly about it then it's best you don't call me again." He never called again, and the rejection devastated Shabana. "If he had rejected me for any other reason, I wouldn't have taken it as hard."

Shabana was born in Pakistan with a vision disability called "retinitis pigmontosa." Retinitis pigmontosa (RP) is a hereditary degenerative disease of the retina. People with RP usually experience a loss of peripheral and night vision. It can eventually lead to blindness. Shabana's disability is invisible most of the time. She does not use physical devices to maintain independence, although her vision is greatly reduced at night.

After the rejection, Shabana rushed into marriage with a good friend who knew of her disability. "…We knew each other from the time we were children. In three months time we were married. Suddenly I realized what I had done and thought, 'why did I do this?'"

Two years later, the marriage produced a healthy baby boy and a divorce. "I felt that I used my first husband, who was also a good friend, to prove to myself that I can be accepted…." In part, Shabana blames her culture for what happened:

> I wish disability could be more open and accepted. It's not something we should feel guilty about. It's not a fault of ours. Once we're made to feel better/good about it then we can feel good as individuals and from there on we can go on to other aspects of our lives. We need this confidence. Marriage is a big issue, a very big commitment.

In Shabana's community, disability is rarely discussed. Lack of education and awareness means that people in the Muslim community will continue to hide their disabilities.

Regaining her confidence, Shabana married again. This time, the couple allowed enough time to learn about each other. She is still married to her second husband and now has three children. "What I have gone through is twice as hard as someone without a disability. I felt I had to try twice as hard." Her second husband knew about her vision disability prior to their marriage, and accepted her the way she was. If it wasn't for her husband's support and sensitivity, Shabana feels she would not have been able to cope as a mother with a disability. She enjoys being a mother, and talks fondly of her three children (none of whom have a vision disability) and passionately about her husband.

The next hurdle is to tell her children about her disability. Though they recognize that "mommy can't see too well," she feels that her children are entitled to education about disability issues. By making them aware of her disability she hopes that they will be openly accepting of all people with disabilities.

> My children help me a lot. When we go out they say, "Mom let me hold your hand, Mom there's a step here," even in broad daylight!... But lately, I want to tell them about what is medically wrong with my eyes. I feel my children should be very secure. Maybe. It's my inner feeling. I want them to know.

She also intends to keep discussing her disability openly at the family dinner table. "[My parents] have been very supportive but the culture is what's preventing them from fully accepting my disability."

Like Shabana, marriage is very important to Aisha, who longs to find a suitable marriage partner. "Men don't look upon us as potential partners or wives, or they don't look upon us as desirable or capable of sex." Myths that women with disabilities are sexless, desireless, and incapable of childrearing and childbearing leaves many women like Aisha in despair.

> ... From a Muslim cultural perspective, culture itself stigmatizes people with disabilities. I have to marry within my religion. That's extremely important to me. It's difficult to get partners within the Indo-Caribbean community because of stigmas toward people with disabilities.

Unlike Shabana, Aisha's disability is very visible. Her electric powered wheelchair is a dead giveaway. Aisha was born with polio in the Caribbean. She talks about her desire to get married, but unfortunately, negative stereotypes of disability within her culture prevent her from finding a suitable partner. "The perception is that, due to my disability, I would not be able to do things like non-disabled women, such as, I won't be able to take long romantic walks, won't have children and wouldn't be able to have as many children as they want."

When Aisha told her parents she was thinking of marriage they were very supportive. They started to talk to friends, family, community members, and others. Aisha looked forward to the "arranged meetings." She eventually decided to return to her homeland in hopes of meeting someone. Aisha did find a suitable partner there. She married him and upon returning to Canada immediately did whatever was necessary to bring him to her. She was devastated, however, when she learned that her perfect partner only married her to immigrate to Canada. Immigrant women with disabilities are vulnerable to being used as a passport to Canada. Nevertheless, she remains optimistic.

> There are good people and bad people. I had to make a decision in a couple of days. I got married. After I got back and we started corresponding on the phone, I realized he wanted to get married to me to come to Canada and nothing else. So I called it off. I stopped the sponsorship....

Fortunately, Aisha's parents supported her decision to end the marriage. Her disappointment has not stopped her from wanting to experience the roles of wife and mother. She wants a partner who will understand and accept her the way she is. But why is marriage so important?

> I have an extended family; people who care about me, lots of friends. What I don't have is a husband. From a religious point of view I can't have a boyfriend. I am not allowed to go on dates. My religion considers marriage as half of fate. For me, marriage means fulfilling half my fate. Also, I have a strong desire to have children.

Loneliness is often a major issue for people with disabilities. Because

Aisha is a wheelchair user, spontaneity is almost impossible. She must book accessible transportation at least four days in advance. Aisha does not go to parties, bars, or other social events or gatherings where alcohol consumption and smoking are practised because they are not compatible with her religious and cultural beliefs.

Western culture does not concentrate heavily on promoting marriage, and the disability rights movement has not concentrated on the cultural impact of disability. The disability rights movement in Canada has done nothing to raise awareness of the marriage-ability of disabled women. They are concentrating on issues such as, violence against women, building self-esteem, sexuality, but not on marriage.

In Aisha's culture marriage is the norm. She has watched sisters and brothers, friends, other family members, people from the mosque and others, marry and have children. She feels that her community should be educated about issues surrounding disability. Perhaps if more Muslim people with disabilities spoke up about exclusion, disabilities would become more acceptable.

Marriage, says Aisha, makes you think about your physical appearance. What is a beautiful body? Can a woman in a wheelchair be beautiful? Can a man be attracted to someone like this? What would make him more interested? What would his concerns be? Will he be open about all of these concerns? And what about inner beauty? These are questions many women with disabilities don't have answers to.

Both Shabana and Aisha have chosen to maintain their identities as Muslim women with disabilities living in Canada. They both agree that the cultural impact on marriage should be discussed more often, and that communities like theirs should be better informed about disability issues. Also, Canadians must be more sensitive and accepting of cultural differences. This will help encourage the acceptance of people with disabilities and most of all, it will promote the marriage-ability of women with disabilities.

The names of the women in this article have been changed to protect their identities.

Originally published in CWS/cf's issue on "Women and Disability," 13 (4) (1993): 49–51. Reprinted with permission.

CARRIE R. CARDWELL

"The Critical Woman and the Space Cadet"

"The Critical Woman and the Space Cadet," 1993, acrylic on canvas.

This painting is about my perception of language as a hard-of-hearing/deaf woman. Moving and transitioning between deaf and hearing worlds is painful. Growing up, I repressed spontaneous verbal communication. Also, external barriers existed, such as lack of exposure to the deaf community and American sign language (ASL).

I developed non-verbal communication primarily through art and dance to compensate. I want mutual understanding and connection, like most people, and can also hate this need. To truly belong requires that I dismantle prickly defences, represented in the painting by the woman on the left.

Otherwise, I may "space out," not really understanding what is being said (signed or voiced). The woman on the right stares vacantly into space. Then, the critical hand on the far rights points at her, calls her dumb. The hand, belonging to the woman on the right with the dunce cap says, "Stop."

The work of dealing with loneliness, a human condition, remains. But forming more satisfying relationships is easier by understanding myself in a deaf context. Relating to deaf people and those in the community, such as interpreters who are also bi-cultural, has been instrumental in maintaining my Self.

Originally published in CWS/cf's issue on "Women and Disability," 13 (4) (1993): 41. Reprinted with permission.

MILANA TODOROFF

"YOU THINK I WANT
TO MAKE FUCK WITH YOU"

Travelling with a Disability or Two

HIRLEY VALENTINE IS A movie about a slightly "overweight," middle-aged English housewife whose children are grown and whose husband has long forgotten that she is a person. In the opening scene, we see Shirley talking to her kitchen wall—the only intelligent conversation she gets. One day Shirley decides that there must surely be more to life and resolves to take a trip to Greece. Once in Greece, Shirley meets Kostos, a restaurant owner. During the beginning stages of their flirtation, Kostos asks Shirley to come with him for a day cruise on his boat. When Shirley resists, Kostos says— "You think I want to make fuck with you. I don't want to make fuck with you. I just want to go out on boat with you...." Kostos and Shirley do get together and for Shirley this is a liberating and exhilarating experience. For the first time in years, she is being seen by another as an attractive, sensual, sexual woman and she is, in that reflection of self, beginning to see herself in a new light.

For Shirley, the trip to Greece turns out to be much more than a vacation. It is a huge step towards facing her fears and a journey within. It is a breaking of domestic chains and a search for an understanding of self as separate from her good mother, good wife roles.

A few days after seeing *Shirley Valentine*, I woke up in the middle of the night, sat bolt upright in bed and said to myself "I'm going to Greece." It was time, like Shirley, to face my chains and my fears. While not tied and tethered in the same way as Shirley (I have never been married and I have no children), I do, like most people, have my own ties that bind. For the past twenty years, I have been "legally blind" as a result of a rare genetic eye problem. What this means to my day-to-day life is that what other people can see at two hundred feet,

I can see at about twenty. (Yes, that is with glasses. Without glasses, my vision is "20/400"—what others can see at about four hundred feet, I can see at about twenty.) As well, reading can be a bit of a chore because I have no central vision. For me, the larger the print, the easier it is to read. More recently, within the past five years, I have been diagnosed with diabetes and am now an insulin dependent diabetic.

I have managed over the years to "pass" as "normal" to most people and have developed sophisticated methods and techniques to hide my physical challenges. Although I had wanted to go to Europe for years, I was extremely concerned and anxious about how I could physically do it. I had long ago given up trying to read maps as the printing was generally too small for me to decipher without an extremely strong magnifying glass. I was also deeply concerned about what would happen if I lost my diabetic supplies. Further, travelling would throw me out of the safety of "the known" and thrust me into situations that I could not control.

Despite the challenges and fear of the unknown, I knew it was time to make my own pilgrimage to Greece. I decided to start in England and work my way down by train. By the time my trip was finalized, it had changed from a ten day holiday in Greece to a thirty-five day, back-packing and hostelling trip through Europe. By mid-May, I was off.

I had packed carefully before leaving, putting diabetic supplies in both my small day pack and my larger knapsack. But, travelling is a confusing, jumbling, and chaotic enterprise. Even the best laid plans go awry. Ten days into the trip, the inevitable happened. After taking an overnight train from Amsterdam, I arrived at the Paris train station at 6:00 a.m. on a Sunday morning. By 6:15 a.m., someone had stolen my small daypack. As I searched frantically through my back pack, my internal body began to convulse and panic. I quickly came to the horrible realization that in the process of travelling, I had managed to transfer my glasses and virtually all my insulin to my day knapsack. I found only two days worth of insulin. As I reflect on this, I wonder, as I often do, about the role of the unconscious in framing parts of our daily lives. Had this happened because it was something that deeply frightened me?

Upon finding a bed at an overcrowded, noisy, and dingy hostel, I made my way to a hospital. French insulin, it turned out, was different from what I was used to. So, later that day, I called my brother in Toronto. I asked him to send more supplies with a friend of mine, Don, who would be arriving in Italy in about ten days. I would pick the supplies up at Don's home near Rome.

Gone now was my dream of going to Greece. The detour to Don's meant that I would have only ten days for a round trip from Rome to Corfu (the nearest Greek Island) and back up through Italy to Paris for my flight home. With this realization in mind, I ended up staying in Paris for five not particularly happy days. I was immobilized and unable to get past my fear of moving on.

Eventually, though, Paris simply got too expensive to stay there any longer. Miraculously, I made my way safely to Italy and to Florence. Florence was awe-inspiring and just the right size for me to negotiate without getting too lost. I found an inexpensive hostel that was in a five-hundred-year-old villa complete with marble statues and frescos on the walls. This trip was finally starting to turn around.

The time came to connect up with Don. It was good to see him, good to talk and laugh with a friend. It was a tremendous treat to sleep in a room by myself and to take off the money belt that I had been wearing day and night for more than three weeks.

From the moment I reached Don's home, I bemoaned the fact that I would be unable to make it to Greece as I had hoped. I had managed to frame my inability to complete my pilgrimage as a personal failure. I had set a goal that I was not going to be able to meet. The subtext was that my disability/illness had "caused" me to curtail my trip. I would just have to accept it. Needless to say, I was having great difficulty with this.

Don eventually managed to convince me that I could indeed make it to Greece. It would be tight, but it could be done. Okay, I thought, it's worth a try at least. The long term ramifications of not trying would be much harder for me to bear.

After two or three days of demanding train and boat travel, I was finally dipping my little toes in the blue waters of Corfu. Once settled in a hostel, I ventured out to the local bar. On my way, I met and started chatting with a man on a pink moped. He, of course, knew a bar that was better than the one that I was heading for and asked me to go for a drink with him. Oh, what the heck, I thought and hopped on. Riding high in the Greek hills, the views were breathtaking. As we rode along, my new friend invited me for dinner at his home that evening. When I declined his offer, he turned slightly and said "You think I want to have sex with you. I don't want to have sex with you. I just want to have dinner with you." What choice did I have? I threw back my head and laughed as the wind whipped through my hair.

Originally published in CWS/cf's issue on "Women and Disability," 13 (4) (1993): 28–32. Reprinted with permission.

KYLA HARRIS AND SARAH MURRAY

"Access-Sex Series"

"Untitled Still #10" (Access-Sex Series). Photo: Kyla Harris and Sarah Murray.

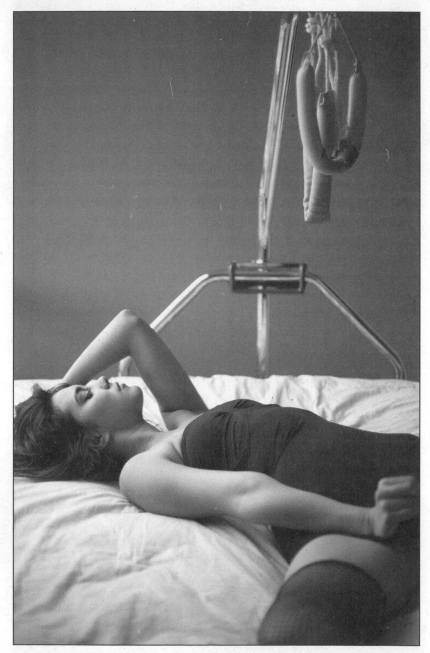

"Untitled Still #3" (Access-Sex Series). Photo: Kyla Harris and Sarah Murray.

"Untitled Still #4" (Access-Sex Series). Photo: Kyla Harris and Sarah Murray.

The concept for the access-sex series and inevitably, the photographs themselves began because I felt there was a need for positive representations of disabled people in the media. To my surprise, as a young, female tetraplegic living in North America, strangers approached me and questioned whether I could have sex or not. I had just graduated from art school and I wanted to make a difference and simply felt there was a need for it. The medium of photography is at the forefront of mass-produced, popularized images, which is why I thought Access-Sex should be photographs. It seemed that I would be challenging the image of the disabled if I could get these pictures seen easily.

I approached photographer Sarah Murray who was recommended to me by my Aunt. It was important for me to collaborate with someone who was "able bodied" so that I could endeavour to change misconceptions they or their supporters would have. Sarah and I committed to fully collaborating on the process and subsequent exhibitions. Cindy Sherman's "Untitled Film Series" was one of the predominant inspirations for the project because of its ambiguous nature. Sherman does not preach the feminist meanings behind the

249

work and it was important for me to do the same. We wanted to be ambiguous about the viewer-subject relationship. Disability is present in the way that Sarah and I "see" my disability; which is most of the time not seeing it, but acknowledging its presence, in the Access-Sex Series.

CHALLENGING THE EDGES

DIANE DRIEDGER

WHEN THE BODY PROTESTS

New Forms of Activism

TO ME, PARTICIPATING IN society has always meant being active and being activist. I have always liked to see the TV footage of the U.S. black civil rights movement and the women's movement from the 1960s. In the early 1980s, I found a social movement—the disability rights movement—and proceeded to work with these organizations as a non-disabled ally. I was twenty and was enjoying seeing people who had felt disenfranchised grab hold of the tools of participation. People with disabilities were organizing to have their own voices heard.

By 1992 I had worked with the disability movement at the provincial, national, and international levels, through organizations such as the Manitoba League of Persons with Disabilities, Council of Canadians with Disabilities (CCD), and Disabled Peoples' International (DPI). At this juncture, I started having mysterious muscle aches and mounting fatigue that I brushed off to continue working on international projects with the Council of Canadians with Disabilities. I found that I was spending more time alone in my apartment recuperating after work and that I was not able to participate in as many volunteer activities. I wondered if I was getting lazy, if I had lost my zeal for causes, if it was all in my head.

Ultimately, I was diagnosed with fibromyalgia in 1996, after four years of floundering in the chronic illness wasteland of doubting myself. Fibromyalgia is a kind of arthritis of the muscles characterized by widespread muscle pain throughout the body and bone crushing fatigue. By this time, my preferred location in the house was the bed or the couch as sitting and standing and doing any prolonged physical activity was excruciatingly painful and debilitatingly tiring. All of my advocacy activities involved just those physical activities. And the Winnipeg winters were piling up in my body—my muscles did not like being cold and my limbs did not traverse snow banks gladly. My body was having a protest—something had to change.

I decided to move to Trinidad and Tobago, where I had been travelling with CCD in the past, to work with the disabled peoples' organizations there and where I had helped in the formation of the Disabled Women's Network (DAWN) of Trinidad. I thought, "I will continue to advocate for change in what little way I can, while I get well." I volunteered to teach a self-esteem and body image course at DAWN once a week. This experience was life-changing to me, as I learned so much from the women with disabilities who came to the class, who ranged in age from twelve to eighty. I learned about being a woman, being a woman with a disability, and still retaining the dignity of who I was. Who I had been as a non-disabled woman was just part of the continuum of me, the making of me, a process. The DAWN women acted out scenes of the discrimination they had faced in their society and they discovered that they had hidden talents for performing.

We wrote poems, stories and essays about being disabled and being a woman. In the end, I edited a small collection of these writings and we launched *From Hibernation to Liberation: Women with Disabilities Speak Out* in 1999 (Driedger). This book was launched at the prestigious Central Bank in Port of Spain and cabinet ministers and the national media attended. The women read and felt empowered in the process. One woman actually became known as the author in her small village, rather than that "lady who walks with a cane" as she had always been known.

I knew that writing one's story had power, as I had been writing my own poetry since the early 1990s. I saw a new kind of activism—it was writing your way into peoples' consciousness, not marching in the streets. I decided to return to Canada and pursue this further. I needed to know more about literacy and theories of writing. I started a Ph.D. in Education in Language and Literacy in 2001 at the University of Manitoba. I wanted to study how writing, and publishing one's work, led to empowerment. I wanted to document this process of empowerment in a systematic way. I began to study and now I had no time to be involved in any community groups for a change. My relationship to the disability movement was now at arm's length, as my arms couldn't carry any more responsibilities. I slugged it out course by course and did a lot of work lying down on my couch. I had started out feeling quite well after I returned from the sunny winters of Trinidad, but now again, the cold and snow began to take its toll on my body. I meted out energy as best I could.

Now, in 2006, I am finishing research for my creative writing, publishing and empowerment project in Baker Lake, Nunavut. I was in Nunavut on a short stint doing research on disability for the J. A. Hildes Northern Medical Unit at the University of Manitoba in 2001. I saw that the idea of writing and empowerment would work very well in the North, a place where orality had been the modus operandi for centuries. And now how did writing fit in to this society where they were looking to combine the traditional and the contemporary ways of life? People in Nunavut were keen to participate in my project.

Again, I packed up and this time went North for a month's time to teach a course with the Elders using traditional songs as our basis to encourage the adult students to write. Everyone produced several pieces of writing and the book, *The Sound of Songs* (Utatnaq), was born. In a few weeks I will return to investigate whether the students felt empowered by seeing their words in print—do they feel that people in the community view them differently now, and does that matter to them?

I see print as a way of extending the little energy I have into the "noosphere," as Pierre Teilhard de Chardin called the amorphous soup of ideas and consciousness that whirls around the world. My body does not need to be physically present at all times to be an activist body. Other ways that I have begun to project my physical body is through visual art. In the last year, I have created two pieces that use my image in the way that the painter Frida Kahlo did. In fact, I see her as my twin activist, as she dealt with chronic pain and disability for most of her life. From her often-prone position in bed, she painted the subject she knew best—the reality of her body and how it appeared to her. Often, these images are raw, stark, and scary. The body is laid bare in all its weakness and despair. Yet, in the process of painting this reality, Kahlo took her body back and propelled it into the world, where it has demanded attention ever since.

I decided to paint myself into Frida's reality—in *Me and Frida Kahlo* I have mimicked her painting, *The Two Fridas*. I have become the

"Me and Frida Kahlo," 2006, watercolour on paper, 19" x 20".

Frida on the left, where she had painted herself in a white dress. In this painting, Frida and I are connected by the arteries of pain, by the blood of being women whose bodies are in protest. In protest of what, we are still unsure. Is it the stress of our societies, is it the disadvantaged position of women, which we rail against, is it the disadvantage of having a weak body in our work-obsessed society, is it the weight of global environmental degradation that has caused our bodies to revolt? In painting myself into Kahlo's picture, I continue to struggle with all these questions thinking perhaps I can find an answer in watercolour.

In my second piece of visual art, entitled, *My Will Remains*, I have created a small installation based on Kahlo's painting, *The Dream*. In this painting, Frida lies in her four-poster bed, sleeping, with vines growing over her. On top of her bed's canopy lies a skeleton. Drawing

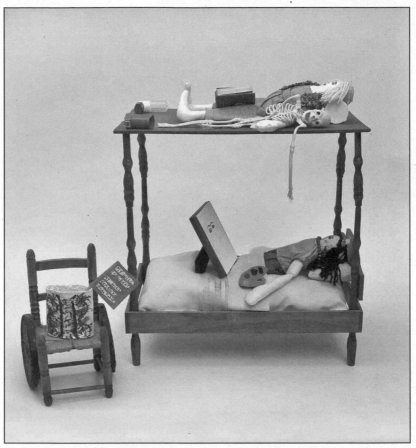

"My Will Remains," 2006, mixed media, 3' x 4'.

on my interest in handmade rag dolls, I fashioned one of Frida and one of myself. Then, I had Frida's four-poster bed, measuring around two feet by three feet, built by a carpenter friend. Frida then is placed in bed, with her easel on her lap, as she often painted, and I am on top of the canopy of the bed, lying down and reading. Next to me, is a skeleton that is reaching down to Frida. This skeleton presents the "Judas figure" that was exploded at Easter time in Mexico and it is a symbol of suicide (Kettenmann). I see it as a symbol of death and the lines of life with chronic pain and immobility as blurred—death waits around the corner. After completing these two pieces, I learned I had breast cancer.

Premonitions. The artery link between Frida and I in my painting *Me and Frida Kahlo* reminds me of the PICC line that I now have implanted in my right arm to deliver chemotherapy. The plastic line goes up inside my arm and into a main artery of my heart. As for *My Will Remains,* this is a partial quote from Frida Kahlo who wrote, "My will is great. My will remains" (qtd. in Herrera 226). I continue to work lying down, and chemo is almost finished. My prognosis is good—but I must do six weeks of radiation yet. Indeed, my will remains.

Originally published in CWS/cf's issue on "Canadian Feminism in Action," 25 (3,4) (2006): 188-190. Reprinted with permission.

REFERENCES

Driedger, D., ed. *From Hibernation to Liberation: Women with Disabilities Speak Out.* Port of Spain: Disabled Women's Network of Trinidad and Tobago, 1999.

Herrera, H. *Frida Kahlo: The Paintings.* New York: HarperCollins, 1993.

Kettenmann, A. *Frida Kahlo 1907-1954: Pain and Passion.* Koln: Taschen, 2000.

Teilhard de Chardin, P. *The Future of Man.* London: Collins, 1964.

Utatnaq, A., ed. *The Sound of Songs: Stories by Baker Lake Writers.* Baker Lake: Nunavut Arctic College, 2006.

CARLA RICE, HILDE ZITZELSBERGER, WENDY PORCH
AND ESTHER IGNAGNI

CREATING COMMUNITY
ACROSS DISABILITY AND DIFFERENCE

Physical difference is looked at from the point that you would never want to have it happen to you. As if it's not something that you could possibly gain from. People need to understand that there are things to be gained from our experiences....

IN OUR SOCIETY, THERE are few positive images of women living with facial and physical differences and disabilities. While contending with discriminations faced by many women, women with physical differences and disabilities also are subjected to the stigma of a body which is perceived as not quite female (Garland-Thomson), "less than whole" (DiMarco), and "not quite human" (Goffman). Women's experiences are directly related to western society's homogenized, naturalized, and patriarchal notions of body and appearance.

Despite growing discourses about diversity issues, ideologies of the body remain embedded within binary oppositions of "normal" and "abnormal" (Davis 1995, 1997). Physical differences and disabilities frequently are positioned as personal tragedy, a burden to self and others, deformity, and inferiority (Rogers and Swadener). Because of medicalization, differences in appearance and ability typically are interpreted as illness or disease. As a result, public dialogue and medical discourse tend to focus on physical difference and disability as something to be shunned or overcome (Zitzelsberger, Odette, Rice, and Whittington-Walsh).

People feel that you owe them an explanation because you don't look like everyone else. They ask, "What happened to you?"

Postmodern and feminist perspectives emphasize how body images and identities are produced and experienced through social interactions. Cultural meanings given to bodies become a basis for identity in interpersonal exchanges. People construct a sense of their bodily self from messages, spoken and unspoken, that they receive from other people throughout their lives. This occurs when they grasp how others perceive their bodies and understand the personal and social significance of these perceptions to their sense of identity and possibility. One of the ways women with facial and physical differences and disabilities are marginalized in our society is through cultural and medical messages about the abject body, such as bodily fragility, dependency, contamination, and sickness, interwoven in their everyday interactions. Many experience negative or inaccurate perceptions about their bodies and lives, encountering judgemental comments, intrusive stares, and questions about their bodies (Keith). These are commonplace, occurring in interaction with family, friends, medical practitioners, strangers, and others.

Sometimes the way health care providers respond to me can have a big impact on how I feel about myself. If I hear words like "deformity" used to describe me then I feel really shitty.

Women with physical differences and disabilities frequently internalize negative judgements about their bodies and lives. They may have learned to view their body as inadequate, unacceptable, and a source of stress and anxiety. This can make it difficult for individuals to develop or maintain a positive sense of self and has important implications for physical and emotional health. For example, many women have experiences of health care interventions marked with a lack of privacy and respect, where difference or disability is the sole focus and other aspects of their identities and health care are not acknowledged (Leigh, Powers, Vash, and Nettles; Veltman, Stewart, Tardif and Branigan 2001a, 2001b). Stresses involved in encountering negative perceptions can deter women's decision-making to access services in health care settings and can leave them feeling vulnerable in social situations (Nosek, Young, Rintala, Howland, Foley and Bennett). At the same time, however, many develop creative strategies to navigate challenging interactions. Women tell how rejecting looks, critical comments, and intrusive touch are everyday experiences, yet they also speak of affirming messages that are features of their relational lives. Through interactions and connections characterized by support, validation, and affirmation, women come to understand and resist cultural meanings of their bodies that position them as "other" within social and medical discourses and relations.

> *I was objectified as a child. At eight years old, they stood me up against a wall in the cold to demonstrate how tall I was, and they were snapping pictures. I didn't start realizing that I was in textbooks until I was a teenager and I was really taken aback.... I went back as a teenager and destroyed all the pictures that remind myself where I was as a child.*

In this article, we describe our involvement with *Building Bridges*, a project that examines everyday experiences related to appearance and ability of adult women with disabilities and other body differences. We outline project activities such as workshops and art-making groups that have been designed to create opportunities for women to share stories, knowledge, and practical ideas with others who have similar concerns and experiences; look at the significant skills that they already use to negotiate stressful and challenging interactions; and build on their existing knowledge and skills together.

IMPETUS FOR OUR INITIATIVE

> *I have so much to say ... a voice muffled by the fears of others. I refuse to stay quiet. I will be heard.*

In August 1999, *Building Bridges,* a partnership project of AboutFace International, the only organization in Canada providing services to persons with facial differences, and the Body Image Project, Sunnybrook and Women's College Health Sciences Centre, was developed. Supported by the Ontario Trillium Foundation, this project was created with, by, and for women living with facial differences, physical differences, and/or disabilities. Quotes embedded throughout this piece are the voices and images of women who have participated in the project.

A vital part of the project was the series of workshops held across Ontario from 1999 to 2004. Women who joined our workshops have included those with visible or hidden differences, such as women with facial and other physical differences or disabilities, which may be present at birth (such as a spina bifida or cleft lip and palate) or acquired later in life through injury (such as a burn or spinal cord injury) or illness (such as facial cancer). Some women may not identify themselves as having a disability, however, there are often overlaps in issues regarding body and self-image.

> *I have learnt the benefits of having a cross-disability workshop. Not only did the participants become sensitive to issues of cross disability but they learnt that their "community" is greater than they had previously thought. I believe that this awareness will create a stronger base for change in society.*

Impetus for *Building Bridges* came from the recognition that there are few spaces for women to explore their subjective and social experiences of living with physical differences and/or disabilities. It was also recognized that there are few places for individual and group resistance to dominant views of body difference. Our objective in the *Building Bridges* workshops has been to provide a place for women to acknowledge their bodies and lived experience as sites of knowledge. The project builds bridges between and across participants' perceived differences and among established and emerging communities of those with disabilities and differences. Liminally situated between a mainstream health care institution and a grassroots community organization, the project also creates opportunities for building bridges between health providers and women with and without differences and disabilities. This is critically important. Active presence of women with disabilities and differences as facilitators gives hope that not all health providers accept conventional accounts of difference conveyed in training. In addition, women living with physical differences and disabilities have insights about operations of cultural meanings of body normalcy and body abjection within everyday life that position them as sites of knowledge for health providers and for all women.

> *We all have issues around appearance. Let's stop looking at each*

*other like we're supposed to be something other than who we are
and start realizing we are on this continuum of difference.*

FROM SKILL DEVELOPMENT TO SKILL DISCOVERY

The workshop sessions used individualized exercises, art making, journaling, small group work, discussions, and large group activities including drama and story telling. Whatever the modality, a key aspect of our workshops and art-making groups has been the cultivation of a positive identity, not in spite of difference and disability, but through incorporating one's body difference into one's positive sense of identity.

> *Surgery is wonderful and it can give people new opportunities, but it is only part of the answer. You still need to find ways to be able to go out there and not let people's stares or comments stop you from doing what you want to do.*

While we began workshop and support group sessions using traditional "skills development" and "solutions-focused" methods (Fiske; Metcalf), we increasingly adopted a "narrative approach" in our facilitation (Drewery and Winslade; White and Epston). This method is a therapeutic application of postmodern theory. Within health promotion, it has emerged as an effective approach for facilitating alternative meanings, identities, and worldviews excluded by dominant accounts and for fostering affinities and actions among marginalized people (Williams, LaBonte, and O'Brien).

Facilitators working from a narrative perspective view participants as having expertise and skills in the challenges of living with body differences, but understand that this knowledge may be hidden by dominant stories that portray them as inadequate or incapable (Silvester). For example, individuals with disabilities and differences often hold important insights about their bodies, health care, needs, and lives that are derived from their everyday experiences but which may be devalued by greater authority given to expert knowledge. From our perspective, because a narrative stance views participants as possessing unrecognized skills in living with difference, it more fully supports them in discovering their own knowledges, and in building on capacities for action that may already work for them in their own lives. A facilitator sums up her perspective on the workshop process:

> *Speaking as a woman with a facial difference, I believe that it is essential that women living with disabilities/facial differences understand that being different is not only negative, but that it has many positive sides (i.e., empathy, strength, courage, etc.). Through the Building Bridges Program, the participants are reminded of what they already know and possess—their survival skills, their inner strength, their communication skills, and their ability to adapt to challenging situations. Women have lived this far in a society that condones attitudinal abuse, and in the workshop context are encouraged to look at the consequences of this abuse and to hone their knowledges derived from their experiences. We offer support so that women may become more comfortable with their bodies and their lives. Through our program, they understand that they are not alone.*

Over time, we have reworked and refined our workshop method to encompass five strategies for helping participants discover and build on individual and communal knowledge and strengths: telling our stories; taking a not-knowing stance; asking purposeful questions; de-centering our expertise; and creating communities across difference.

BUILDING BRIDGES WORKSHOP METHODS

> *What is positive for me about the group is to see that I am not alone and I can share my life experience with others.*

Telling Our Stories

One of our most significant workshop methods has been the use of storytelling within a group context. Storytelling invites description and explanation on the who, how, why, what, and then what (LaBonte and Feather). It enables women to see themselves as authors in their own lives. Most activities are designed so participants can look at what has worked well in social and health care interactions and what they could do differently. Through telling stories and witnessing storytellings, participants are able to remember and reclaim the knowledges and skills that they already possess, gain insights, and identify alternative actions in challenging situations. Others' reflections on their stories amplify participants' awareness of knowledge and skills they already use to handle difficult interactions. When women recognize the ways their stories resonate with each other, this creates movement, or new understandings of common experiences and new energy for action. Telling stories within a group context moves participants to recognize the collective knowledges and skills that are present within the group. Many women have commented that they have felt more empowered through recognizing their abilities to make choices and by expanding their choices within interactions.

> When I was younger, how I got though those experiences was by developing a sense of humour.... I was tired of these solemn faces looking at my body. Why did I have to make them comfortable? But I did. That has always been the way that I approach the world in terms of dealing with some really difficult times.

Taking a Not-Knowing Stance

Using a narrative approach to group work, facilitators begin from the assumption that women in the workshop have knowledge, skills, and insights about moving through difficult situations, and that these knowledges can provide alternatives for actions. Narrative facilitators uncover people's stories by taking a curious or "not knowing" stance, asking questions without having preconceived ideas or theories about what the outcomes should be (Drewery and Winslade). The facilitator's expertise lies in looking for the meaning and effects of problems in people's lives and listening for alternative stories, or examples of their responses and actions in constraining circumstances.

Facilitators use questions to assist participants in accessing what they know about dealing with difficult social and medical encounters and to share this knowledge within the group. For instance, those who have experienced a high degree of medicalization and institutionalization often have been placed in passive roles in health care interactions and given limited opportunities to share information with providers and others about their bodies, health, needs, and lives. This can undermine women's confidence and abilities to access and communicate their knowledge and to collaborate with others in their health care.

In *Building Bridges* workshops, facilitators are influential not by imposing interpretations or making interventions that could reinforce participants' relinquishing of agency but through using their questions and reflections to guide women toward the knowledge and skills they have of their lives that are relevant to addressing the challenges at hand.

> *The exercises were ones we could apply to everyday life. Also, looking at things the way others see them, was very valuable to me. Thus, I learned not to make myself the victim before I enter a situation.*

Asking Purposeful Questions

A key aspect of the method is to support participants in recognizing and validating their own knowledges by the questions facilitators ask and the ways they phrase these questions. Rather than giving emphasis solely to the problem, this approach to asking questions stresses the multiple facets of each person that they bring when dealing with challenging clinical and other social interactions. The method assists participants in deconstructing oppressive identities and in claiming subjugated knowledges marginalized by dominant medical and cultural views. Questions facilitate generative processes of exploring other possibilities of embodiment and preferred accounts of selves.

> *A wheelchair can be seen as something positive. It's a tool that's liberating. I always thought of it as a prison on wheels. Now I see it gives me freedom.*

De-Centering Our Expertise

Facilitators have found that the more they "decentre" themselves by not taking the expert role (White), the more participants in the group speak openly, and direct the focus according to their own interests, desires, and solutions. When facilitators are "decentred," women are recognized as having expertise and "primary authorship status" over their own lives. Participants, not facilitators, hold knowledge and skills generated over the course of their lives that can become important tools for addressing the predicaments they face (White).

My goal was to see myself as a sexual and beautiful person. Now when people flirt with me, I accept it as a compliment and I don't automatically think that it's impossible for someone to flirt with me.

Creating Community across Difference

The facilitator's role is to build a collaborative group learning process. Group responses are structured to give participants the tools to witness, affirm, and inspire each other. While most participants are initially more conscious of differences within the group, openness to safely ask questions eventually sparks interesting conversations about people's affinities. Encouraging individuals to share with others who have similar concerns and experiences helps end feelings of isolation. This is important, as many people with differences and disabilities may have limited opportunities to learn or talk about their bodies and lives or examine possible intentions and actions within social situations.

It is fascinating how powerful we feel with each others' support; there's nothing like knowing we have shared experiences and outlook. I really think that since we have a social problem, having social support is part of the solution—both in the workshop and afterwards.

Within the workshop settings, participants have opportunity through activities and discussion to question and resist cultural meanings related to their bodies that position them as "other" in interactions. Through seeing themselves as members of a group that is rejecting its position as marginal, many participants move to cultivating new or preferred views of their difference. As they revisit medical meanings received in clinical settings, collective recollection of past responses and actions often motivates women to revision the value and possibilities of living with disabilities and differences. While enhancing individual agency within and without health care situations, women develop connections that build bridges with other women and create commonality around physical difference and disability. This not only helps participants to challenge perceptions of themselves, but it builds a sense of community across physical difference and disability.

IMPORTANCE OF FACILITATORS WITH "INSIDER KNOWLEDGE"

In our culture we're all raised with the idea of being independent and being strong and especially people who have facial differences. I know a lot of times when I grew up I got these messages all the time, "oh you are so strong and coping so well." So that kept me from wanting to talk about any problems or issues.

In our workshops, women with physical differences and disabilities are facilitators. Having facilitators who can become part of the group, while remaining aware of group process, is highly effective. For example, many people with physical differences and disabilities have learned that they should not speak of the difficulties that they encounter in their day-to-day lives. Friends and family members often feel they have little experience to draw upon when responding to women confronting stressful and challenging interactions. It may be difficult for friends and family to know their loved one is experiencing daily intrusions they can do nothing to change. Consequently, when trying to discuss a troubling social moment, many women have encountered subtle cues suggesting that it was a topic best avoided. In communicating their stories to a facilitator and a group who also live with body differences or disabilities, women do not have to succumb to societal pressure to make their story telling more palatable. Facilitators who share their own challenges of living with a difference and/or disability can support participants to speak of painful situations and vulnerabilities. In this way, facilitators with "insider knowledge" can act as role models, mentors, and advocates (White). Participants in our workshops have commented on how comfortable they were made to feel by the facilitators and how much they appreciated the personal sharing by the facilitators.

I am so glad to have had this quality experience with a group of women of all ages and backgrounds. Their diversity made it a rich learning experience. Also, it is amazing that this was free! I value that the facilitators were women with physical differences.

IMAGINING NEW MEANINGS OF DIFFERENCE

Over the past two years, we have held several creative expression workshops, including an art making series called *Being and Becoming* and a photography workshop series entitled *See Me*. *Being and Becoming* featured four themes: love, sexuality, spirituality, and possibilities. In the *Being and Becoming* workshops, women were encouraged to do anything that came to mind relative to each theme with any of the art materials available, including paint, clay, magazines for collage, textiles, and other craft materials. The *See Me* workshop sessions focused on participants' examining, through photography, social and clinical moments of looking and being looked at; exploring what was concealed and revealed in interactions; and recollecting old and imagining new ways of seeing their bodies and themselves. For many women with disabilities and differences cameras have an association with pictures taken in medical settings. In *See Me* workshops, participants have opportunity to take their own pictures, creating images that resonate with and reflect on their different senses of self.

In our art and image making groups, participants are introduced to a process for witnessing and participating in the group. Facilitators introduce this process by telling group members that it is not their role to give opinions, or place positive or negative judgements on other participants' art or images. As witnesses, their task is to engage with others about what they have heard and seen, and link and build on each other's expressions. Participants are also encouraged to reflect on what they have learned and/or how they have shifted as a result of viewing others' artwork and listening to them talk about their expressions of creativity. This approach helps facilitators and participants to shift from evaluating or interpreting the artwork to allowing themselves to be affected and moved by each other's art making. For example, one participant who created two clay sculptures of her body differences said about her art pieces, "my nose and my spine are issues that are very hard for me to look at." Once her pieces were done she expressed to the group: "it felt so liberating to feel the clay nose, and to trace my clay spine with my finger." Another participant who depicted a woman in a wheelchair voiced of her work, "that woman is in action, with her arm out showing movement."

In many images created throughout the sessions, the women illustrate how possibilities for their lives are constrained in some ways by body limitations. Yet, the more recurrent locations of the limitations they encounter are external barriers, including attitudinal and literal walls others have built to exclude them. Unlike traditional support group exercises that are highly structured, the creative processes women partake in are more fluid, without sharp beginnings and endings. Often participants undertake exploring possibilities for their bodies and lives in informal conversations as they pick out a paint colour or learn how to set up a shot with the camera. Comments from workshop evaluations suggest that while women view the art and image making as valuable, the most meaningful feature of these groups is the sense of connection they feel in sharing their images, artwork, and stories with other women. One woman wrote what inspired her most was "the joy" she felt in witnessing participants discuss their creative work, where others wrote that they were most moved by learning other women were dealing with similar issues.

Building Bridges creates an opportunity for shifts in meaning of difference and disability to occur. Shifting meanings of difference has important implications for increasing individuals' capacity to collaborate in their health, and for enabling them to expand their options and choices in challenging health care interactions. When women perceive health providers' increased openness to understand their unique experiences of disability and difference, this enhances practitioner-client communication, comfort, and competency in clinical situations. The project does not deny the challenges of others' and our own perceptions of body difference, but it does open up the possibility to imagine. Imagining becomes a resource that allows women to make new meanings and create new connections through art, image, and metaphor, and in so doing, envision new images and interpretations of difference.

The Building Bridges Project has produced two resources: Talking About Body Image, Identity, Disability, and Difference: A Facilitator's Manual *and* Building Bridges Across Difference and Disability: A Resource Guide For Health Care Providers. *If you are interested in ordering your own copies of the Resource Guide or Facilitator's Manual, please call AboutFace International at 416-597-2229 or toll-free 1-800-665-3223 or email to info@aboutfaceinternational.org. Copies of both documents in* PDF *format can be downloaded for free from <http://www. carlarice.ca/publications.html>.*

Originally published in CWS/cf's issue on "Women and Health," 24 (1) (2004): 187-193. Reprinted with permission.

REFERENCES

Davis, L. *Enforcing Normalcy: Disability, Deafness and the Body.* New York: Verso Press, 1995.

Davis, L., ed. *The Disability Studies Reader.* New York: Routledge, 1997.

DiMarco, L. C. "Disabled Women are Doubly Discriminated Against." *Women's Education-Education Desfemmes* 12.2 (1996): 6-10.

Drewery, W., and J. Winslade. "The Theoretical Story of Narrative Therapy." *Therapy in Practice: The Archaeology of Hope.* Eds. G. Monk, J. Winslade, K. Crocket, and D. Epston. San Francisco: Jossey-Bass, 1997. 32-52.

Fiske, H. *Workshop in Solution-Focused Counselling.* Toronto: Office of Advanced Professional Education, University of Toronto, 1999.

Garland-Thomson, R. *Extraordinary Bodies: Figuring Physical Disability in American Culture and Literature.* New York: Columbia University Press, 1997.

Goffman, E. *Stigma: Notes on the Management of Spoiled Identity.* Englewood Cliffs, NJ: Prentice Hall, 1963.

Keith, L. "Encounters with Strangers: The Public's Response to Disabled Women and How This Affects Our Sense of Self." *Encounters with Strangers: Feminism and Disability.* Ed. J. Morris. London: Women's Press, 1996. 69-88.

LaBonte, R., and J. Feather. *Handbook on Using Stories in Health Promotion Practice.* Ottawa: Health Promotion and Development Division, Health Canada, 1996.

Leigh, I., L. Powers, C. Vash and R. Nettles. "Survey of Psychological Services to Clients with Disabilities: The Need for Awareness." *Rehabilitative Psychology* 49.1 (2004): 48-54.

Metcalf, L. *Solution Focused Group Therapy.* New York: Simon and Schuster, 1998.

Nosek, M., M. Young, D. Rintala, C. Howland, C. Foley and J. L. Bennett. "Barriers to Reproductive Health Maintenance Among Women with Physical Disabilities." *Journal of Women's Health* 4.5 (1995): 505-518.

Rogers, L. and B. Swadener, eds. *Semiotics and Dis/ability: Interrogating Categories of Difference*. Albany: State University of New York Press, 2001.

Silvester, G. "Appreciating Indigenous Knowledge in Groups." *Narrative Therapy in Practice: The Archaeology of Hope*. Eds. G. Monk, J. Winslade, K. Crocket and D. Epston. San Francisco: Jossey-Bass, 1997. 233-251.

Veltman, A., D. Stewart, G. Tardif and M. Branigan. *Perceptions of Primary Healthcare Services Among People with Physical Disabilities. Part 1, Access Issues*. Toronto: DisAbled Women's Network of Ontario (DAWN), 2001a.

Veltman, A., D. Stewart, G. Tardif and M. Branigan. *Perceptions of Primary Healthcare Services Among People with Physical Disabilities. Part 2, Quality Issues*. Toronto: DisAbled Women's Network of Ontario (DAWN), 2001b.

White, M. *Intensive Training in Narrative Therapy*. Toronto: Brief Therapy Training Centres, Gail Appel Institute, Oct. 21-25, 2002.

White, M., and D. Epston. *Narrative Means to Therapeutic Ends*. New York: W.W. Norton, 1989.

Williams, L., R. LaBonte and M. O'Brien. "Empowering Social Action Through Narratives of Identity and Culture." *Health Promotion International* 18.1 (2003): 33-40.

Zitzelsberger, H., F. Odette, C. Rice and F. Whittington-Walsh. "Building Bridges Across Physical Difference and Disability." *Ways of Knowing in and Through the Body: Diverse Perspectives on Embodiment*. Ed. S. M. Abbey. Welland, ON: Soleil, 2002. 259-261.

WALKING A WOMAN'S PATH

Women with Intellectual Disabilities

SEVERAL YEARS AGO THERE was a study called "*When Bad Things Happen*" (excerpts from this study appear in an article earlier in this book). It looked at the kinds of things that were happening to women with intellectual disabilities. When we read about the things that were happening to women and heard about experiences from women that we knew, we decided we wanted to do something to help. There are many resource books for people about keeping safe, feeling better about yourself and laws and rights, but we couldn't find one that specifically focused on bringing women together and talking about how it feels to be a woman, the joys and hurts, the difficulties and challenges and what we need to do to keep ourselves safe.

Our facilitators invited seven women with and without intellectual disabilities to be part of a group that would meet regularly and start looking at those things. Each woman was paid $20 at the end of each session. After talking about things together the plan was to develop this workbook about our experiences and then go out and invite other women in Manitoba to think about and talk about the same things. We hope to start many other groups and provide them with this book and our experiences so they can do the same.

We knew that we wanted to write this book together and do it as creatively as possible. Some people like words, some people like to draw; some people choose to use pictures that are already available. Our facilitators had already gone to the store and brought a huge basket full of markers, stickers, feathers, hearts, scissors, glue, and dozens of old magazines. We each received our own private journal.

Our group started meeting one Sunday afternoon in the Fall of 2007. We developed a few **traditions** (things we would do each time we met). Here's how each of our sessions happened:

- •We started with soft music which helped quiet us down from the outside world.
- •Each woman was invited to talk for two minutes about how her week was or how she was doing.
- •We had a little carving of a woman that we used as our "talking stick." We passed it around as we shared—when the carving was in front of you it meant it was your turn and everyone else sat quietly and listened. When you were done you passed the carving to the next woman. It helped us to be respectful.
- •After everyone had a turn we talked about the theme of the group that day. In our first group, we started by talking about what it meant to be a woman.
- •We kept making notes and decided as a group what topic should come next and each week as we talked, we wrote.
- •We ended each session by standing in a circle, holding hands.
- •We took turns saying something that would officially close the group.
- •At the end of each session, we each took a turn thanking each woman and presented them with their $20 honorarium.

Our discussions were varied. We talked about life and death and sex and parents and our bodies and how to keep safe. One week we celebrated one woman's birthday and used that session as an opportunity to each bring something about our own childhood or birth story. We made posters and used pictures and words and colourful images to make sure that everything was documented.

We invite you to use this book. We hope that our discussions and work will be as fun, difficult, hopeful, sad, happy and ultimately helpful in your life and as you grow and learn how to feel more comfortable being an empowered, strong, healthy and safe woman. Use it on your own or use it to bring together your own group.

**We CAN be strong women
and we can live our lives the way we want as we
walk our own woman's path.**

women are nice people to get together and go out for supper
or birthday parties
or dances
or go to a show
bowlers, prime ministers
women can be pastors and doctors
day care workers and friends
some women are very strong
like Margaret Thatcher
but I don't think she's soft inside
women can be everything except a man
man I feel like a woman!

—A woman's group participant

WHAT DOES IT MEAN TO BE A WOMAN?

We decided to start our book by talking together about what it means to be a woman. It means something different to each person and we thought it was important to start by coming up with a description in common. Most of us hadn't really thought much about this and yet it is such an important part of our experiences and stories.

We put a huge long piece of paper on the wall and in the middle of the paper wrote "I am woman." Then we went to our craft boxes and brought out magazines, stickers, hearts, feathers, scissors, glue and markers. Each of us started going through the craft supplies and chose some things that we thought of when we thought about being a woman. For an hour we filled up the wall. One of the facilitators listened to our discussions and wrote down important words like "beautiful, sexy, powerful, and vulnerable." She also drew some images of things that we were saying. It was a very exciting and busy afternoon.

We talked about the good things about being a woman (being a mother, being beautiful, taking care of our bodies, doing important jobs) and then we talked about the not so good things like being abused, feeling vulnerable, feeling powerless, being with men (and sometimes other women) who did bad things—like hitting, hurting and rape.

After about an hour we sat back and looked at the whole picture and all the different messages that we included. We realized that all the magazine pictures that we had glued on were of skinny women.

We searched through the magazines for pictures of women that were chubby or even fat and couldn't find any! Our facilitator began to draw some pictures of larger size women to make sure that women that looked like some of us were on the poster. We were all very pleased by the end of the session and decided that we would put up the poster each time we met and continue adding to it.

IMPORTANT WOMEN IN OUR LIVES

For this next section we decided to start talking about the important women in our lives. Women can get stronger by being with other women—sharing and supporting their experiences. It was a good way to spend some time really exploring some of the women who have been important in our lives and to think about why they were important.

Each of us spent some time before the meeting thinking about it and came to the meeting eager to share! Here's how it worked. We went around the table and we each talked about one woman. We thought we'd go round a few times and each talk two or three times but we ended up spending so much time the first round, sharing and remembering. Our facilitator wrote down our words on a poster.

Here are some specific things that we each shared:

One group member talked about her grandmother and she said with tears in her eyes, "my grandmother was strong on the inside and I just knew she cared about me."

Another group member talked about her foster mom who took her in when she was ten days old!

Another group member talked about her older sister. Even though they fought like crazy when they were younger, they had become such good friends and supports to each other over the years, so much so that they lived in a house together.

Another group member talked about her doctor who was a woman. This was a doctor she hadn't seen for a long time and didn't even live in Winnipeg anymore. She had such an impact on the group member that it was the first woman that she thought about sharing with the group. She said "she just knew what I struggled with all the time and she was there to help."

Another group member talked about a staff person who she described as "beautiful and kind."

Still another group member talked about her mom who died last December and she said, "I'll never forget her."

The last group member talked about her mom who had also died. She told us how her mom was often sick and "she would rub her legs in the middle of the night to try and help her feel better."

We passed around the Kleenex a lot during this discussion. There were tears and smiles and memories and it felt at times like all these women were sitting there with us. The facilitator put each woman's name on a list. It was great to meet all these women that we had just talked about. It felt comforting to remember that we were not alone even when some of the important women in our lives had already died. Talking about the important women in our lives was sometimes hard work. It brought back different kinds of emotions. Even though it was hard work everyone agreed that this exercise was worthwhile.

Unfortunately along with the good memories came some bad ones. One woman talked about the abuse that she had suffered with her mother. As we will talk about in the next section it's not just men who abuse us, sometimes it is women.

IT'S ALL ABOUT POWER

One of the first serious discussions our group had was around the topic of power.

> What does power feel like?
> Who has power?
> Who doesn't have power?
> What do we do to get power?

Power is about having choices about who we are and what we do. It is the ability to make things happen in our lives. We thought about at least two ways to think about "power" – either having it (being **powerful**), or not having it (feeling **powerless**).

Feeling Powerful

Feeling **powerful** means that we feel confident and strong and able to speak about what is on our minds. We feel safe and able to make our own choices. We are likely to feel pretty good about ourselves.

277

Feeling Powerless

Feeling **powerless** means that we feel frightened or hurt and we feel unable to do anything about it. It may feel like other people in our lives don't let us do what we want to do or they make us do things that we don't want to. We are likely to feel pretty bad about ourselves.

Feeling Powerful

Those are the times we feel safe and secure and able to do things and make decisions. We feel good about ourselves. Here are the things that we talked about when we thought about feeling powerful.

When we feel **powerful** we think of:

- Not feeling scared and hurt;
- Advocating (speaking out) for ourselves or others;
- Not having as much stress in our lives;
- Feeling so much better after prayer and meditation;
- Doing things better: dusting, other housework, being with friends;
- Being with other people at church—getting together and talking and just having fellowship (sisterhood?);
- Doing things together;
- Working;
- Reading a book that inspires us or better yet writing one!
- Waking up in the morning especially on a Sunday.

One group member thought of the image of "two women holding each other, having a candle in the middle."

It's human nature to feel good about ourselves when we have our power and bad about ourselves when we don't. Nobody feels good all the time. Everyone feels bad inside sometimes. What we want to do is increase the times we feel good and learn some ways to get better at decreasing the times we feel bad. And most of all we want to feel safe to live our lives and speak our minds.

Feeling Powerless

This was a more difficult discussion. It brought back memories that some of the women didn't like. We all could think of lots of times that we felt powerless. We explored three different possible reasons:

a. Because we are women. There are many books, movies and stories about women feeling powerless, being hurt and scared. It used to be that women had no rights in our country. That was so many years ago when our grandmothers and great grandmothers were living. That has changed. Being women may still make us feel more powerless but there are many women who are learning how to change that. In Canada we have a law called the Charter of Rights and Freedoms. It says that all people (men and women) have the same rights in Canada.

b. Because we have disabilities and people haven't learned to respect us. It used to be that people with disabilities had no rights but that too has begun to change. We now have laws that make sure that people with disabilities have the right to make decisions about their lives, with support if needed. In Manitoba the law is called *The Vulnerable Persons' Living with a Mental Disability Act.*

c. Because we haven't learned to find ways to be STRONG and speak OUT. In other words we may think we are powerless but we really aren't. We just haven't practiced those skills yet. Here is an example.

> *Judy has had a weight problem all her life and people would say things to her that would hurt her feelings. Sometimes her boyfriend nagged her. She never said anything but just kept all the bad feelings inside. One day Judy's boyfriend said "you are so fat—why do you have to eat so much food!" This time Judy decided to be brave and she said, "do you know how much it hurts my feelings when you say that to me?" Judy's boyfriend apologized. He didn't know how badly it made her feel about herself when he said things like that. Judy ended up feeling so good that she had found her voice and spoke up. Instead of feeling bad and powerless, she felt strong and powerful.*

This is a good example of someone who felt powerless and just by speaking up began to feel more powerful. Judy's weight problem didn't go away because she spoke up, but she just didn't feel so badly about herself and she even felt closer to her boyfriend. Judy hadn't realized that she could have the power to say those kinds of things to other people.

Here are some of the things that we talked about in our discussion about the bad power. See if any of these things sound familiar to you. When we are **powerless**, we think of:

- Our voices being taking away and we don't feel safe to speak;
- The times that someone tells us "not to tell";
- People threatening us, taking advantage, neglecting or abusing us;
- Not being able to defend ourselves and feeling physically weak;
- The things we can't do, not the things we can do;
- People who don't listen to us or respect what we believe;
- Feeling so tired and worn out;
- Not being able to make good decisions;
- Not being able to take care of ourselves.

Later, we'll start talking about the things we can do to feel powerful and safer. It's important that we remember that talking about being powerless and writing things down doesn't make things different.

We may still feel powerless. But starting to talk about it is the first step to understanding it and trying to find ways to change how we act and how we feel.

And then there are the times that we hurt other people.

Along with power comes responsibility. It's important to think about the ways in which we might misuse our power and hurt someone else. We all know what it feels like to feel powerless and to be hurt. But have we thought about the times that we have hurt others?

Maybe we didn't do it on purpose. We may have yelled at someone and said mean things that hurt them. We might even have hit someone else when we were angry or frustrated. We may have used mean words by calling someone else negative names.

**EVERYBODY HAS THE POWER
TO EITHER HELP OR HURT OTHERS.**

A story about Janie helps us understand this.

Janie and Sam are good friends. They spend lots of time together. Janie lives in her own apartment with one other person. One day Janie was really upset about something that happened at work and she wanted to talk to Sam. She called and left a message. Then she called again an hour later. The next morning she called two more times. She was becoming very upset that Sam wasn't calling back. When she got home from work there was still no message from Sam. She called three more times but still no Sam.

The next afternoon when Janie got home from work there was finally a message from Sam. She called him and as soon as he said hello she started yelling. She said some very mean things. She said he wasn't her friend and then she banged the phone. Sam tried to call again but Janie was still so angry she wouldn't talk to him.

What Janie didn't know is that Sam had been feeling very sick. He hadn't been avoiding her at all; he just wasn't able to call her back! When Janie heard this she started feeling really badly about all the mean things she had said to him. Because she was feeling hurt, she yelled at him and ended up hurting his feelings. She thought he was being mean to her but she realized that she was the one who had been mean. *Janie misused her power and ended up hurting her best friend. It made Janie feel badly that she hurt Sam.*

It's so important that we not misuse our power. The thing is … we know it feels bad to be hurt, but it might feel just as bad when we know we have hurt someone else. When we hurt someone else we might be misusing our power.

WHAT'S PUBLIC AND WHAT'S PRIVATE?

Public Places – Private Places

There are some parts of our body that others can touch and some that are private. There are people we share private things with and others we don't. There are places that are public and places that are more private. So we felt it was important to include a chapter in our workbook that addresses these important issues. First let's look at places where we spend time.

Public Spaces are places where we are likely to see people who we may not know very well or at all. Not only do we see all the people, but in a public place people can see us too. Here are some examples:

- a shopping mall
- a city bus
- a grocery store
- at school
- in a movie theatre
- at a community event or day program.

Private spaces are places where we are usually by ourselves or with someone else that we are comfortable with. People we don't know cannot see us when we are in a private space. Here are some examples:

- your bedroom
- your bathroom.

Public Talk – Private Talk

It's important that we are able to speak about the things that are on our minds. In an earlier section, we learned that it is one way to get back our power. Sometimes we are sharing happy things, sometimes we have sad, scary or angry things to say. We all need to learn who the people are that we can have these more personal conversations with.

Public talk is what we say to other people we don't know very well or what we say when we are in a public place where other people can hear us. Such as:

- talking about the weather while riding the bus
- talking about a sports event with someone we work with
- talking about a movie that you have seen with your cousin
- talking about your volunteer job with a staff that works in your home.

Private talk is when we are talking about personal things or feelings.

When we are talking about private things we take care to only do that with people that we know and trust. We talk privately with someone in a private place. We may be talking about:

- how much money you have with your close friend
- a physical problem you are having with your body with your doctor
- sex with your boyfriend, husband or very close girlfriend
- a situation where someone has hurt or abused you with someone who can help you.

Here are some examples of people in your life you might share private talk with:

- a very good friend that you have known for a long time and who you trust
- a partner
- a helper like a doctor, teacher, police officer who you feel comfortable talking to
- a priest, minister, pastor, counsellor, lawyer or rabbi or someone else whose job it is to help or guide you.

Remember—do not talk to strangers or acquaintances (someone you don't know very well) about private things unless they are community helpers who you are comfortable talking to.

**If someone asks you something private
just say NO—and then leave.**

MY BODY IS MINE

Each of us owns our own body and we decide who can touch it. We need to understand which parts of our body are private. We need to think about who touches those private parts of our bodies and who doesn't.

There are two very important words that we need to learn and practice when other people want to touch our bodies.

They are YES and NO.

But we also need to understand which parts of our bodies are public and which are private so … let's look at our bodies and list all the parts and talk about which parts are public parts. That means that everyone can see them.

For example, everyone can see our:

- •legs
- •arms
- •nose
- •toes (if you are wearing sandals)
- •fingers
- •hair on your head

Think about the parts of your body that you keep covered. Here are some examples:

- •your breasts
- •your vagina
- •your bottom

Are there other parts of your body that feel private to you? Remember—it is your body and only you can decide if other parts of your body feel private to you. For example, you may not want people to touch your face or give you a hug.

❖It's sometimes confusing to know the difference between public and private.
❖We need to understand what is a private space and what is a public space.
❖We need to understand what is public talk and what is private talk.
❖We need to understand what is public and what is private about our bodies.

We will be doing a good job of keeping ourselves
safer when we really begin to understand and practice what
is public and what is private.

WHEN BAD THINGS HAPPEN

During our discussions about power and about public and private things, we came back to the difficult discussion of **when bad things happen.** Pretty much everyone around the table talked about times that they felt hurt and abused. We remembered that in the first chapter (on our poster), we used the words "unsafe" and "vulnerable" to describe what it means to be a woman. It is so important that women talk about why we are sometimes hurt and what we can do to make ourselves stronger.

These are different kinds of abuse situations that we shared:

•In some cases it was a parent who hurt us. Parents are supposed to take care of us. Most do. Some don't.

•Sometimes it was a staff person who was there to protect us but what they actually did was hurt us.

•Sometimes it was a boyfriend or girlfriend that we trusted— or a husband or a partner.

•Sometimes it was just a stranger that we met on the street.

•Sometimes we told someone about being hurt and sometimes we just kept it to ourselves.

The one thing that was pretty much the same for all of us was agreeing that being hurt or abused ALWAYS made us feel badly about ourselves.

We learned that being abused is someone else misusing their power over us. And, we began to understand that we needed to find a way to stop that from happening.

Let's use Mary's story as an example.

Mary takes the bus home from her work program every day. Last Monday a man got off the bus when she did and started following *her home. He tried to talk with her; he asked her if she wanted to go to a restaurant for coffee or come to his house to watch television. She didn't want to go. She just wanted to go home and get away from him. He was bigger and stronger than she was and he wouldn't leave her alone. He told her he needed $5.00 and she gave it to him. She was frightened but what could she do?*

In this situation someone is misusing his power over Mary. When one person misuses his/her power over another it is abuse.

Does Mary have to give money to the man who was following her home?

Mary is feeling threatened by the man who has followed her home. She gave him money even though she didn't have to or want to. She could have said "NO" but was afraid or didn't even know that she could refuse. She felt powerless—he was misusing his power.

The best way to know if someone is abusing you is to think about how you feel in a given situation.

- is someone touching you in a way that makes you uncomfortable?
- is someone holding you down and not letting you move?
- has someone threatened you and said, "*if you don't do what I say then I'll…?*"
- has someone taken something from you, like money or something you own?
- has someone hit you?
- has someone stopped you from eating, sleeping, having a bath or going out?
- is someone doing something that makes you feel uncomfortable or angry but you feel afraid to tell them?

If you answered yes to any of the above questions, then you are being abused and you need to tell someone.

LEARNING TO SPEAK FOR OURSELVES

There is one very important way that we can help keep ourselves safer. We've already talked about the fact that sometimes being a woman means feeling vulnerable and powerless. Remember, those were some of the words that came out in our first meeting when we talked about what it means to be a woman? When we feel powerless it's really difficult to talk to people that we think are more powerful. We may feel angry, frightened, sad, threatened and ... really really small.

We must learn how to speak for ourselves.

It's hard to speak up for ourselves especially when we haven't had the experience of doing it. The first thing we have to do is recognize that we are feeling uncomfortable and powerless. We ask ourselves – am I being abused by this person?

The next important step is to tell someone if we think we are being abused. Did you know that? Sometimes it's about saying NO and sometimes it's about finding someone we can trust to describe what is happening.

Here are some things we have learned and we hope you will think about.

What if you are afraid to talk about it when something bad happens?

It's okay to be afraid—telling can be scary. It is **never** okay to just be silent when you feel that someone is doing something to you that is hurtful. You have a right to speak up for yourself but you also have a responsibility to do something about it.

What can you do?

Find someone you feel safe with. Ask them if they would be willing to listen to some things that are bothering you and to get some help sorting through what YOU should do about it. When you are looking at what you should be doing that means that you are taking the responsibility to try to make the situation better. Sometimes that means saying NO. Sometimes it means talking to a person with whom you are feeling powerless. Sometimes it means talking to someone else who can help you. Maybe they can practice with you ahead of time or perhaps they could go with you and support you when you tell. Remember it is your right to be safe and your responsibility to talk about times that you think you might be experiencing abuse.

It is really hard to do something that you have never done before so … practice … practice … practice.

Even though these are VERY difficult things to talk about, it gets easier each time you try it.

Who are the people that YOU know that you could talk to about feeling powerless or abused? Can you think of someone? Someone who would be willing to help you practice? Perhaps you could talk with them about something that has been bothering you but that you have been too nervous or afraid to talk about. Perhaps you can ask their advice or just ask them to listen.

Why is it so important to speak up?

- Because you are important and you have a voice.
- Because you have the right to be safe.
- Because you have the right to tell people what you are feeling.
- Because when you talk to someone you get help to feel better.
- Because when you talk to someone about how you feel you are practicing and getting stronger at taking responsibility.

We can learn to be stronger women!

THE JOY OF BEING A WOMAN

What an experience this has been—talking together with other women about ourselves, our power, our bodies, our hurts, our rights and, of course, our responsibilities. We are so lucky to be women. We are so lucky to have each other as we walk our woman's path. It took us almost a whole year to put together this workbook. We worked hard having the same discussions that we hope you have. We lost a few women along the way, but a few of us have stuck it through right to the very end. We had lots of fun; we definitely shed a few tears and we challenged each other along the way.

Before we finish this part of our journey, let's do two more exercises to celebrate ourselves, our hard work and one another.

For the first exercise you will need a mirror, the bigger the better. Stand in front of it and look at you – look at all of your body parts, your legs, your arms, your face, your hair, your hips, your breasts, etc. Say into the mirror, "I love every part of me. I am perfect, I am beautiful. I am a perfectly beautiful woman." It may be hard to say, but practice. So often we are critical and feel bad about parts of our body. It is time to celebrate everything about us. Even though there may be things we want to change, it doesn't mean we don't accept and love who we are. **Being a strong woman means:**

- •We *can* be powerful
- •We *can* be strong
- •We *are careful* not to hurt other people
- •We *can* become comfortable talking to other women (and maybe men) about how we feel
- •We *can* be safe and when we don't feel safe we can ask for help
- •We *can* learn together and grow as we walk our woman's path.

EPILOGUE

Excerpted from the book, *Walking a Woman's Path*. The book was completed in early 2009.

Walking a Woman's Path (2009) was collectively written by a women's group brought together intentionally for this purpose. The women's group included: Clare McCarthy, Janet Forbes, Jennifer Gallant, Marsha Dozar, Melissa Martin, Ruth Wyn Dopson, and Valerie Wolbert.

Walking a Woman's Path was sponsored by Community Living-Winnipeg and funded by the Status of Women Canada. The intent was to initiate discussions with women with intellectual disabilities that would focus on self-esteem, self-development, assertiveness, and keeping safer. Following the publishing of the book, women around the province of Manitoba were invited to several sessions and retreats to begin "the walk." The challenge for the facilitators was presenting the material in an accessible way, given the diverse abilities and disabilities of the women. Simple language and concrete examples and discussions were required to ensure that women were engaged. The work continues.

DIANNE POTHIER

THE FIRST STEP IS TO BE NOTICED

"WE DON'T THINK OF you as disabled because of what you have accomplished." My friend thought she was paying me a compliment; both our friendship and my degree of shock got in the way of my bluntly explaining that her comment was instead very insulting. And it was particularly ironic that her comment was prompted by her knowing that I was in the final stages of writing an article[1] about disability from my perspective as a person with a visual impairment (close to legal blindness).

What was so offensive about my friend's comment? The explicit assumption was that persons with disabilities are not expected to accomplish anything of significance. If you have achieved anything of note, you cannot really be "disabled." A clearer statement of able-bodied insensitivity to people with disabilities would be hard to find.

In a different way, that same point had been brought home to me a few days earlier at an academic conference. Again the point was made more poignant by the fact that the incident in question arose in a context in which disability was expressly under discussion. There was significance not only in the incident itself, but also in the differences in the reactions to it.

The location of the conference was itself disturbing. It would be difficult to imagine a building more wheelchair inaccessible. The only apparent access to the building was by stairs; there were no elevators between floors; the floors themselves were not level, with mezzanines connected by stairs; and many of the conference sessions were in steeply tiered classrooms. In two days at the conference, I had heard no comment, either apologetic or critical, about the building layout.

There was a session at the conference devoted to a discussion of a committee report on equality in access to education which included disability issues. The program involved a short opening plenary, a series of workshops, and a closing plenary. At the opening plenary, one of the authors of the report gave some background on its preparation and introduced the other authors. He explained that one of the committee members was unable to be at the conference because she was away training a dog. Several people in the audience laughed at that remark. I thought to myself: what is so funny about someone training a guide dog? I resolved to myself that sometime before the end of the session, I would comment on the inappropriateness of the laughter.

Shortly thereafter we broke into workshops. The facilitator in my workshop was one of the members of the committee. She had arrived late at the plenary and had not been present at the time of the laughter. She started the workshop discussion by saying that we all knew the nature of the problem, and it was only the solutions that needed to be addressed. I decided I could not let that pass. I said that what had just happened in the plenary was an indication to me that there still was difficulty in recognizing the problem. People with disabilities are clearly not fully accepted and integrated if people thought it was funny that a blind person would need to train a dog. Moreover, no one had yet expressed concern about the inaccessibility of the building in which we were discussing equality.

My comments did not generate any particular response. However, there was good discussion on other points in the workshop, and I was satisfied that I had made my point. At the start of the closing plenary, I felt no particular need to repeat my comments. But the tone of the closing plenary was far too complacent and self-congratulatory for me to keep silent. Near the end, I decided to say my piece.

I again noted the inaccessible nature of the building we were in, and my offence at the laughter in the opening plenary. I added a comment about my own frustrations in sitting through days of people reading their papers. I know that I, a person with a visual impairment, would have been judged very harshly for such a performance, given the way I read.[2] I was attempting to jolt people out of their complacency, and the only way I knew how to do that was to let my anger show. Showing anger carries with it the danger of simply alienating people, but I had reached a point where I was prepared to take that risk. At least, I got people's attention. The range of reactions to my point about the laughter was very interesting, from apology to denial.

An Aboriginal woman friend who had been sitting next to me in the opening plenary, and who had been one of those who had laughed, immediately came up to me with a profuse apology. I found that gratifying, because it showed she had understood my reaction. It was obvious to me why she understood so readily. She had just done to me what had been done to her many times before—displayed an insensitivity that conveyed a message of exclusion.

At the other extreme, a white male friend started our conversation by doubting that there had been any laughter at the opening plenary. I gave a very curt response to that comment. I had no patience for the attitude: "since I didn't notice it, it can't have happened." There had been clear and unmistakable laughter; that point was not open for debate. My friend backed off, and moved from denial to defensiveness. He said that while he had not himself laughed (which I had no reason to doubt), he had found the comment about training a dog odd. He had not been thinking of a guide dog, but of training dogs in the way that one trains horses. My response was that, even accepting, as I was prepared to do, that this sort of explanation accounted for the laughter, it was still offensive. That is because it means that the notion of needing a guide dog is simply not part of people's thinking. Even in a setting in which access to people with disabilities was the topic for discussion, they could not comprehend a reference to a dog as meaning a guide dog. In an able-bodied perspective on the world, guide dogs do not figure prominently. My friend did not seem convinced that I had a point. My interpretation of this is that someone who is not used to being marginalized has a harder time recognizing it when it happens to others.

Later that day, this same friend and I happened to be sitting next to each other at a session on Aboriginal rights. The person giving the presentation was Mohawk. In the course of his discussion, he asked the audience if we could name the six nations of the Iroquois confederacy. To our embarrassment, we collectively could not do so. My friend recognized the parallels to our earlier conversation, and its significance started to hit home. He recognized and commented to me that this was the kind of insensitivity that I had been talking about. I agreed, feeling humbled by the fact that this time I had been among those displaying the insensitivity.

A slight need not be intentional to be hurtful. Indeed, where there is a simple failure to notice, the very absence of intention may itself constitute the problem. People cannot feel that they really belong unless they are made to feel that other people at least recognize their existence.

Originally published in CWS/cf's *issue on "Women and Disability," 13 (4) (1993): 16-17. Reprinted with permission.*

[1]Since published, D. Pothier, "Miles to Go: Some Personal Reflections on the Social Construction of Disability," 14 *Dalhousie Law Journal* 526 (1992).
[2]For elaboration, see above mentioned article.

NANCY E. HANSEN AND DIANE DRIEDGER

ART, STICKS AND POLITICS

D ISABILITY, POLITICS AND ART belong on the same continuum although they are not usually perceived as such. Traditionally, over the past thirty years, the Disability Rights Movement in Canada has identified legislation as the principle mechanism for effecting social change. Disability art and culture is slowly emerging and the nondisabled majority often views it as a curiosity, on the fringes of mainstream society (Garland-Thomson 2010). Typically, most crutch users, and society in general, have simply treated crutches as a medical or assistive device designed as an instrument to assist movement from place to place. Academics, physicians and therapists seldom explore the relationship between the crutches and the user except insofar as the mechanics enhance utility. Aesthetics have rarely, if ever, been a part of the discussion.

Tracing an unexpected journey, this paper examines the connections and intersections between and among diverse elements through a plain pair of wooden crutches.

BEGINNINGS

In the Spring of 2007, two friends, Nancy, a disabled academic activist, a crutch-user, and Diane, an artist, writer, and academic, and a woman with invisible disabilities, met at a journal launch at a local bookstore. Diane's art and writing appeared in the issue. We began discussing the possibilities of crutches as fashion, art and a reflection of individuality for people with disabilities.

Nancy said to Diane, "How boring, dull and utilitarian my crutches are." Wooden crutches are austere, varnished wood with brown or

Photo: Christine Blais-Kerr

black straps. In Nancy's case, the straps are just above the elbow, the functional equivalent of a pair of dark, horn-rimmed spectacles. Nancy exclaimed how it would be great to have colourful, sexy ones. Not since secondary school and her very early university days had she decorated her crutches to reflect some sense of her individuality or style. At that time, she applied various colours of electrical adhesive tape in strips depending on colour trends and wardrobe choices. She once decorated them with Canadian flags in honour of Canada Day and when traveling abroad. Nancy abandoned the practice when she first entered the job market in a bid to display professionalism—to reflect a more polished look, to move away from a "casual student" appearance. We discussed crutches as fashion, art and a reflection of individuality and personality. Nancy saw "fashion" and Diane saw the opportunity for something more. Diane said "Why not make a real fashion statement using disability rights phrases?" And so we began.

ART STICKS

We collaborated over a period of many months to transform the crutches. Diane applied multiple coats of cherry-red paint to the crutches and began the transformation of wood to canvas utilizing a "graffiti art" style. Diane painted disability rights phrases in black on the crutches. Little did we know that this was only the beginning. A simple pair of crutches became an unlikely vehicle for shaping the mainstream gaze. The crutches' presence shifted perceived boundaries of space and place in a positive manner.

In some ways, this was a reclamation project, of taking ownership on our own terms. We moved against powerful silencing cultural norms. As Bonnie Sherr Klein states: "To give permission to the artist within your disabled body is an outrageous act of defiance" (5). As a culture, Western society has often pushed disability into the background and thus assistive devices have been hidden and, until recently, strictly utilitarian. The only element regularly displayed on such devices is the company trademark of the manufacturer. (Nancy's, husband Peter, a wheelchair user, was often called "Jay" in law school, as "Jay," the wheelchair seat-maker, is emblazoned across the back of the chair). Wood was a new canvas for Diane, as she had never before painted on a pair of crutches.

Diane painted the crutches in a "graffiti art" style, where powerful, public text is emblazoned on everyday objects or spaces that society docs not usually perceive as valuable. We brainstormed disability rights terminology. We chose favourite words and disability and human right phrases such as:

- A Voice of Our Own (Council of Canadians With Disabilities)
- Education is key
- The Last Civil Rights Movement (Diane Driedger, Author)
- Ignorance Is not Bliss
- Human Rights
- Vegetables of the World Unite (Ed. Roberts, American Disability Rights Advocate)
- Nothing About Us Without Us (James I. Charlton, Author)
- Reject Ableisim
- Be the Change You Wish to See in the World (Mahatma Gandhi)
- Peace, Truth, respect , dignity, Inclusion, unique
- Beauty in Everything
- Knowledge is Power (Sir Francis Bacon)

Photo: Christine Blais-Kerr

Photo: Christine Blais-Kerr

•Question Crip Phobia
•Access is a State of Mind

These are only a few. They became a literal fashion statement that Diane printed in black paint on top, thus transforming the crutches into an artistic creation. Now an everyday object had artistic worth and power. Other Canadian artists, notably, the late Maud Lewis, also an artist from Nova Scotia with a disability, who had polio and rheumatoid arthritis, painted on items of daily life from baking utensils to barn board.

Diane sees her art as her children. Once created, the art takes on a life of its own, going out there on its way, without Diane expecting anything, not knowing how it will be received.

TRANSFORMATIONS

Nancy cried tears of joy when she saw the finished product for the first time. The crutches touched her on a deep emotional level that she could never have imagined. Nancy's crutches looked sharp and fashionable. For the first time in her life, culture, function and fashion intersected—a literal manifestation of her pride as a disabled person. The graffiti crutches provided the finishing touch fashion element to her professional look. If Nancy had a difficult meeting, she would take the red and black crutches. She felt greater confidence, as they constituted an integral part of her power suit. It was a truly liberating experience, as the graffiti crutches gave her a much different feeling than her "everyday" wooden crutches, which were nondescript in comparison. In addition, the graffiti crutches quite literally changed attitudes, and generated confidence, conversation, communication and change.

It was subtle at first. Nancy started to notice people reading her crutches as she rode the elevator. Security officers would read the graffiti crutches as they passed through the x-ray machine at the airport. Total strangers would say, "Those are the nicest crutches I have ever seen," or "nice decoration" or "cool crutches." These comments were very positive as opposed to them making no comment or a negative comment about the everyday crutches. About her other crutches she hears comments such as: "Wouldn't it be easier to use a wheelchair?";

"Those are really old"; "It must be really hard to use those"; or "How come you don't use the metal ones?"

When she moves through everyday spaces with the regular crutches people ask, "How come you haven't got the red ones?" Many people think that the graffiti crutches are autographs, or "'Did you do that yourself?" before closer examination and Nancy explains that they are actually "commissioned art." This phrase itself is a point of interest and people take a closer look. The reader smiles. Often the interaction will result in the observer reading the phrases out loud followed by, "Why not?" Others comment: "Those are really fashionable"; "You should get a different colour made"; "really pretty"; "sharp"; "really neat"; or "really great." Nancy never knows when these encounters will take place. The most memorable, to date, happened at an international conference on human rights late last year, when the Keynote Speaker stopped in the middle of her prepared text and said, "I don't need to talk about this subject any further. Nancy's crutches say it all. Be sure to read them." At a break point in the conference, several people made a point of coming up to read the crutches. And so it continues…

We discussed why the crutches had this unforeseen impact. We talked about staring and the representation of disability. The crutches had become an unexpected player in the question of the social representation of disabled people. They had become a new way of being the "voice" of persons with disabilities. Indeed, gradually the voices and knowledge of disabled people have been building a more realistic and complete picture of disability in daily life (Sandell and Dodd). Over the past several decades, public perceptions of disability have been slowly shifting away from "helplessness" and "victimhood" influenced, in part, by a growing rights-based understanding demanded by other equality seeking groups. Sandell and Dodd reiterate: "As human rights discourses have gained increasingly global influence, as the politics of difference has brought about greater sensitivity over depictions of a range of minorities, and as the disability rights movement has gathered momentum, so these pernicious stereotypes have become less publicly acceptable and widespread" (6).

In her recent book, *Staring: How We Look*, Rosemary Garland-Thomson details the power of the normative gaze and the cultural invisibility that disabled people historically experience. According to society, those individuals labelled as "different" should blend into the background— be present, but socially invisible. Society often perceives the presence of visible disability as disruptive to the natural social order. Staring is a form of visual snooping. The social landscape is slowly shifting and the stare is being repositioned to a form of engagement with the emergence of disability culture and politics. According to Garland-Thomson:

> When people with stareable bodies… enter into the public eye when they no longer hide themselves or allow themselves to be hidden, the visual landscape enlarges. Their public presence can expand the range of bodies we expect to see and broaden the terrain where we expect to see such bodies. This new public landscape is in part a product of the laws, social practices, and changed attitudes wrought by the larger civil rights movement—including the disability rights movement. (Garland-Thomson 2009: 9)

In addition, the narrative is being quite literally re-shaped and shifted toward worth and dignity. People with disabilities reclaim the stare and the nondisabled majority learns and recognizes new knowledge. (Garland-Thomson 2009). Nancy and her graffiti crutches quite literally reclaimed that stare on her terms.

Similarly, the new book, *Re-Presenting Disability: Activism and Agency in the Museum* (Sandell and Dodd), documents how portrayals of disability are changing as perceptions change and the understanding of difference shifts. Cultural representations of disability (or the lack thereof) have a direct impact on how mainstream society understands disability: "[P]ublic portrayals of disabled people have effects and consequences which—though slippery, diffuse and difficult to trace—are nonetheless ubiquitous and capable of powerfully shaping disabled people's lives in innumerable and very tangible ways" (3).

The emergence of the disability politics rights cultural narrative is slowly shifting the mainstream lens away from stilted representations of naturalness of bodily difference (Garland-Thomson 2009). They revalue devalued people, the kinds of people society has only glimpsed at in institutions or in medical pictures with black boxes over the disabled persons' eyes. As Garland-Thomson explains: "As more people with disabilities become visible in the public eye, so too have varied images emerged that tell a broader range of stories about people with disabilities ... that do not replicate the corrosive old stories of suffering, inferiority, pity or repugnance" (23).

Nancy's own experience with the phenomena of staring and representing disability was quite unexpected. All she set out to do was to complete a fashion statement, not create teachable moments. Neither of us dreamed that a simple pair of red and black crutches conceived as a fashionable alternative to a utilitarian walking aid would turn into a movable art installation.

We never thought that these crutches could be so transformative. They literally help rewrite society's existing cultural narrative of disability one chance encounter at a time.

REFERENCES

Garland-Thomson, R. "Picturing People With Disabilities: Classical Portraiture as Reclamation Narrative." *Re-Presenting Disability: Activist Practice in Activism and Agency at the Museum.* Ed. R. Sandell and B. Dodd. New York: Routledge, 2010. 23-40.

Garland-Thomson, R. *Staring: How We Look.* New York: Oxford University Press, 2009.

Lewis, M. *Canadian Artist Biography Database: Maud Lewis.* Online: <http://www.edu.pe.ca/threeoaks/art/601/lewis.htm>. Accessed: 06/05/2010.

Sandell, R. and B. Dodd. *Re-Presenting Disability: Activist Practice in Activism and Agency at the Museum.* New York: Routledge, 2010. 3-22.

Sherr Klein, B. "The Art of Disability: Some Ideas About Creativity, Health and Rehabilitation." John F. McCreary Lecture, University of Toronto, October 11, 2000. Online: <http://www.philia.ca/files/pdf/bskdisability.pdf>. Accessed 6 May 2010.

ANJALI DOOKERAN

"Untitled Drawing"

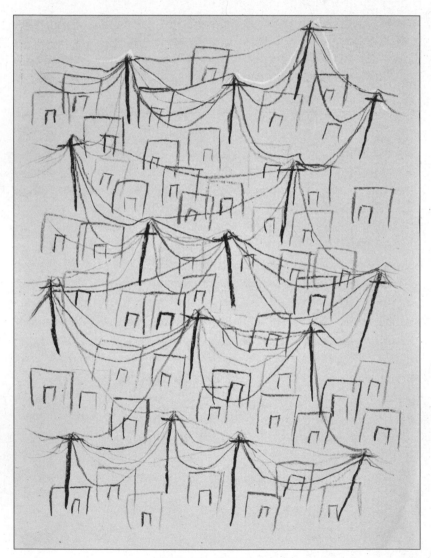

"Untitled," c.2006, drawing.

JOSÉE BOULANGER, SUSIE WIESZMANN AND VALERIE WOLBERT

THE FREEDOM TOUR DOCUMENTARY

An Experiment in Inclusive Filmmaking

MAKING *THE FREEDOM TOUR* documentary is an experience we will never forget. The three of us, along with three other People First Winnipeg members worked together for over two and a half years to create a documentary about what it's like to live inside and survive an institution for people labelled with an intellectual disability. We are very proud of our work and it still keeps us busy as we continue to talk about the need to close down institutions and provide supports for all people to live in the community. We all met for the first time in February 2005 at a rally held at the Manitoba Legislature to protest our provincial government's decision to invest more money into the Manitoba Developmental Centre (MDC), an institution located on the outskirts of a small town an hour's drive from Winnipeg. Over the last one hundred years, MDC has had different names like Home for Incurables, Manitoba School for Mental Defectives and Manitoba School for Mental Retardates. Parents were encouraged to put their children in places like MDC. They were told their son or daughter would get an education and specialized health care nobody else could provide in the community. We know from survivors that this didn't happen. People suffered, they didn't get an education and once you were placed in there, it was very hard to get out. Some never made it out at all, they just died there. So you can imagine how we felt at the rally.

Our hearts were filled with sadness and anger: How could our government support this institution?

> We were very upset with the government wanting to spend that forty million dollars on the Manitoba Developmental Centre. It was a very cold day. I remember Josée did some

Top: Jonathan Bland, Joe Macdonald, Josée Boulanger, Mark Blanchette. Middle: Valerie Wolbert. Bottom: Kevin Johnson, Susie Weiszmann and David Weremy

interviewing after; there were lots of people. People First of Canada members were there. We were really riled up because they decided to spend that money without consulting with anybody [with intellectual disabilities]. (Valerie Wolbert).

Yeah, I was holding a sign. I remember about the candle light vigil. Richard Ruston [President of People First of Canada] was there. (Susie Weiszmann).

People with intellectual disabilities, support workers, family members and allies were holding signs that said "The safest place is my home," "Set them Free!," "I like my freedom," "Institutions give us no choices," and "There's a place for people like me, it's called my home!" People were shouting "Free our people!" and "Shame on you!"

Terrilynn, the president of People First Manitoba at the time [of the rally] gave a great speech. She even asked the Minister to give her [deinstitutionalization] pin back! There was lots of support. I was just there to help people out, to make sure that people could get there. I was there supporting Susie at the time. (Chris Currie)

*2005 rally against further investment into
Manitoba Developmental Centre in Portage la Prairie.*

Nobody at the rally cared that it was minus 40 degrees outside; we all knew that being stuck inside an institution would be much worse! Josée set up her video camera inside the Legislature and Valerie and many other self-advocates approached her to tell their story.

> I had been interested in the People First movement thanks to my mother who is an adviser for a French speaking chapter in Ontario and my brother who is a member. When I heard there was a rally to protest this decision, I knew I had to be there to see people in action, to record their stories. I wanted to become part of this movement somehow. (Josée Boulanger)

We didn't know it then but the video interviews done during that rally became our starting point for *The Freedom Tour* documentary.

A year later, Josée presented the footage to People First Winnipeg members. She explained that she was a student in Disability Studies at the University of Manitoba and a community filmmaker interested in working with people who have been labelled with an intellectual disability to make videos. She asked us if we would be interested in working with her. She recognized Valerie and David Weremy from the rally and said she would bring the video footage for us to watch. After the first issue of *Institution Watch* (a newsletter to raise awareness about institutions for people with disabilities) was handed to members, some of us suggested we make a long video about closing institutions. Then Josée was invited to attend the provincial People First meeting to show the rally video. As members watched it, the atmosphere in the room was charged with emotion; there were tears and anger.

> I remember feeling nervous as I saw people's reactions. I was afraid to promise something I could not deliver. This was a very serious and difficult situation, people's lives were involved. Some people there had lived in institutions and others had friends who were still stuck there. One member was very insistent about following through on making a film. Dave Weremy had survived eighteen years of confinement at the Manitoba Developmental Centre. As I listened and observed the reactions, I felt very strongly that we could find funding to help us make this happen. I suggested that the National Film Board of Canada (NFB) should be supportive of a film about deinstitutionalization. I promised that I would call the NFB and let People First know how it went. (Josée Boulanger)

Luckily, Joe MacDonald, the documentary producer at the NFB at the time, was interested in our film idea. He was especially supportive of our participatory or collaborative approach. Our documentary project took on a new focus when People First of Canada (PFC) got wind of the film we were planning. It just so happened that PFC had a grant to make a video about deinstitutionalization across the Prairies and the PFC administration approached Josée with the idea of combining our energies.

> During our first meeting, I explained that the documentary that I was planning on making with People First Manitoba was going to be inclusive. I wanted members to be part of making the documentary, perhaps even as co-directors. How else would a film be made by a self-advocacy movement? The administration was initially sceptical about this idea but I assured them that with guidance, we could make this

documentary using a participatory approach. Working with a small group of People First Winnipeg members, we could make our film collaboratively. To my relief, they took the leap and agreed to go along with the experiment! (Josée Boulanger)

Josée then got permission from People First Manitoba members to work with PFC on the film. She explained that working with People First of Canada meant we would have more money but we would have to include stories from survivors living in Saskatchewan and Alberta instead of just focusing on Manitoba. We agreed to work with PFC and started to dream even bigger! Josée announced the new partnership to the NFB producer and a contract was written up to develop the script for *The Freedom Tour*. We were all excited to have the opportunity to tell people about institutions. Most people don't know that they still exist in Canada and have no idea what it's like to live in one of those places.

I knew that people with intellectual disabilities could live outside institutions with proper help and funding. Video is good for telling people's stories and getting the message out. It lets the government know that we can live in the community. It's very educational. A video is more expressive, you can tell expressions, moods. In a book, some people wouldn't be able to read it and we tried to make our video plain language. Sometimes books aren't plain language. We could actually show our feelings. (Valerie Wolbert)

Why the government doesn't get people out of there. Why people are trying to fight them to get the money. The money can go to everyone, People First. Why people go to the institutions, we gotta get people out there. We're trying to help David and Freddy,[1] who passed away. I like to be independent, on my own. I can go to the movies, people in institutions: nothing. (Susie Weiszmann)

GETTING STARTED

For over a year, Valerie, Mark, Kevin, and later Susie, met on a weekly basis at Dave's apartment to work on the film proposal. Sometimes we went on trips or visited people we thought we would like to include in our film. Josée would write things up based on what we'd talked about and we would read it out loud and tell her if it was ok or not. This is also the way we're writing this article.

> We watched a lot of movies. We talked about how we would connect with other groups across the prairies. We were all watching that documentary [entitled] "How's your news?" and Kevin and I were wondering if we could get an RV and some banners. I was making lots of lists, and [came up with the idea of] the balloons. That could've been me asking do you think we could put some signs on the sides of the RV too? (Valerie Wolbert)

Everyone worked together and had an important role to play. Dave had the first hand experience of living in a large institution, and Kevin made sure we included as many stories as possible. It was very important for him to make sure that we didn't just focus on one person. He wanted to show that lots of people have survived institutions and that the People First movement has many active members. The Provincial Archives had pictures of MDC and Valerie decided to go find them:

> I found original pictures so I brought all the information back [to the group]. The original bathrooms of MDC, the bedrooms, the kitchen, I think there were about twenty-one pictures. We see those pictures right at the beginning of the film and People First of Canada also used those pictures at that conference, "Closing Institutions: Opening Communities." The lady at the archives in Winnipeg told me that out in Portage la Prairie, they have an archive at MDC, so we went there.

As we looked at the photo albums of people who had lived at MDC, and others who still did, we were shocked that none them had names to let us know who was in the picture. Family photo albums are such an important part of a person's life story, and it was sad to see that nobody took the time to put down the names. They were just pages and pages of anonymous faces looking back at us.

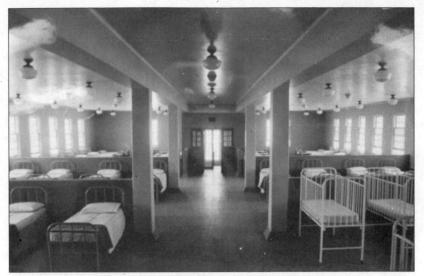

MDC *Dormitory, 1960s. Manitoba Provincial Archives*

Kevin was asking where the CEO was because we wanted to
ask her some questions, and they said she was in a meeting and
so Kevin thought they were not being truthful and Josée, and
I went downstairs and lo and behold guess who was there in
that cafeteria? None other than that CEO from MDC! (Valerie
Wolbert)

We weren't surprised that she didn't want to talk to us. We were starting
to get a reputation as troublemakers because we wanted institutions
shut down.

We went back to MDC a few more times. Dave wanted to visit his
friend Freddy and we asked him if he would like to be interviewed
for our video. He said that he would like that but he was under the
Public Trustee, a substitute decision maker appointed by the Province
of Manitoba. He didn't have the power to say yes or no. We had to
make a formal request for permission to the Public Trustee. Dealing
with them was like a roller coaster. They refused our first request
without even knowing anything about our movie! Josée called the
Public Trustee's office to ask how they could make a decision without
having all the facts. We were invited to send in a new request, which
they granted. Our victory was short-lived because a day before our
interview with Freddy, they told us they had changed their minds: it

311

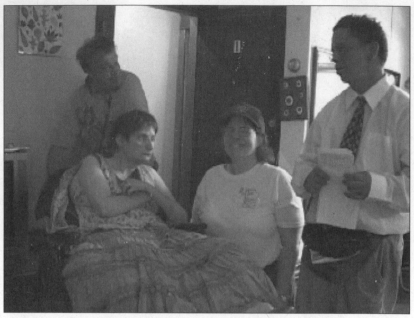

*Dave, Valerie and Kevin interview Catherine Shaefer while
Josée and Mark are behind the camera.*

was not in his best interest to participate in our film project.

Our first opportunity to actually film together as a team was on a
very hot summer day in 2006. We showed up for a huge celebration
with our video recording equipment and asked our questions.

> I remember our first time interviewing was at Catherine
> Schaefer's house. We got to meet Catherine. It was great
> to celebrate her birthday. It was a very hot day. She lives
> independently with live-in staff. [During the party] one
> of the MLAs was rude to us. We asked him if we could
> interview him and he was against it. But I remember Kevin
> interviewed the leader of the Liberal Party; he was nice.
> (Valerie Wolbert)

Susie hadn't joined us yet and it felt as though something was missing.
"In the beginning there was Kevin, Mark and David and I thought
we needed another woman so, we invited Susie" (Valerie Wolbert). In
the Fall of 2006, we approached Susie Weiszmann. She accepted and
became one of the co-directors of *The Freedom Tour*. Susie brought

312

with her a gift for performance, a good sense of humour and a warm personality:

> I'm funny, I like to joke around, I like to laugh, I like gospel songs; it cheers me up and I like Chris a lot [support worker driving RV]. (Susie Weiszmann).

In preparation for our two week Freedom Tour, the NFB funded the production of short video stories by all five People First members. Josée showed us some examples of video stories. We brought pictures of ourselves and our families and shared some personal stories about ourselves. Josée took notes and we made storyboards to give us an idea of what we would like to show in our video self-portraits. At first, we didn't know if we would put these videos in *The Freedom Tour* documentary or if they would just stand on their own.

For her video, Valerie filmed the small town where she grew up: "I felt it was so shocking when we went back to Poplar Point, it was a ghost town, the last time I went there was ten years ago" (Valerie Wolbert).

For Susie, making her video self-portrait was one of the highlights of The Freedom Tour process:

> I liked the short stories, the big church. And I sang "Amazing Grace." About David, I was concerned. My roommate too; she's been in institutions. Just tell people how to get families to get along. Why people don't learn about understanding feelings? Why do people have to be inside institutions? I'm going for it [closing institutions]! (Susie Weiszmann)

There was a lot of practising before we went on The Freedom Tour. We wanted to feel confident for our big trip. During the 2007 provincial election, we organized a candidates' debate where we showed our short video self-portraits and asked the candidates questions related to community supports and their position on the Manitoba Developmental Centre. There were over one hundred people in the audience. We were all up on the stage and Valerie kicked the evening off by talking about People First and the documentary we were working on:

*Susie and Josée prepare to film her video at the Westminster Church
in Winnipeg. This is where Susie sang "Amazing Grace."*

Still from Susie Weiszmann's video self-portrait.

I showed the map about where we were going to go [during
the Freedom Tour] and I was the master of ceremonies. Susie

· asked the candidates great questions. (Valerie Wolbert).

Remember, I sang "Amazing Grace" in the video on the big screen. (Susie Weiszmann).

And everyone was calling us movie stars after that! (Valerie Wolbert)

On another occasion, Valerie invited a community news reporter to ask us questions about our film and the tour. We took that opportunity to make a list of the questions media would most likely ask us during The Freedom Tour. This was also a very important exercise because it helped us prepare answers for the media with which we felt comfortable, and reflected People First values; thus we felt more confident when talking to the media. As a group, we prepared the questions we would be asking survivors about their experiences with institutions.

It was very exciting planning and I would call you [Josée] and ask did we forget this or that? I remember we did that video booth even before we went on the tour. I was upstairs in the PFC office booking that bus for the Walk and Roll for Freedom in Portage la Prairie. (Valerie Wolbert)

Valerie was a driving force throughout the entire process.

ON THE ROAD FOR FREEDOM

We spent a lot of time planning but we didn't really know how things would turn out once we went on the road. It was certainly a whirlwind Tour! We all remember very long days of driving to get from one place to the next, getting lost so many times! "Chris got stuck in the ditch!" (Susie Weiszmann). One time we got stuck after an especially long day of interviewing and a beautiful vigil organized by People First Saskatchewan at the old Valley View Centre cemetery. It must have been close to 11:30 pm. It was pitch black outside and Chris backed up the RV and it got stuck in the ditch! We were literally in the middle of nowhere. It had taken us hours to find this cemetery. How would we ever get out of here? Some of us were ready to cry! But instead of crying,

Valerie and Susie consult the schedule.

Chris slammed her foot on the gas pedal and the RV shot out of the ditch. What a sight that was. We were really lucky that night. A few other times we weren't so lucky, like when we crossed a very narrow bridge in Saskatoon and the awning of the RV ripped right off! We had to use duct tape to put it back together. We were so relieved that the RV rental company didn't charge us for that!

The Freedom Tour brought out strengths and weaknesses in everyone; there's nowhere to hide during these intense productions. We all had to depend on each other and the lines between paid support staff and people requiring support were often blurred. Valerie helped Susie with her diabetes. Shane Haddad, past president of People First of Canada, supported John Cox when he became ill during the Tour.

> Everybody gets experience working together as a group. We got to know people inside and outside and everything about them. There were difficult times too. We tried to help each other. I tried to help Susie as much as I could with her diabetes. I would push David in his wheelchair. (Valerie Wolbert)

Richard Ruston, the People First member representing the National Task Force on Deinstitutionalization, gave advice to our camera man who was not used to working in an unpredictable collaborative process: The film was important, but people and relationships had to come first. It was a constant balancing act trying to make sure everyone got what they needed with the expectation and responsibility to produce a documentary that we would all be proud of. We really had to have faith in our process, trust our hearts and our gut feelings.

Near the end of the Tour, we conducted an interview in Lethbridge Alberta with Michener Centre survivor Tedda Kaminski. Tedda told

Video still of Tedda Kaminski during an interview.

us how she saw staff hitting other residents. She also talked about all the work she and other residents did without getting paid. After the interview, we all went for coffee at Tim Horton's and talked about how the People First movement was doing in Alberta. As we drove Tedda back to her apartment, she asked if she could come with us to Calgary. Josée said if she didn't mind sharing a bed, she was more than welcome. Tedda responded "Give me thirty minutes"! She got her things ready in a flash and jumped into the car with us. Once in Calgary, Tedda spoke at our closing ceremony and came along with Susie and Josée to interview Judy Heward, another Michener Centre survivor. Tedda mostly listened while Josée and Susie asked questions about what had happened to Judy in that institution.

> Oh, and I really miss that woman and she died. I'm really sad that she died [Judy has since passed away]. And I remember that other lady [Tedda Kaminski] that came with us. You're supposed to be out of the institution! Why do people do that? Broken bones.… (Susie Weiszmann)

We were all upset to learn about the horrible abuses Judy had survived. Like many other people who were institutionalized in Canada, Judy was sterilized without her consent. Her Public Guardian had the power to authorize such things even without consulting with her family. Judy was so traumatized by her experience at that institution that she could not bear to hear the words "Michener Centre." To avoid making her feel scared and anxious, her sister Bonnie answered our questions while Judy went upstairs with one of her support staff.

All People First members on the Tour participated in the production process. Some of us asked questions, others helped out with loading and unloading equipment but everyone had the chance to see for themselves the amount of work that goes into making a film. "We weren't able to interview anybody that lived in the institutions so we interviewed people who lived outside the institutions" (Valerie Wolbert). Getting permission to interview a person inside an institution is not easy, especially since we don't like them and want them to shut down. Most people who live on the inside don't have the power to make their own decisions because, like Dave's friend Freddy, they are under the Public Trustee or Public Guardian. Permission has to be granted and since we are critical about the institutions, this permission is not easy to get. Another reason that led us not to pursue trying to interview residents was that some People First members told us they were worried that people living inside the institutions might not be safe if they said something negative. We got worried about that too and decided that talking to survivors was the best strategy to take.

> I think a lot of it was skill development. There are not a lot of professional opportunities for people [who have been labelled] with intellectual disabilities, to see the behind the scenes. I saw a lot of the emotional impact of being involved in the interviewing and hearing people's experiences in institutions. There was nothing about protection there, it was very real, very raw. You're not gonna get that in segregated settings. And all the community connections that have happened because of this. That's your goal as a support worker, you spend a lot of time protecting the people you support from stuff without wanting. Unfortunately, we keep people from living those experiences. (Chris Currie, Community Support Worker)

BEYOND THE FREEDOM TOUR

Once we got back from The Freedom Tour, it took us awhile to recover. We were all exhausted. It had been a demanding experience for all of us but we made it through! And, we still wanted to see each other after everything we'd been through. The process of editing our documentary took about seven months. Erika MacPherson was our editor and she was wonderful to work with. Josée spent a lot of time with her in the editing room and Valerie, Susie, Mark, Kevin, David and Chris would come in periodically to view the progress and give input. We even gave a rough copy to the Executive Committee of People First of Canada to see what they thought about it. We would make changes and consult each other again. We did our best to make sure that all People First members would be happy with *The Freedom Tour*.

We were very lucky when it came to music for the film. Musicians from within our community, some who had survived institutions themselves, wrote some especially for us:

> [It] was authentic, original because the Scott-Tones wrote the music and that other gentleman did the songs especially for us. And Peter Bourne sang especially for us too. He's a gentleman who has lived in a institution for a long time, Woodlands. (Valerie Wolbert)

> I really like the Scott-Tones, and Scott, I really like him. I want more music, I don't have enough, they're welcome to come to by birthday. (Susie Weiszmann).

Now that *The Freedom Tour* is out on DVD we often get invitations to present it and talk about it. It's keeping us and Chris, our advisor, very busy: "They say over a million people saw it!" (Valerie Wolbert) Some agencies providing support for people who have been labelled with an intellectual disability have started using *The Freedom Tour* as a tool to train their staff, so they can know what people have been through in institutions. It has been shown at different festivals, disability events and conferences and we are very proud of our work. As the new president of People First Manitoba, Valerie has been especially busy:

> I've been invited to do presentations and to get the word out there that nobody needs to live in institutions, they need to live in the community. It doesn't matter about the severity of their disability, we think about our abilities. I say labels belong on jars not on people. (Valerie Wolbert)

Our work has been recognized by our peers through awards from the Council of Canadians with Disabilities and Community Living Manitoba and People First of Canada's Pat Worth award. Susie received an honourable mention for her video self-portrait and travelled to Calgary Alberta to the Picture This ... International Disability Film Festival. "There were about 200 people over there! I was on the speaker, I sang my song 'Amazing Grace'" (Susie Weiszmann). It's a wonderful feeling when something you've worked so hard on is appreciated and useful.

I was interviewed for the [proposed] Canadian Human Rights Museum to share my personal story. I gave them a copy of *The Freedom Tour* when they had a gathering of the public. I'm hoping they're going to have a display of it and show it there. I've been getting lots of invitations to speak and things which is great. I got to show *The Freedom Tour* at the Global Justice Film Festival. I was nervous, a lot of people were there and they seemed to be happy to have a real person talking. We all went to Calgary together to show *The Freedom Tour* at the Picture This ... International Disability Film Festival, oh and Minneapolis! We all showed *The Freedom Tour* there, too. (Valerie Wolbert)

MAKE ANOTHER FILM?

Yes. I agree with that. About jobs, Handi-Transit. I'd like to go on the radio. How about making a story about me and my diabetes, a story about my life and part of the family? Maybe make a video about my roommate. I have good roommates, we like to go out, they're good workers, we do cooking in the house, the laundry together. (Susie Weiszmann)

Kind of like life outside of the institution: To tell people about their rights. That we can all live in homes and get married, have a job. We can talk about transportation. (Valerie Wolbert)

...or losing your job. I think we should interview Kathleen (Susie's house manager). I want to interview all my staff. (Susie Weiszmann)

The pride and the memories that have come out of that. You'll

Video still of Valerie Wolbert's video self-portrait.

forever be the people who helped people with intellectual disabilities' voice be heard. Friendships were developed. It was a beautiful journey to see from a support worker's point of view. (Chris Currie)

We went through a lot of stuff together. Some of the motels were pretty seedy and we had to eat on the road sometimes, we were on a very tight budget. We certainly got to know each other really well! (Josée Boulanger)

A lot of people went on that Tour. I'd like to go again. (Susie Weiszmann)

Well before [The Freedom Tour], things weren't very exciting, then things just really took off. I would do it again in a heartbeat! (Valerie Wolbert)

[1]David survived eighteen years at the Manitoba Development Centre and wants to see it be shut down. Freddy, David's friend at MDC, passed away. He never got out.

For a copy of *The Freedom Tour* documentary, contact: People First of Canada, Suite 5, 120 Maryland Street, Winnipeg, Manitoba, R3G 1L1, Canada. Phone: 1-204-784-7362; Members' Phone: 1-866-854-8915; Fax: 1-204-784-7364; Email: <info@peoplefirstofcanada.ca>.

To watch Susie and Valerie's video self-portraits, as well as other videos by people who have been labelled with an intellectual disability, visit: <www.labelfreezone.ca>.

PAT ISRAEL AND FRAN ODETTE

THE DISABLED WOMEN'S MOVEMENT

From Where Have We Come?

O
VER THE PAST TWENTY years, women with disabilities have organized and strategized to ensure that our "equality" rights were highlighted and addressed within the realm of both the women's movement and the disability rights movement. The kinds of organizing that have taken place over the past two decades has resembled that of a social movement, in which it's strength was in numbers and new ideas. The Disabled Women's Movement grew and flourished, demonstrating the creativity and initiative needed to have our voices heard. Even before DAWN Canada met in 1986, women with disabilities began organizing through writing about our own lives, in our own words. *Voices From the Shadows: Women with Disabilities Speak Out* by Gwyneth Matthews was one of the first Canadian publications dealing with issues for women living with disabilities. Also, in 1985 an issue of *Resources for Feminist Resources* dedicated an entire issue on "Women and Disability." For the first time a mainstream women's journal provided women with disabilities a forum in which to have their voices heard. This marked the beginning of an era in which women with disabilities demanded the right to take their place in the women's movement.

The momentum continued to swell when, in June 1985, women with disabilities from across Canada gathered at a national meeting to form DisAbled Women's Network Canada (DAWN Canada). This was an historic event since it was the first time that we had received funding to actually organize and come together to deal with our issues separately. Prior to this, disabled women's issues were ignored by both the disability rights movement and the women's rights movement. Many feminists did not seem to regard women with disabilities as women at all, while the disability rights movement failed to acknowledge that many of our issues were different from the issues affecting men with disabilities.

Both Canadian and U.S. feminist researchers and writers have highlighted the work of women with disabilities internationally (i.e., Laura Hershey; Diane Driedger; Susan Sygall and Cindy Lewis). Today, women with disabilities around the world continue to challenge stereotypes, participate in community life and politics, and lead organizations for social change. Women with disabilities encounter multiple barriers and in spite of these barriers they continue to work to become full and equal participants in their communities. While we represent up to twenty percent of the world's female population, many of us continue to experience the same problems and oppression faced by women everywhere. These critical concerns are also compounded by discrimination and inaccessibility related to disability. Education, training, employment, transportation and housing are oftentimes more difficult for women and girls with disabilities to access than our non-disabled sisters (Sygall and Lewis). Today, despite much of our work, the contributions and concerns held by women living with disabilities is not on the agenda of the many organizations that make up the global women's movement. Women with disabilities offer a powerful untapped resource to the movement for women's human rights. Women's organizations can enrich their programs if they take proactive steps to include disabled women by creating opportunities for all women in their communities.

Laura Hershey writes, "like other women around the world, women with disabilities are emerging from isolation to organize and fight for their rights and empowerment. Disabled women are reframing their individual struggles in a larger political and social context. As they meet in grassroots groups and exchange experiences across national borders, they are forming networks of support and a new culture of shared experience and pride." Sygall and Lewis list in their work some examples of how groups of women with disabilities are organizing for equality, some of which include:

•A national network of grassroots organizations of women with disabilities in Nicaragua, that works cooperatively to maximize support and political power throughout the country.

•The Uganda Disabled Women's Association operates a

revolving loan program for women with disabilities to initiate
small businesses. A travelling drama group raises community
awareness about women with disabilities.
•Women with disabilities in Russia are leading seminars on
sexuality and reproductive health.
•In the UK, Deaf women are providing peer support, materials
and training to enable Deaf women to obtain information and
access to health care; and finally,
•Women Pushing Forward (formerly Whirlwind Women) an
international women's wheelchair project, works with disabled
women to build and repair their own chairs, and earn additional
income to support their families. Women Pushing Forward
currently works with women and women's organizations in
Uganda, Mexico and Nicaragua.

Prolific feminist writers living with disabilities (many of whom
are part of DAWN Canada) write about the kinds of organizing and
advocacy related work that we are undertaking on our own behalf.
For many of us, this work is needed more than ever before. On every
continent, new leaders are emerging to oppose double discrimination
based on sex and disability. Whether we are working within existing
male-dominated disability groups to form women's groups, or
creating brand new women's organizations from the grassroots up,
many determined activists are bringing a gender perspective to the
international disability-rights movement. As well, many of us are
trying to meet the social and political agendas of the women attending
the meetings, creating opportunities for eliminating the barriers that
contribute to our isolation and offering ways by which we can nurture
our own self-respect and pride. Regardless of the points that bring us
together, we are developing and moving forward agendas for change,
and look toward the future where inequities that are associated with
disability are also inclusive of gender. There are new and emerging
leaders within our communities.

While progress has been made women's NGOs must work more closely
with disabled women to find creative, practical solutions to problems
of access that prevent them from developing and contributing their
expertise and skills. Leadership training and community projects must
undertake specific outreach efforts to include women with disabilities

at every level, as staff, consultants, participants, board members, and evaluators.

Both here in Canada and internationally, the women's community can no longer afford to overlook the immense resources that women with disabilities offer. We invite the global women's movement to expand the gender dialogue, to reach out and include women with disabilities in all efforts to achieve justice and women's human rights.

More than ever, issues for women with disabilities cannot "disappear"and need to remain on the agenda. DAWN women are not afraid to uncover the realities of our lives; proud to use the word "feminist" in our literature, and strive to be inclusive of all women with disabilities. Embracing diversity and our understanding of inclusion goes beyond that of gender and disability, as we know there is so much more about who we are that needs to be recognized and acknowledged in the work we do.

However, despite our work, the issue of ableism within the women's community and the movement as a whole still exists.For example, when workshops are offered that focus on issues for women with disabilities, the number of participants remains low. However, when our issues are included alongside the issues of other communities of women who experience marginalization, oftentimes, the attendance increases … it's hard to know if they're really coming to hear us or not. The reality is that although our lived experiences may be different, there are threads common to all women that bring us together. It is crucial that our concerns from the multiple locations and identities that are part of all women's experiences are not merely heard but are acted upon by those from the various movements of which we are a part, including the lesbian, gay, bisexual, trangender/transsexual, intersex, and queer (LGBTTIQ) communities, the movement of women of colour and women from various ethno-specific communities as well as the disability rights movement. We still cannot assume that workshops or women's conferences will be accessible or that our once non-disabled sisters who might be experiencing changes in their health and are living with disability will acknowledge or recognize our presence and the multitude of resources that we bring to these meetings.

The "social movement" of women with disabilities challenges the women's movement and the disability rights movement to begin acknowledging differing definitions of equality. Women who have been traditionally "marginalized" still need to be more welcomed by and included more within the women's movement and the disability rights movement. However, is this enough? More than seventeen years ago, Fran Odette interviewed 25 Canadian women with disabilities regarding their experiences with both the women's movement and the disability rights movement. Many women expressed frustration and isolation in their attempts to organize within these two movements. The notion that "difference is equated with inequality" captured many of the women's feelings of exclusion. Thus, one's "physical difference" can be and has been seen as a tool to be used against us in numerous ways.

Strides have been made, victories won, however, in writing this article, we know that there still needs to be much more work done in order for many women living with disabilities to feel that they are truly part of the movement of women—all women. Potential partnerships can exist without the appropriation of disabled women's voices. Academic women's journals are more reflective of diversity, however, more effort is needed to reflect the lived experiences of the communities of women whose voices we have not yet had a chance to learn from, including our sisters with disabilities, or who are Deaf/hard of hearing, who still find themselves on the fringes because of race, ancestry, sexual identity, age, poverty, ethnicity, and immigration status.

On May 19-21, 2006, DAWN Canada, with the generous support of Status of Women Canada, sponsored the Sowing the Seeds Conference. This conference came about to address issues impacting women with disabilities who "are one of the most economically, socially, legally and politically disadvantaged groups in the community. This disadvantage contributes to isolation from support networks and exclusion from decision-making processes that impacts on their lives, increasing their vulnerability to all forms of systemic discrimination and violence. For many women living with disabilities, it has been suggested by anecdotal evidence that "the recent cutting of social programs, has resulted in the increased exclusion and isolation of women with disabilities, across Canada" (DAWN Canada).

Sowing the Seeds Conference was organized to focus on enhancing effective needed strategic development to be undertaken by DAWN Canada in order to work towards ending the isolation and exclusion of women with disabilities and to assist them toward mobilizing community, developing local strengths and leadership, and effectively participate in policy and program developments aimed at improving their social conditions. This will be done in cooperation with community partners, which will facilitate the effectiveness of actions undertaken by DAWN Canada.

Along with many women's organizations across Canada, DAWN Canada has also experienced ongoing challenges in obtaining sustainable funding. However, it continues to do much work in ensuring equality rights for women living with disabilities across Canada. Some of the activities that DAWN has carried out recently are:

•Fundraising for the Sowing the Seeds Project and preparing for the 2006 Annual General Meeting;
•Participation with LEAF in the VIA Rail court case;
•Participating in the Status of Women Canada meeting—Gender equality consultation;
•Participating in Service Canada meeting ;
•Participating in an e-list on United Nations Convention on Elimination of Discrimination for Persons with Disabilities and a second e-list on women's articles;
•Attended equality national conference;
•National Shelter Survey to determine levels of access for women with disabilities entering women's shelters and transition houses.

Through the participation of diverse women in the Sowing the Seeds Conference (2006), we have witnessed the development of women's leadership skills, which over time have been enhanced and strengthened, thereby enabling Canadian leaders to organize local, provincial, territorial grassroots groups of women with disabilities and support their effective participation both in the national organization as well as in Canadian society.

Change is around the corner. We are women first and belong with women's communities in the struggle to fight all women's oppressions; we have lots to offer and will not stay on the sidelines. We also need to relish in our difference. Diversity along the continuum of movement and experience is critical for our work and for our movement to survive and be true to all women. The experiences that women with disabilities bring to the women's movement are invaluable. Join with us to ensure "equality" for all women.

Originally published in Canadian Woman Studies: An Introductory Reader *(Toronto: Inanna Publications, 2006) pp. 589-594. Reprinted with permission.*

REFERENCES

DisAbled Women's Network (DAWN) Canada. Online: <www.dawncanada.net>.

Driedger, Diane and Susan Gray, eds. *Imprinting Our Image: An International Anthology by Women with Disabilities.* Charlottetown: Gynergy Books, 1992.

Hershey, Laura. "Disabled Women Organize Worldwide to Build Unity and Power." Crip Commentary.

Matthews, Gwyneth Ferguson. *Voices from the Shadows: Women with Disabilities Speak Out.* Canada: Women's Educational Press, 1983.

Odette, Francine. *Women with Disabilities: The Third "Sex"—The Experience of Exclusion in the Movement Toward Equality.* Independent Enquiry Project in partial requirement for Masters of Social Work Degree, Carleton University, Ottawa: Faculty of Social Work, 1993.

Stewart, Houston, Beth Percival and Elizabeth R. Epperly, eds. *The More We Get Together: Women and Disability.* Charlottetown: Gynergy Books, 1992.

Sygall, Susan and Cindy Lewis. "Tapping into the Power of Women with Disabilities in the International Women's Movement." *Raising Our Voices: The Newsletter of the Global Fund for Women* July 2000.

BONNIE BRAYTON

LEADERSHIP, PARTNERSHIP AND NETWORKING

A Way Forward for the DisAbled Women's
Network of Canada

I N JUNE 2010 THE DisAbled Women's Network (DAWN) began our
twenty-fifth year in service to women and girls with disabilities in
Canada—in another book we hope to chronicle and reflect on the
whole of our history, but this is about the years 2007 to 2010 and what
those years have brought us to—our new DAWN.

A NEW DAWN

In December 2006, our President, Carmela Hutchison, together with
a dedicated group of women with disabilities activists/volunteers, who
are the Board of DAWN Canada, successfully secured funding for a
national project with Status of Women Canada focused on violence
and housing for women with disabilities. The Board determined that
a key step in truly establishing a national presence was to establish a
new national head office in Québec and to rename the organization to
reflect a bilingual focus in our work.

On May 1, 2007, the National Head Office of the DisAbled Women's
Network/Réseau d'action de femmes handicapées (DAWN-RAFH)
Canada was opened in Montreal in the Maison Parent Roback. The
Maison is unique to Québec—a feminist collective that provides office
space, shared meeting rooms, resources, and a wide range of supports
to some of the largest women's organizations in the province.

A new (leadership) position was created, National Executive Director.
A strategic plan for our organization to sustain itself over the medium
and long term required an individual with experience in management,
administration, and fundraising. My background in both the public
and private sector as a manager is combined with a definite bent for

the entrepreneurial qualities needed to "re-vision" and to re-postion our organization in a leadership role and appears to be moving us in the right direction.

In my early days as the National Executive Director, Shelley Breau, our PEI representative, called about once a week. Yesterday, when Shelley telephoned me, it was to tell me that Sherrill is dying. I began to weep. "She said your name Bonnie. I think she wanted me to tell you good bye." Sherrill Ing is a founding member of DAWN-PEI, a small group of women with disabilities from the Charlottetown area who, under the defiant spell of Peggy Reddin, began a disabled women's dance group in the mid 1980s. Today, Sherrill is the Co-chair of our Prince Edward Island Affiliate. I have been weeping on and off since yesterday. Maybe I am a little over-tired as we have had a lot of long days and deadlines lately, but I cannot shake the image of Sherrill and Shelley with me in a photograph I have—smiling over a business lunch of fish and chips we enjoyed at a local pub, when I visited them in 2007. It was a golden day. The DAWN meeting had been a great success, with music, pizza, prayers, a turn around the table to talk about the journals we had presented to each of the members, and the magnificent blanket hand-made by Shelley and presented to me.

Sherrill faithfully sent reports to the head office, detailing the meetings, who she drove, who attended, the balance in the account, and little bits of information until the spring of this year. Sherill lost both her parents, just months apart, and now her own life is slipping away.

Sherrill has been our rock—mine and Shelley's. I first met Sherrill and Shelly when I was invited by our DAWN Nova Scotia representative, Jane Warren, to a conference called "Tools for Life" being held in Wolfville in October 2007. I planned a road trip to meet Jane and attend the Conference and decided to take a side trip so I could also meet Shelley, our Prince Edward Island rep, and our membership face-to-face. I was still new and trying to feel my way around our work by attending meetings, accepting invitations and attending conferences, which is still the very best way to do our work—networking.

Shelley's hands have knitted and crocheted many blankets over these years. We presented one to the only women's shelter on the Island, Anderson House, for the disabled mothers' room on the first floor. Blankets have been made to raffle off at the local Walmart where Shelly and Sherrill set up tables together and sold raffle tickets. Raffling the blankets helped offset the cost to have meetings and the transport necessary to bring the women together once a month.

As resourceful and independent as she has always been, Shelley has recently had to move to assisted living outside of Charlottetown. Shelley's carpel tunnel syndrome is so severe now it hurts her to knit and crochet and she misses it. When she called me earlier this week, we knew Sherrill was sick but it sounded like it might be fine somehow, so we mused about knitting machines for future raffles. I was working on this article when I learned that Sherrill had passed away.

I want to honour Sherrill and Shelley today by telling you about them—these incredible and yet ordinary women. I have the blanket that Shelley knit, and the women of DAWN Prince Edward Island gave me, wrapped around my legs as I write this.

From a room in Lower Montague, Prince Edward Island and in each province and territory of Canada there are incredible and ordinary women and girls with disabilities—forgotten sisters, mothers, daughters and neighbours *living the edges*. I write this to honour them all.

2007—A NEW NATIONAL HEAD OFFICE AND RE-ESTABLISHING OUR VOICE

In our first year at the new head office in Montreal, and my first year as our National Executive Director, we were encouraged by the level of support we found waiting for us in both the feminist and the disability communities, where social justice and social inclusion are a central focus.

DAWN-RAFH Canada plays a unique role as the only national organization led by and for women with disabilities—bridging the gaps between the two. In both the feminist and disability sectors, millions of Canadians face systemic barriers, discrimination, increased rates of violence, a complete void of affordable, accessible housing, alarming rates of poverty, and the lowest employment and literacy levels. Among them, women and girls with disabilities are at the greatest risk—despite this, recognition, research and resources related to us remains virtually non-existent.

At the heart of our mission and our strategy these past three years and going forward, is our urgent call to every leader in every corner of this country, mayors to Members of Parliament, CEOs and NGO Directors, Coordinators, Chairs, City Planners, to First Nations Leaders—bring us to the table! A review of the places we have been and the networking and partnerships we have been building on, speaks to the effectiveness of that strategy—one we continue to build on (see our Annual Reports at <www.dawncanada.net>).

The unanticipated but very real result of these years of work, has been the number of calls and requests for assistance we have received from women with disabilities in crisis from all corners of Canada—with no mandate, resources to offer referrals or crisis support in place, we made no attempt to undertake such outreach, but women continue to call because they desperately need assistance and do not know where else to turn. This disturbing phenomena speaks to the core of our mission and the reason we continue to exist as an organization and to speak for the millions of women with disabilities who have been waiting their whole lives now for their share of equality, justice, and prosperity.

2008—NEW WORK LINKED TO OUR PAST AND OUR FUTURE

The most significant undertaking of its kind since DAWN Canada's ground-breaking work on access to shelters for women with disabilities from the late 1980s and early 1990s, "Bridging the Gaps—Violence, Poverty and Housing: An Update on Non/Resources for Women with Disabilities" (DAWN-RAFH Canada) is a summary of an eighteen-month project funded by the Status of Women Canada's Community Fund that brought our organization back to a leadership position for the women we serve. The response to this first phase, in what we anticipate will be a multi-year project, affirms our unique position as the only national organization in Canada working on reducing the alarming rates of violence against women with disabilities, improving our access to community resources, shelters and housing, and addressing the extreme poverty, particularly that of single mothers and senior women and women who face triple jeopardy: Aboriginal, racialized, immigrant, and LGBT women with disabilities.

The tool developed during this project, the National Accommodation and Accessibility Survey (NAAS), which surveyed just over ten percent of all women's shelters in Canada, provided valuable information to us and to the Government of Canada while also providing very clear, current guidelines to shelter workers and administrators on how to make their facilities more accessible, from installing the right kind of doorknobs to the need for TTY technology for deaf women and everything in between. This very transferable "tool for change" will be used and expanded in the next phase of this work.

The idea of an International Panel at the First World Conference of Women's Shelters was as epic a journey as any who come after us will take. The whole thing started with a Skype call with Carolyn Frohmander, my counterpart from Women with Disabilities Australia (WWDA). Their work on violence prevention is a good decade ahead of ours. Sue Salthouse, the rep from WWDA, came to attend the conference from halfway round the world. Eudalie Wickham, came to Canada from Barbados to share the Podium with Sue and our representative, Dr. Michelle Owen. (In an absurd sidebar that only women with disabilities can appreciate, note that there was no Podium to share because it was not accessible—no ramp; ah, but that is another story). More than seven hundred delegates and presenters from around the world attended the conference—the only voices from among many to speak for two hundred million women around the world.

2009—TIME TO REFLECT

In a report to our funders last year, on a particularly tough day, I wrote that oppression was the meeting place between gender and disability. It was a heavy statement and still resonates when I say it because it is the truth, our truth.

Not long after, on a particularly good day, our new mantra came to me, as naturally as if it had always been there. Leadership, partnership and networking—this simple expression of hope for our future suggests an open strategic approach that reflects our wider vision of inclusion and working on social justice issues beyond our mandate to serve women and girls with disabilities. We gave our goddess logo an update and added the Canadian Maple Leaf as her backdrop. DAWN Saskatchewan and RAFH Québec have added the Prairie lily and fleur-de-lys to theirs respectively, to great effect. We plan to add a special banner for June 2010 to July 2011 in celebration of our Silver Anniversary.

(C) E.J. Miller-Towle

DAWN ♦ RAFH
Canada

25 ans au service des femmes handicapées
25 years of service to women with disabilities

PEER MENTORS: "PROMISE LESS, DELIVER MORE"

Carmela Hutchison is the DAWN-RAFH President. We first met on the Hill, about thirty minutes before entering Centre Block and presenting a Brief on Economic Security to the Parliamentary Committee on the Status of Women. Carmela was prepared, with a written statement that included statistics and some powerful anecdotes to frame the situation of our women, presented in that way our dear Parliamentarians appear to prefer. This was my third day in service and I had *no idea* of the meaning of "appearing." I had originally suggested to Carmela in one of our first (of hundreds) calls, that I could take notes and give her a call after the meeting. If she laughed to herself, she never let on to me. She just told me crisply (years before Carmela had been a nurse in the military) that we would be fine. Carmela is a multiple, brain-injured, mobility-challenged, and brilliant woman. She had come prepared.

She had written a wonderful, simple statement for me to read that day as well. It included a greeting and thanks to the Haudenosaunee Six Nations People—another one of her "teaching" moments that I have come to appreciate more fully with time.

I have lost track of the number of Boards Carmela serves on and stopped counting after ten. Her years of governance experience have benefited DAWN-RAFH Canada. We continue to grow and the governance instruments and structure that are in place now, reflect this process as we go through it. We have had our share of growing pains. This is evident as we struggle with the complexity and tensions of trying to realize the expectations and aspirations of a nation of women who have been oppressed in so many ways that trust is in short supply.

I met Pat Danforth for the first time when I accompanied Carmela to the 2007 Annual General Meeting of the Council of Canadians with Disabilities. I knew some of the names from reading bits of our history, Yvonne Peters and Pat Danforth among them. Big dossiers were on the Agenda as the ink was still drying from Canada's signing of the Convention of the Rights of People with Disabilities and the Via Rail case had just been won at the Supreme Court.[1] It was a good place to learn and allowed me, for the first time in my post, to do what I do exceedingly well: working a room (I come from a management and fundraising background).

Carmela and I were both struck by how the women across the room began unconsciously gathering. By lunch time we were many. Pat was at the table next to ours.

Meeting Pat Danforth, much like when I met Carmela and so many of the other women (and men) who have supported us these past three years, was like meeting another long-time friend. Because she is one of the founding members of our organization, I think I expected her to be older, but she is young in appearance and has an energy that is almost palpable. We talked that day and planned a meeting in Montreal—she was presenting at an international transportation symposium. We met over lunch in Chinatown across from the Convention Centre that had just been redressed in multi-coloured glass, our choices limited by the usual absence of accessible restaurants.

"Promise less, deliver more." Perhaps not her own words, but this was the sage advice Pat offered me that day when I pressed her on how I should approach our work. Intellectually I understood her point when she said it, but it has taken a long time to take hold of this advice in practice and is all the more complicated to apply when you are trying to re-establish your credibility, which is where we were at the time.

We must always project bigger if we are going to be taken seriously and "inserting" our organization in places we've been forgotten, was and continues to be an important way in which we do our work. The next challenge that arises is maintaining our position once the divide is bridged.

Our longevity and earlier work established our voice but it is not enough in this digital and global age. Our relevance is still tied to the same issues as it was by the women who first claimed our earthy goddess as a symbol for our cause, with her fists raised in hope and defiance—stopping the violence and ending the poverty of women with disabilities.

THE CENTENNIAL FLAME AWARD 2009

The women involved in the founding of our organization remain an inspiration to me, to our staff, our Board, our members, and to many young women in university studies in Canada and beyond our borders. We regularly receive requests for information about the founding members and would be much better able to respond to these enquiries with this important piece of our history properly documented. We were delighted to support the nomination of Diane Driedger for the award based on her application to research and then write about the seventeen women with disabilities who met in Ottawa, which resulted in the founding of our organization in June 1985. We hope to organize a large conference later in the year to celebrate both our new and founding leaders and to share Diane's insights from this research.

On June 22, 2010, with great honour and reverence, I stood with Diane beside the Centennial Flame on Parliament Hill in Ottawa and listened as she spoke the names of each of the seventeen women who came together twenty-five years earlier to bring this organization and our movement to life.

Diane's work has been important to me. Above me, on the wall in my office, is an enormous portrait of Frida Kahlo with the words "PASION" emblazoned in red. I bought this painting after a show of Frida's work here in Montreal, a decade before I began this work. I also have a watercolour print, painted by Diane, which is a portrait of her and Frida Kahlo—their hearts are visible and connected. This painting is a re-working of Kahlo's painting, "The Two Fridas," and evokes Diane's connection to another woman, another artist, with a disability. Frida painted until her death. I am quite sure Diane will paint for as long as she lives, giving artistic expression to many of the issues and barriers that women with disabilities face on an ongoing basis.

2010—CONVERGENCE

How do we go forward? After twenty-five years so much has changed, yet so much remains the same. It seems at every gathering and conference these past years there has been much debate about where we've come from and how far we have to go. We are experts on inclusion and exclusion and this is our legacy and our way forward.

In March 2010 Canada finally ratified the CRPD the Convention on the Rights of Persons with Disabilities and the Feminist Movement apparently turned 50!? We now hold two international legal instruments in our hands that demand equality for women and girls with disabilities in Canada as a fundamental right.

In June 2010, we hosted a Provincial Round Table at the Montreal Head Office. Our theme was violence prevention and women with disabilities. It is our new mantra in action—a first in Québec—and it brought together the leadership of some twenty-five organizations from the disability and women's sector to share ideas, concerns, and contact information. It was a huge success and the first of many. We will be looking to undertake similar activities in other regions across the country during this pivotal year.

The 2011 Women's World Conference, which this year will be held in Ottawa, will begin as we end our 25th year in July 2011. The opportunity to be a part of this, the largest feminist gathering in Canadian history, is another leadership story. We have been brought in as consultants to ensure that it is the most accessible and inclusive global women's conference ever held. Thematically the conference is about the women from the margins and bringing us to the centre—*inclusions, exclusions, and seclusions*—women in a globalized world. How can one not be hopeful with this bright moment in our near future. Our women, at the podium, on the stage, presenting and collaborating—from the beginning process to the closing ceremonies, we will be there.

I often feel the presence of our "ghost and gone sisters"—with fists raised and bread and roses they break down those invisible walls that have separated us from our freedom for so very long now. They drop little miracles into our days to keep us hopeful and determined. I resist the temptation to add the word "strong"and have come to a point where I choose my words with much more care.

Leadership, partnership and networking. Staying on message and focused is beginning to show real, tangible results. Seeing our future in a medium and long-term context and not from grant-to-grant and project-to-project basis, and recognizing the depth of experience and knowledge we bring to the table, also shows results. DAWN-RAFH Canada is not about building a network—the network is already there. We are about building leadership and good governance among our own women and engaging leadership to partner with us in the places where we work, where we learn, where we worship, where we mother, where we love, and where we live.

[1]This was a Charter Challenge by the Council of Canadians (CCD) with Disabilities. DAWN Canada was an intervener. Via Rail bought inaccessible passenger rail cars and CCD went to court to prevent a publicly-funded Crown Corporation from buying new equipment that was inaccessible to people with disabilities. The Court ruled that persons with disabilities are members of the public and Via Rail is responsible to ensure that its services are accessible.

REFERENCES

Council of Canadians with Disabilities vs. Via Rail Canada Inc. Via Rail Supreme Court Appeal. Online: <http://www.ccdonline.ca/en/transportation/rail/supreme-court-appeal>.

DisAbled Women's Network/Réseau d'action de femmes handicapées (DAWN-RAFH) Canada. "Bridging the Gaps—Violence, Poverty and Housing: An Update on Non/Resources for Women with Disabilities." Prepared by Jewelles Smith. Montreal: DAWN-RAFH Canada, November 2008.

CONTRIBUTOR NOTES

Jancis M. Andrews was born in the UK in 1934. At fourteen years of age she ran away from her violent home and refused to return to school. In Canada, she enrolled in grade nine, finally obtaining a BFA from the University of British Columbia. She is the award-winning author of *Rapunzel, Rapunzel, Let Down Your Hair and Other Stories* and *Walking on Water and Other Stories*. Jancis is a community volunteer living in Sechelt.

Joy Asham is a Cree Storyteller and Storymaker and a cultural activist. Before being slowed down by disabilities, she was an exuberant performer/playwright and freelance writer. For the last fifteen years, she has been a columnist for the *Thunder Bay Chronicle Journal*, writing about the Aboriginal experience. In her work she has found that people are not so much that different, as we all smile, cry, laugh, and feel deep loss when our loved ones hurt. Asham has been the recipient of many arts awards and has achieved critical success for much of her work. Her arts achievements followed a sensitive social work career where her specialties lay in community and organizational development while also working one-on-one with victim healing issues.

Marie Annharte Baker was born in 1942 in Winnipeg where she is working on a manuscript which explores Indigena silence. She believes that life story and contemporary storytelling are ways of making metissage out of fragmentary identities. Her poetry collections include *Being on the Moon* (1990), *Coyote Columbus Cafe* (2004), and *Exercises in Lip Pointing* (2003). She is a member of DAWN Winnipeg and a grandmother of three. Her son is Forrest Funmaker, educator and writer.

The **Association for Community Living-Manitoba** is an advocacy group dedicated to the full inclusion in the community of persons of all ages who live with an intellectual disability.

Maria Barile has more than thirty years experience as a community worker with women with disabilities. She is one of the original group of seventeen women who started the DisAbled Women's Network (DAWN) Canada, and one of the founders of Action des femmes handicapées (Montréal). Having published in the area of disability, feminism, and technology, Maria offers workshops and lectures on issues of ableism/disableism. In the past twenty years, she has presented to various commissions on the use of depo provera, violence, and other issues that affect women with disabilities and advocated to improve access to the health care system and women's shelters (for women with disabilities). She works as a consultant in her company Eco Access and is co-director of the Adaptech Research Network based at Dawson College.

Josée Boulanger is a community filmmaker and graduate student in Disability Studies at the University of Manitoba. She uses collaborative video storytelling as a way for people who have been labelled with an intellectual disability to share their knowledge, express themselves, and teach others from lived experiences.

Bonnie Brayton is the National Executive Director of the DisAbled Women's Network of Canada (DAWN-RAFH). DAWN Canada has been focused on advancing the rights of women with disabilities for twenty-five years in Canada and internationally. She is also the President of Coup de Balai-Clean Sweepers, a social economy organization in her community. Bonnie also serves on the Boards of the Canadian Centre for Disability Studies and La Maison Parent-Roback (a Quebec feminist collective) in Montreal. Bonnie lives in Montreal with her partner, Delmar, and their two daughters, Leah and Virginia, their two cats, Bowser and Felix, and Tsoukie the wonder poodle. Originally from a small town in Northern Québec, Bonnie Brayton's career spans more than 30 years in the private and public sector.

Carrie R. Cardwell is an artist and an Expressive Arts therapist (since 1985). Currently she enjoys working with Deaf, hard-of-hearing, and hearing individuals, couples and families in her private practice in the west end of Toronto; as well she works part time in a community-based Deaf and hard-of-hearing children's mental health program in Milton. She lives with her two teenage sons. For more information, see her website <carriecardwell.com>.

Charlotte Caron is currently Acting Principal of the Centre for Christian Studies in Winnipeg. She has written several articles on living with chronic illness including "Water Wearing on a Stone: The Role of Shame in the Social Construction of Chronic Illness" in *Dissonant Disabilities: Women with Chronic Illnesses Explore Their Lives* (2008). She and Gail Christy worked together in the Barbwire Collective to write *Not All Violins: Spiritual Resources for Women with Disabilities and Chronic Illnesses* (1997).

Gail Christy, whose mobility impairment is the result of Cerebral Palsy, is a recently retired member of the Order of Ministry of The United Church of Canada where for twenty-seven years she served pastorates in Saskatchewan and eastern Ontario. She has written for children about living with disability and now tries to educate her grandsons about these challenges. She thoroughly understands living on the edge and despite retirement continues to do so as she ministers as United Church chaplain at Elisabeth Bruyere Hospital, does consulting for Bereaved Families of Ontario-Ottawa Region, and acts as Spiritual Director.

Community Living-Winnipeg is an organization that focuses on enhancing the lives and status of people living with an intellectual disability by promoting full inclusion and participation in the community. The Women's Group, comprised of women with intellectual disabilities and non-disabled women, came together to develop a process of self-exploration that came to be called "Walking a Woman's Path."

Doreen Demas has been active in the disability consumer movement and the First Nations community for many years. More recently, she has been involved in the First Nations disability self-help movement, at an international, national and regional level. She is currently Executive Director of the First Nations disABILITY Association of Manitoba Inc. Her personal experience as a Dakota woman with a visual impairment has helped shape her skills and abilities as an activist, researcher, and policy analyst in both the First Nation and disability communities.

Julie Devaney is a health activist who advocates for patient and disability rights through her writing, performances, and workshop facilitation. Her memoir, *My Leaky Body*, will be published by Key Porter Books in 2011. She has a Master's Degree in Critical Disability Studies from York University in Toronto. Find her online at: <www. myleakybody.com>.

Prior to her death in August 2004, **Tanis Doe** was a respected Fulbright scholar, mother, gay rights activist and Canadian who identified as having Aboriginal ancestry. As an academic and activist Tanis's work in Canada and in the United States was situated in some of the historic centres that were part of the revolution and evolution of the Canadian and American Disability Rights Movement. Her accomplishments included work with the DisAbled Women's Network, Council for Canadians with Disabilities (formally known as the Coalition of Provincial Organizations of the Handicapped), University of California: Berkeley, Gallaudet University, the World Institute on Disability and the Ryerson University, School of Disability Studies. Working from her own lived experience, personal and political, Tanis contributed to the development of disability studies programs, challenged barriers to post-secondary education, worked to draw attention to the issues of violence against women with disabilities, and communicated her perspective of motherhood and parenting from the lens of a person who identified with multiple racialized communities.

Anjali Dookeran was a gifted visual artist, whose forte was watercolour painting. She had a Bachelor of Fine Arts and a Master's of Library Science. Her work was shown in solo and group exhibitions in Winnipeg. Recently, her painting from the Red Series graced the cover of *Dissonant Disabilities: Women with Chronic Illnesses Explore Their Lives* (2008). Anjali had chronic illness. She passed away in 2007.

Kelly-Jo Dorvault is a multi-media artist who uses her personal experiences as a reference point for her art and as a tool for creating dialogue. Combining different techniques, materials and processes is one way she uses to explore how everything is connected and to deal with the crossovers between reality and fantasy.

Diane Driedger has written extensively about the issues of women and people with disabilities over the past thirty years. Her book *The Last Civil Rights Movement: Disabled Peoples' International* was published in 1989. She has co-edited two international anthologies by disabled women and, most recently, co-edited with Michelle Owen, *Dissonant Disabilities: Women with Chronic Illnesses Explore Their Lives* (2008). Diane is an educator, administrator, activist, and researcher in the area of disabled women's issues in Canada and internationally. She is also a visual artist and poet, and holds a Ph.D. in Education. She lives in Winnipeg.

Jane Field, a former high school teacher and literacy worker, is a writer and singer-songwriter, a speaker and performer in the Toronto area. She was a wheelchair user for fifteen years, quadriplegic for six of those years, before she met a doctor in 2002 who told her she had a treatable nerve disease. Since undergoing extensive treatment, she no longer requires a wheelchair, but continues to straddle the boundaries of identity and belonging in the disabled and non-disabled communities. Her lesbian identity remains unchanged.

Cheryl Gibson worked as a psychologist for the Ontario Ministry of Education until she was labelled permanently disabled after a "failed back operation" in 1989. She continues to work in her profession by giving workshops on journalism and running a small private practice from her home. She has two children and two grandchildren and lives in a small community in Eastern Ontario where she has learned what the term "community" really means.

Nancy E. Hansen, Associate Professor, is Director of the Interdisciplinary Master's Program in Disability Studies at the University of Manitoba. Nancy is researching in the areas of literacy, culture history, health care, ethics, and human geography as they relate to disability issues in daily life.

Kyla Harris grew up in Canada with a family history of artists. Her work and life took a dramatic turn when she had a diving accident in 2000. Since then she has been interested in the viewpoints of minorities. She now predominantly paints figurative work in oils at her studio in East London.

Laura Hockman, BSW, RSW, MA, is the Executive Director of Independent Living Vernon. Her nickname is Betty Rubble because of her giggle, and she has four dogs (Gabbi, Armegeddon, Nightmare, and Kilo) who help her keep her sense of humour.

Esther Ignagni is an Assistant Professor in the School of Disability Studies at Ryerson University. A former community health worker, she was an organizer and advocate in the anti-violence and HIV/AIDS action movements during the late 1980s and 1990s. As someone with lived and work experience in the area of disability, her academic work involves the use of sociological theories to explore citizenship as a determinant of disabled people's health. She is also involved in several projects exploring the use of new media in constructing new knowledges of disability and in constructing new ways for disabled people to transform their personal and collective realities.

Pat Israel is proud to be a disabled feminist. She lives in Toronto in a barrier free house with her partner of many years, John, and her dear mom, Helen. Emma the wonder dog, along with Sarah and Phebe, the cats extraordinaire, also race around in this house.

Sally A. Kimpson is a disabled nurse, disability activist, and scholar with direct experience of living on income support, and a deep interest in how public policy constructs the lives of disabled women with disabilities in ways that create barriers to social and economic equality. She is currently completing her Interdisciplinary Ph.D. (Nursing and Education) at the University of Victoria. With its focus on the socio-economic well-being of disabled women, in particular how they live with the policies and practices to which they are subject, Sally's dissertation makes links between poverty, health and social justice in disabled women's lives.

Sarah Murray is a portrait and documentary photographer, who lives in Vancouver, B.C. At the age of twenty, she began her studies in manual photography at Focal Point. By 1996, Sarah was shooting professionally. She is constantly exploring her fascination with the human condition through her camera lens. Sarah has balanced her love of portraiture and travel through her photography, and a career that allows her to be a global citizen with an eye on the world.

Lynda Nancoo is currently working in the financial industry as a technical analyst. She spends her spare time encouraging young girls to write about their life experiences especially if they have been touched by disability.

Renee Norman is an award-winning poet, writer, and teacher. Her most recent collection of poetry, *Martha in the Mirror,* was published by Inanna Publications in the spring of 2010. Her first volume of poetry, *True Confessions,* was awarded the prestigious Helen and Stan Vine Canadian Jewish Book Award for Poetry in 2006. Her second volume of poetry, *Backhand Through the Mother,* was published in 2007. Renee's doctoral dissertation, *House of Mirrors: Performing Autobiograph(icall)y in Language/Education,* received the Canadian Association for Curriculum Studies Distinguished Dissertation Award and was published in 2001. She lives in Coquitlam, British Columbia.

Tracy Odell lives with her husband, David, in Scarborough, Ontario. Married for twenty-three years, they are now grandparents, thanks to her daughter, Katie, who was mentioned in this article. Their younger daughter is studying classics in her third year of university. Tracy is currently employed by the province of Ontario as their Director for Accessibility Program Design and Delivery. Despite all predictions to the contrary, Tracy and her many relationships are still alive and well.

Fran Odette is a disabled, queer, feminist activist who has been actively working in the area of equality rights for persons with disabilities for more than eighteen years. Fran works with the women's community around issues of access to services for women with disabilities, particularly with regards to services for survivors of violence. Trainer/ educator, researcher and writer, much of Fran's work has been supporting service providers in the violence against women sector as well as social service agencies to make the linkages needed to ensure that all women have access to services.

Michelle Owen is an Associate Professor in the Sociology Department at the University of Winnipeg and Acting Coordinator of the new Disability Studies Program. Current projects include an investigation of how Canadian academics with multiple sclerosis negotiate the workplace. She co-edited, with Diane Driedger, *Dissonant Disabilities: Women with Chronic Illnesses Explore Their Lives* (2008).

Alexandra Pasian is a poet, freelance writer, and professor of composition and professional writing living with her family in Montreal.

Wendy Porch has a M. Ed. from the Ontario Institute for Studies in Education/University of Toronto. Most recently, she was a Research Fellow at The Open University UK where she was engaged in European research projects aimed at ensuring access for people with disabilities to Lifelong Learning. She was a facilitator in the Building Bridges Project in 2003 and 2004.

Dianne Pothier of the Schulich School of Law at Dalhousie University has been a member of the law faculty since 1986 (Full Professor since 2001). Teaching and research subjects include: constitutional, conflicts, public, labour, human rights, equality, and disability. Previous employment includes being legal counsel to the Canada Labour Relations Board (1984-1986) and a Supreme Court of Canada law clerk to Justice Brian Dickson (1983). Litigation experience includes being the appellant's co-counsel in the Supreme Court of Canada in *R.D.S. v. The Queen*, [1997] 3 S.C.R. 484, and being counsel for the joint intervention of LEAF and DAWN in *British Columbia v. Auton*, [2004] 3 S.C.R. 657. Awards include the University Medal in Law

(Dalhousie Law School, 1982) and the Frances Fish Women Lawyers' Achievement Award from the Nova Scotia Association of Women and the Law (2005). Publications include being the co-editor, along with Richard Devlin, of *Critical Disability Theory: Essays in Philosophy, Politics, Policy and Law* (2006).

Carla Rice is Associate Professor in Women's Studies at Trent University in Peterborough, Ontario, where she lectures in culture, health, and psychology. A leader in the field of body image and difference within Canada, she is a founding member or former director of innovative initiatives such as the National Eating Disorder Information Centre, the Body Image Project at Women's College Hospital in Toronto, and Envisioning New Meanings of Disability and Difference, an Ontario-wide arts-based partnership project with the YWCA. Her research explores representations and life history narratives of body and identity.

Sharon Dale Stone is Professor of Sociology at Lakehead University. Her current research and teaching focus on critical disability studies, social gerontology, and qualitative research methods. She has also taught and maintains a keen interest in feminist studies, queer studies, and critical media studies. She recently published the book, *A Change of Plans: Women's Stories of Hemorrhagic Stroke* (2007) which was based on SSHRC-funded research, and she is working on producing another book-length manuscript based on that research. She is also a co-investigator on a project examining the workplace experiences of academics with multiple sclerosis, and on another project examining the consequences of workplace injury.

Milana Todoroff continues her traveling adventures. Since her trip to Europe, she has been to China and Tibet and has recently returned from a trip to Turkey.

Susan Wendell is Professor Emerita of Women's Studies at Simon Fraser University. She wrote *The Rejected Body: Feminist Philosophical Reflections on Disability* (1996) and several articles on disability and illness. She is currently working on a book about ethics and the value of suffering. She has lived with ME/CFIDS since 1985.

Joanna M. Weston has had poetry, reviews, and short stories published in anthologics and journals for some twenty-five years. Her publications include, among others, a middle-reader, *Those Blue Shoes*, and a volume of poetry, *A Summer Father*.

Susie Wieszmann is a member of People First Winnipeg. Her love of singing brings people together in the spirit of fun. Susie has a great sense of humour and is always quick with a joke. She wants all people to enjoy the freedoms she does living in the community.

Winsom: As a person of many cultural heritages—with African, Maroon, Arawak, Spanish, and Scottish ancestries—I bring to my work a spirituality which manifests itself through a syncretism of African-based religion and deeply personal experiences. *"I evoke the powers of ancient alchemy, for love, from my hands and heart, my mind, my body, my spirit. I transform these elements into the power of love."*

Valerie Wolbert is President of People First Manitoba. She is unstoppable in her committment to making life better for all people who have been labelled with an intellectual disability. Valerie gives of her energy, time and skills to many organisations in the Winnipeg area.

Hilde Zitzelsberger is a Ph.D. candidate in the Lawrence S. Bloomberg Faculty of Nursing and alumni of the CIHR Ph.D. training program Heath Care, Technology and Place at the University of Toronto. She also is a lecturer at the University of Ontario Institute of Technology where she teaches in Health Sciences. Her interests include children's and adult's embodiments, gender issues, and health care technologics and places.

Photo: Gary Annable

Diane Driedger has written extensively about the issues of women and people with disabilities over the past thirty years. Her book *The Last Civil Rights Movement: Disabled Peoples' International* was published in 1989. She has co-edited two international anthologies by disabled women and, most recently, co-edited with Michelle Owen, *Dissonant Disabilities: Women with Chronic Illnesses Explore Their Lives* (2008). Diane is an educator, administrator, activist, and researcher in the area of disabled women's issues in Canada and internationally. She is also a visual artist and poet, and holds a Ph.D. in Education. She lives in Winnipeg.